COVENANT ESSAYS: *Two*

COVENANT ESSAYS: *Two*

T. HOOGSTEEN

RESOURCE *Publications* • Eugene, Oregon

COVENANT ESSAYS: TWO

Copyright © 2022 T. Hoogsteen. All rights reserved. Except for brief quotations in critical publications or reviews, no part of this book may be reproduced in any manner without prior written permission from the publisher. Write: Permissions, Wipf and Stock Publishers, 199 W. 8th Ave., Suite 3, Eugene, OR 97401.

Resource Publications
An Imprint of Wipf and Stock Publishers
199 W. 8th Ave., Suite 3
Eugene, OR 97401

www.wipfandstock.com

PAPERBACK ISBN: 978-1-6667-3863-6
HARDCOVER ISBN: 978-1-6667-9960-6
EBOOK ISBN: 978-1-6667-9961-3

MARCH 29, 2022 9:44 AM

Scripture quotations are from the Revised Standard Version of the Bible, copyright © 1946, 1952, and 1971 by the National Council by the National Council of the Churches of Christ in the U.S.A. All rights reserved.

"Scripture quotations are from The Holy Bible, English Standard Version, copyright © 2001 by Crossway Bibles, a publishing ministry of Good News Publishers. All rights reserved."

J. Medema 1918–2010
B. Medema-vanLingen. 1921-2015
Ann 1950–2016

For remembering

CONTENTS

Introduction | ix

MANY SON-OF-MAN NAMINGS | 1

MANY SON-OF-GOD NAMINGS | 43

LEFT, LEFT, LEFT | 67

CONFESSIONAL STUDIES | 71

JONAH EXPOSITION | 133

THREE ARRESTING THEMES | 149

ERRORS IN THE NICAENO-CONSTANTINOPOLITAN | 170

EXEGETICAL STUDIES | 191

FOLLIES AT FUNERALS | 200

SEXUALITY ON AND OFF THE MAIN ROAD | 210

INTRODUCTION

Essay collections provide interesting thematic varieties as brief concentrations on specific signature subjects.

MANY SON-OF-GOD NAMINGS opens up the Christ's judging office.

MANY SON-OF-GOD NAMINGS separates the names for believers from the Son of God and God the Son.

LEFT, LEFT, LEFT in a picturesque manner expands on the gates in Matthew 7:13–14.

CONFESSIONAL STUDIES begins with a personal journey, moves into a critical evaluation of the Forms of Unity (the Reformed confessional foundation), and enlarges into a contemporary statement of faith focused on holiness, sanctification.

JONAH EXPOSITION struggles with the work of this Old Testament prophet.

THREE ARRESTING THEMES concentrates on hopeful Bible expositions.

ERRORS IN THE NICAENO-CONSTANTINOPOLITAN focuses on pagan philosophical entries in the popularly recognized Nicene Creed.

EXEGETICAL STUDIES continues opening up the immediate background started with *The 2014 Tradition of the Elders*.

FOLLIES AT FUNERALS takes a stab at eulogizing.

SEXUALITY ON AND OFF THE MAIN ROAD separates the biblical from the pagan relative to marital union.

On the whole, COVENANT ESSAYS: TWO creates thematic variety as well as memorable concentrations on pertinent subjects.

MANY SON-OF-MAN NAMINGS

Uneducated interpretations trouble the Son of Man in his identity. These affronts to his Person distort his majesty, glory, honor, and thereby unavoidably flout his judgeship. The title, the Son of Man, with its origin in the Old Testament dispensation, revealed Jesus' least recognized office.

Consider the following distortions with *conservative* roots:

"Christ's self-designation."[1]
"The bond between heaven and earth."[2]

Others mangled the meaning of the name similarly: finite man, mere man, a reference to his human nature,[3] the ideal man, messenger of God, image of God,[4] God's representative, even a foreign figure.

Consider the distortions with *liberal* roots:

"the messenger and agent of God,"
"eschatological salvation-bringer,"
"redemptive agent,"
"agent of God's New Age,"
"final agent and plenipotentiary,"
"inaugurator of the true Israel."[5]

---

1. Hendriksen. *Mark,* 91. Ibid. *Luke,* 298. Jones. *Knowing Christ,* 214.

2. Pentecost. *The WORDS & WORKS of JESUS CHRIST,* 162, "'The Son of man' is the bond between earth and heaven, belongs in an equal degree to both; He is the medium through which God reaches man and man reaches God. As the One who unites and unifies earth and heaven, He is the Source of the Divine life in man, is the Light that creates, the Bread that maintains, life in the world."

3. Spykman. *Reformational Theology,* 396, " . . . Jesus' most typical way of identifying himself as 'the Son of Man,' emphasizing the integrity of his human nature." McGrath. *Christian Theology,* 278, "It is an affirmation of the humanity of Christ."

4. Perhaps with reference to Hebrews 1:3p, "the exact imprint of his nature."

5. Kee. *Jesus in History,* 138, 203, 141, 146, 150.

Somehow the Son-of-Man naming may have identified Jesus as an apocalyptic figure, a distinct being. Misrepresentations know no limits. "The problem confronting the early believers was that of finding a connection between the humble life, rejection, and death of Jesus, and the glory of the exalted Son of man of which he had spoken. They solved this problem by making the Son of man concept the chain which linked together in a logical sequence the Lord's life among men of humiliation and renunciation, his shameful death on the cross and his resurrection, and his subsequent exaltation to incomparable majesty at the right hand of God."[6] With such speculative misrepresentation the ongoing Church in the twenty-first century identified the Son of Man.

V

According to Matthew 12:1–8, Mark 2:23–28, and Luke 6:1–5, men of the Oral Law, Pharisees, with spite-full exaction misjudged the Son-of-Man naming. They accused the Twelve of threshing on that Sabbath. Actually, what Jesus' disciples did, eating kernels of grain out of hand, followed a legitimate activity during harvest weeks, Deuteronomy 23:25. The Lord condemned the pertinent Pharisaic rule, judging that only " . . . the Son of Man is Lord of the Sabbath." Of every Sabbath. Never despotic Pharisees lost in the securities of self-righteous endeavors. Thus the Son of Man condemned a legalistic—however inconsequential—deformation of the Seventh Day, and led foundational followers, the Twelve, into the time to come, living each Sabbath to honor him, the Son of Man, preparatory to the eternal Sabbath.

Wherever in the Bible, foremost in the Gospels, authors inserted the Son-of-Man title, through the Author they recorded that Jesus shattered interpretative conflicts and accusatory crises by means of breakthrough judgments.[7]

---

6. Higgins. *Jesus and the Son of Man*, 13.

7. Note: neither Matthew, nor Mark, nor Luke, nor John identified Jesus in every conflict with the Jews as the Son of Man, though fitting, Matthew 12:9–14, 15:1–9, 16:1–4, 19:3–12; etc. Each of the four Gospelers expressed the Son-of-Man designation with discrimination: instances 1) in which Jews impressed the Oral Law upon the Church to exclude Jesus from the covenant community and 2) in which they with destabilizing forces of conformity compelled the covenant community into the Tradition of the Elders.

MANY SON-OF-MAN NAMINGS
IN THE OLD TESTAMENT

From genealogical Numbers through jarring Ezekiel the Scripture's Author revealed numerous sons of man, predominantly positive, as types of the Son of Man; if these sons of man agitated against the LORD, as anti-types they hindered the historical progress of the Old Testament's Gospel manifestation. Leaders during the first dispensation, positive or negative, represented or mischaracterized the Son of Man.

Prophecy

Balak, King of Moab, had purchased Balaam's prophetic services, therewith fatally to condemn the LORD's Israel journeying toward Canaan. The LORD, however, foiled the son of Beor's covetousness and issued through his mouth only blessings upon the sprawling covenant community. A part of these blessings, Numbers 23:19,

> God is not man, that he should lie,
> or a son of man, that he should change his mind.
> Has he said, and will he not do it?
> Or has he spoken, and will he not fulfill it?

Whereas Balaam in the name of Moabite gods intended Israel's condemnation the LORD God honored his promise to Abraham, Exodus 3:13–17; hence, to Balaam's shame and Balak's chagrin, he preserved his people. Moreover, he embarrassed Moab's idolatry terribly.

In effect, this Numbers-saying, prophetically charged, revealed the LORD's judging office; unbiased,[8] he condemned all who violated Israel's integrity. Balak, and the Midianites with him, attempted to offset with cursing the covenant community's progression, Numbers 22:4p, "This horde will now lick up all that is around us, as the ox licks up the grass of the field." Thus Balak perceived Moab's sobering future, which in due course also happened.

Given the temptation, a *man* and a *son* of *man* may take a bribe to commit injustice, such as Balaam's fees for divination. The LORD, however, according to his inviolable righteousness refused to recant, no matter the circumstances, his promise to Abraham and allow a temporary king to rout his as if shepherd-less people.

In fact, the LORD God created the historical bearings of Balaam's blessings, in the process establishing his fidelity as the unbribable *man* and

---

8. Exodus 23:1–3, 6, 8; etc.

son of man. As this strange to Israel prophet addressed Abraham's seed, God obstructed the idolatries of Moab and Midian from achieving Balak's goal; those partisan pantheons as well as military authorities lost, reeling in disarray. The Almighty, through Balaam's blessings rather judged venal Balak, therewith condemning Moab and also Midian, then to lead Israel away to the Land of Promise. Never under the influence of avarice, Yahweh moved Israel under messianic authority to his covenant inheritance.

Wisdom's Judging

Job and the Psalms include a divergent range of teachings on the son-of-man revelation, each one laden with or contrary to the way-into-tomorrow momentum.

1–2

Take Job 25:5-6. Bildad the Shuhite had not listened to Job 23—24 and through a gross generalization (again) accused the arduously suffering man of more unspecified unrighteousness. The accusation pointed to a truth that no man living naturally attains to righteousness before the LORD. But with this unwise verbal assault Bildad sinned, blasphemed.

> Behold, even the moon is not bright,
> and the stars are not pure in his eyes;
> how much less man, who is a maggot,
> and the son of man, who is a worm!

Thus Bildad grilled Job and further suppressed the blameless and upright man under indefinite guilt in order with sly prodding to elicit a false confession of sin. Yet, Job, the *man* and the *son of man*, a type of the Son of Man, ably defended himself against this *friend's* insinuation of evil. In his own defense Job prophesied, and righteously so, 26:1—31:40, thus curbing Bildad's sham concern. Job at some length judged the man's inopportune wisdom as error.

Also consider Job 35:7-8. Here the blameless and upright man shielded himself against Elihu's indictment of internal and thus still secret sinning, one of the mind, perhaps pride, perhaps self-righteousness.

> If you are righteous, what do you give to him?
> Or what does he receive from your hand?
> Your wickedness concerns a man like yourself,

and your righteousness a son of man.

Herewith Elihu, fourth of the alleged friends, claimed Job misjudged himself; the *man* and the *son of man* had given nothing worthwhile to God, and therefore suffered inordinately much. In this very long attack calculated to hurt, Elihu with his pronounced one-sidedness intensified the stress in the oppression of a *son of man* for whom the LORD by grace had a better destination; in fact, the last of the condemning judgments reflected badly upon the accuser who withheld hopes for Job's tomorrows. Yet the LORD himself freed Job—a ruler in his time and place—for his divinely intended destiny; as a type of the Son of Man, Job in the work ahead revealed the righteousness of living in the merciful presence of almighty God.

Quietly, the Author unfolded two features common to the son-of-man terminology:

One: The *son of man* and *man* in such linguistic structures served reciprocally, *son of man* interpreting *man* and *man* interpreting *son of man*. Each reflected the judging function with which the LORD God originally endowed Adam; all who committed themselves negatively to this office, misusing it by opposing the divine will, received unbending condemnation. All men who judged in conformity to the Lord's competence received high commendation. Thus the two terms—*man* and *son of man*—interacted; before the Lord the one equaled the other.

Two: The *man* as well as the *son-of-man* naming in its combinative format articulated eschatological force; each instance reached for a conclusion, a judgment. Thus, this terminology interpreted further evidence of the LORD's creative shaping of history.

The Spirit mobilized in the Old Church sensitivity to the son-of-man naming, which intensified in the pull of history.

2–2

Psalm 8:3–4 framed the hope of a forward-thinking son of man[9] moving out to conquer the foes exposed in verse two.

> "When I look at your heavens, the work of your fingers,
> the moon and the stars, which you have set in place,
> what is man that you are mindful of him,

---

9. Against the biblical grain: Taylor. *The Names of Jesus*, 26, minimized the significance of the *son of man* title by calling it merely a synonym for *man*.

and the son of man that you care for him?"

The Psalmist *remembered* the creation mandate with which Adam as first image bearer applied dominion, dominion suffused with judging to determine the right way from the wrong as he faced the tree of the knowledge of good and evil. David confronted by an enemy incursion, the untenable tension of which generated this entreaty, with awe recalled the original dominion mandate. As the LORD God had created Adam to rule over all earthworks, part of which to forestall the encroachment of sin, so he in a much later age commissioned the son of Jesse to govern at the head of all Israel, part of which included judging swells of military transgressions escalating on Canaan's borders.

At the turning point in the psalm David, judging, believed his dominion authority; then in the strength of divine care he crafted also the fifth verse, "Yet you have made him a little lower than the heavenly beings and crowned him with glory and honor." Sensitive to this escalation of hope David amplified his unifying dominion in Israel against threatening militarily superior anti-covenantal forces.[10]

V

Psalm 80:17 revealed a nation-wide confusion in shame that Israel suffered following a military defeat; responsive, the Psalmist, reaching out, implored the LORD for a favorable judgment upon his people, one to the enemy's undoing.

> But let your hand be on the man of your right hand,
> the son of man whom you have made strong for yourself!

To break the deep collective despair and the broad national woe, this son of man, a positive type, called for the LORD's gracious judgment in a visceral victory for the covenant nation. The Psalmist thus with penetrating insight supervised the recreation of Israel's eschatological hope.

V

---

10. Against the biblical grain: Crossan. *Jesus,* 49, "The Hebrew or Aramaic translated as 'son of man' is simply, like *mankind* in English, a chauvinistic way to describe all humanity, a patriarchal way for the part to describe the whole in its own exclusive image."

Psalm 144:3–4 revealed another son of man, one shouldering the burdensome fears of his people; under the unpredictable heel of foreign domination Israel's misery impoverished covenant liveliness. Similar to Psalm 8:3–4,

> O LORD, what is man that you regard him,
> or the son of man that you think of him?
> Man is like a breath;
> his days are like a passing shadow.

In that manifestation of insignificance and transitoriness the Psalmist pled for release from enemies' malicious designs. Driven to dismay, this son of man as psalmist, judging, recognized that only through divine supremacy his people journeyed into an emerging epoch. Hence, due to the LORD's renowned mercies the destination of the first dispensation enthused him with covenant vitality.

\/

According to Psalm 146, the LORD himself had humbled short-sighted Israel for seeking a victory according to an unfaithful monarch's plans, his earth-bound energies in the first dispensation disconnected from Israel's destination. Therefore, succinct, to reverse disintegration of covenant meaning, verse three,

> Put not your trust in princes,
> in a son of man, in whom there is no salvation.

This *son of man*, an indeterminate type paralleling an unworthy prince, offended the LORD and damaged Israel through spurious judging. Yahweh condemned such subversive Davidides[11] in Israel and alone moved his people into the projected covenantal freedom.

\/

In patience-exuding Job and throughout intermeshing Psalms the Author revealed several sons of man, either positive or negative types with respect to the Son of Man. If the latter, an idolatrous Davidide, misjudging, he concocted dissolutions of covenant order; with consequent loss of divine beneficence, such a king flaunted forbidden obstacles, images of wood and

---

11. A Davidide, one of King David's legitimate successors.

stone. If the former, a Davidide forerunner, judging, envisaged the flow of history in which the LORD himself broke all sinfully acute torments.

Both namings, paralleling *man* and *son of man*, equaled each other, impressing upon exegesis/interpretation that every ruler, specifically in the Davidic lineage, carried the office of kingship crucial to which the function of judging. Unbelieving princes forced this dominion into idolatry. Believing men served the LORD and, nation-building, his people. The *man* and the *son of man* emancipated headship, responsibility first, from idolatrous gratifications, in all ages applicable politically to Israel's kings and princes.

Prophetic Hope

Among the prophets the son-of-man naming followed the historically tempered pattern of meaning, for Ezekiel much more intensively. Israel's idolatry wearied the LORD, Isaiah 1:14; nevertheless, judging, he broke the corrosive impact idol-worshipers imposed and frustrated these barriers to salvation. He had predestined the great Day and thus and then conformed history to his glory.

1–2

Reflection on Isaiah 51:12–13a. The LORD called the covenant people to account for the worship of Babylonian idols; rather than irreducible and unwavering covenant faithfulness, his own trusted these crude devices, Isaiah 41:5–7, 44:9–20; Psalm 135:15–18. King Hezekiah's unbelief poisoning the covenant nation turned the LORD God against his own; he refused to tolerate such idolatrous fearfulness, such unbridled covetousness, which inhibited reliance upon his omnipotent trustworthiness.

> I, I am he who comforts you;
> who are you that you are afraid of man who dies,
> of the son of man who is made like grass,
> and have forgotten the LORD, your Maker?

The untypical *man=son of man* populating this frame of reference was a retrograde Davidide who through governing powers led Israel into restive and superstitious anti-covenantalism, demoralizing the people of the Lord. Hegemonic Babylon had turned the faith of God's appointed king away from his destiny in grace, generating fire-like friction between the LORD and Israel, all the while imposing impending retributive punishment upon the unfaithful covenant nation. To fear the enemy more than to trust in

Israel's Maker? In stark contrast to this enmitous *son of man*, a princely creature who falsified the Faith, the LORD God condemned such a judge, a king deaf to the word of the Lord. Yahweh calculated his worth no more than grass that withered and died.

V

Reflection on Isaiah 56:1–2,

> Thus says the LORD,
> Keep justice, and do righteousness,
> for soon my salvation will come,
> and my deliverance be revealed.
> Blessed is the man who does this, and the son of man who holds
> it fast,
> who keeps the Sabbath, not profaning it,
> and keeps his hand from doing any evil.

Isaiah hereby contrasted the earlier son of man who compelled fearful Israel to forsake the Commandments, Isaiah 51:12–13a, to this son of man who maintained in a distracted world the righteousness of the Law even under preponderant greed for preservation of life. Untypical political leaders directed either a herd mentality to increase covenantal disobedience or compelled Israel into an outdated illusion, both celebratory of idolatry. Typical Davidides mobilized Israel for the covenant way.

2–2

In addressing Ezekiel, a non-Davidide, the LORD GOD titled this prophet numerous times as *son of man*, thus he pressed the judicial office upon his heart, soul, mind, and body for nearly two decades, 592–570 BC. Ezekiel 2:1–3,

> And [the LORD] said to me, "Son of man, stand on your feet, and I will speak with you." And as he spoke to me, the Spirit entered into me and set me on my feet, and I heard him speaking to me. And he said to me, "Son of man, I send you to the people of Israel, to nations of rebels, who have rebelled against me. They and their fathers have transgressed against me to this day."

By the time of Ezekiel's commissioning, the depraved and totally subverted fixation of Israel's heart had excited the accelerating progress of the divine wrath gathered for the Exile. This fury, unless satisfied, held the envy-charged people of the covenant bound in idolatrous bondage. In fact, against Ezekiel,[12] the LORD's messenger to unfaithful Israel—Israel in Exile!—the people of the covenant rebelled with fearsome insurgences. Nevertheless, the prophet laid the divine judgment upon Israel.

V

Israel before and during the Exile edged closer to indiscriminate brokenness; for the covenant people with deadly forces of religiosity rivalled insubordinate nations and irremediable empires in the surround. Ezekiel 2:4–7,

> The descendants also are impudent and stubborn: I send you to them, and you will say to them, "Thus says the LORD God." And whether they hear or refuse to hear (for they are a rebellious house) they will know that a prophet has been among them. And you, son of man, be not afraid of them, nor be afraid of their words, though briers and thorns are with you and you sit on scorpions. Be not afraid of their words, nor be dismayed at their looks, for they are a rebellious house. And you shall speak my words to them, whether they hear or refuse to hear, for they are a rebellious house.

The LORD lacked no foresight when he day by day pressed the levelheaded prophet to persevere in his task, the condemnation of Israel first, specifically all now quartered in Babylonian lands, casualties of idolatry.

Throughout, Ezekiel as son of man ruled as Israel's judge. At the command of the LORD GOD the prophet handed down irrevocable condemnation upon the covenant people as a whole. When none of David's lineage reigned in Jerusalem, Yahweh assigned another to accomplish his judgment.

V

At LORD's command Ezekiel also issued the revelation of the final covenant formation coming. Jeremiah 31:31–40; Ezekiel 36:22–32,

> Therefore say to the house of Israel, Thus says the LORD GOD: It is not for your sake, O house of Israel, that I am about to act, but for the sake of my holy name, which you have profaned among the nations to which you came. And I will vindicate the holiness of my great name, which has been profaned among the nations, and

---

12. Against the biblical grain: Rosen. Y'SHUA, 34, "'Son of man' was a term first employed in Ezekiel. There it seems to be little more than a stylized equivalent of 'man.'"

which you have profaned among them. And the nations will know that I am the LORD, declares the LORD GOD, when through you I vindicate my holiness before their eyes. I will take you from the nations and gather you from all the countries and bring you into your own land. I will sprinkle clean water on you, and you shall be clean from all your uncleannesses, and from all your idols I will cleanse you. And I will give you a new heart, and a new spirit I will put within you. And I will remove the heart of stone from your flesh and give you a heart of flesh. And I will put my Spirit within you, and cause you to walk in my statutes and be careful to obey my rules. You shall dwell in the land that I gave to your fathers, and you shall be my people, and I will be your God. And I will deliver you from all your uncleannesses. And I will summon the grain and make it abundant and lay no famine upon you. I will make the fruit of the tree and the increase of the field abundant, that you may never again suffer the disgrace of famine among the nations. Then you will remember your evil ways, and your deeds that were not good, and you will loathe yourselves for your iniquities and your abominations. It is not for your sake that I will act, declares the LORD GOD; let that be known to you. Be ashamed and confounded for your ways, O house of Israel.

By way of this disquieting messenger the LORD God upheld the conscious intent of the son-of-man nomenclature.[13]

V

Isaiah and Ezekiel, when ruling Davidides submitted to the Babylonian hegemony, in different ways honored the titular son-of-man naming. Each gathered in respective person the implacable tensions and radical ruptures agitating Israel. Both thereby glorified the LORD God and bonded the faithful remnant with perseverance. Simultaneously, the son-of-man naming thus far qualified as typology; the princes of Israel and the prophet Ezekiel served as types or anti-types of the Son of Man.

IN THE NEW TESTAMENT

Halfway the Daniel-book the son-of-man revelation solidified in a Person of the Trinity, the Seed of the woman promised since the verbal formulation

---

13. Against the biblical grain: Taylor. *The Names of Jesus*, 26, "In Ezekiel the phrase is used frequently by the prophet as a human self-designation."

of Genesis 3:14–15. Stereotypical enemies within and without the covenant community on account of arrogant intolerance had built idolatrous barriers to hamper and hinder the Lord Jesus from completing his earliest prophecy.

Daniel's Son-of-Man Visions

Daniel dreamt. Starting at Daniel 7:1a, "In the first year of Belshazzar king of Babylon, [the LORD's man] saw a dream and visions of his head as he lay in his bed." These night visions, which prophesied of the time to come, troubled this mentally and emotionally sound servant of the Lord as he perceived the nations and the world's empires as a restless sea, violent in turmoil and vehement in confusion, the whole conflicted by highly charged winds roaring in simultaneously from four directions. In the brute and bloody militaristic struggles the peoples worldwide—moved by deep secrets unleashed in ancient traditions—thrashed about to obtain constantly dying glories, each swept away and drowned by insurmountable waves.

Isaiah, *circa* 760–701 BC, had addressed these manmade lands and realms, 13:1—23:18, Babylon, Assyria, Philistia, Moab, Syria/Damascus, Ethiopia, Egypt, Medo-Persia, Edom, Arabia, and Tyre. Jeremiah, *circa* 626–580 BC, had addressed these erratic peoples and dominions, 46:1—51:64a, Egypt, Philistia, Moab, Ammon, Edom, Elam, and Babylon/Chaldea. Ezekiel had addressed these explosive empires and peoples, 25:1—32:33, Amnon, Moab, Edom, Philistia, Tyre/Sidon, and Egypt. Under these storm-swept waters Assyria, congested by ruthlessness, had sunk forever into remote depths. In the overlapping welters of storm-driven winds, nation fought nation and empire defeated empire to steal the wealth of victim-neighbors and gather in the notoriety of infamy—only to disintegrate under fiercer violence. Individually and collectively all strove again the Kingdom/Church to defeat Yahweh, the King of kings and the Lord of lords.

Each listing of the nations 1) tallied the tyrannies and peoples inhabiting Daniel's visions and 2) revealed the sinking of imperialistic hegemonies. In Isaiah, Jeremiah, and Ezekiel's prophecies the LORD God with respect to the nations made suddenly and comprehensively visible in the night the historical confusion and dehumanization opposing his covenant way; throes of militaristic violence culminated initially over the near horizon competed for the still scarcely credible defeat of Babylon and impelled the fateful rise of the more religiously egalitarian Medo-Persian Empire, soon geopolitically huge, from India to Ethiopia, Esther 1:1. Yet Medo-Persia's complex and bloody lust for wealth as well as power also represented only a massive eddy in a roiling ocean churning agitatedly from deep down with storms of mutual hatred.

The LORD opened Daniel's eyes to the envious tyrannies rising and falling. Daniel 7:2–3, "I saw in my vision by night, and behold, the four winds of heaven were stirring up the great sea. And four great beasts came up out of sea, different from one another." From the passé center of foundering Babylon and at the cusp of the rival Medo-Persian swell of international sway the LORD commanded Daniel's dreaming: beasts[14] representative of the empires driving cataclysmic conflicts and conspiracies against the Almighty.

Of the beasts remorselessly emerging from the anti-rational sea of nations, the fourth caught and held Daniel's attention most bleakly; in its ferocity it differed from the others. Dan 7:7–8, 19–27. This monstrous obscenity represented first of all Rome's imperial signature.

The beast-vision differed largely from Nebuchadnezzar's dream, Daniel 2; in and through the king's colossal statue with its precious and glistening metals the LORD God revealed a governing movement in history still protective of the covenant community; in that idol's sequential civilizations he promised a measure of order. In contrast, the aroused beasts characterized extreme brutality and violent chaos immeasurable, destructive of all civilization, anarchy supreme, the fourth the most.

As the fourth beast's manifold horrors—in appearance as well as in tirading—rolled into Daniel's consciousness, 7:9–10, astonishment and fear multiplied.

> As I looked,
> thrones were placed, and the Ancient of days took his seat;
> his clothing was white as snow, and the hair of his head like pure wool;
> his throne was fiery flames; its wheels were burning fire.[15]
> A stream of fire issued and came forth from before him;
> a thousand thousands served him,
> and ten thousand times ten thousands stood before him;[16]
> the court sat in judgment, and the books were opened.

On the one hand, Daniel perceived the glory of the Ancient of Days seated on his distinctive throne; on the other, he saw the major consequence

---

14. Dodd. *The Founder of Christianity*, 117, indicated that the beasts characterized the brutal pagan empires which successively oppressed Israel.
15. Ezekiel 1:4–28.
16. Psalm 68:17; Revelation 19:14.

of a divine judgment on the earth, the targeted defeat of the tumultuous beasts, notably the fourth with its blasphemous horn, 7:8, 20. In effect, Daniel in the vision foresaw also the downfall of the Roman Empire, its beast yet evolving in womb-like tensions. Daniel 7:11–12, "I looked then because of the sound of the great words that the horn was speaking. And as I looked, the beast was killed, and its body destroyed and given over to be burned with fire.[17] As for the rest of the beasts, their dominion was taken away, but their lives were prolonged for a season and a time." Upon that judgment, not by the Ancient of Days, for such work was not attributed to him, appeared the "one like a son of man," the Victor even over the worst of the now anachronistic beasts, and strode to the Ancient of Days.

V

This ineffable courtroom setting and the centrality of the Ancient of Days (thus identified for the first time and in the Old Testament further unidentified) prophetically and typologically foretold the unveiling recorded as Revelation 4–5. First, in the Revelation-document, the One seated on the throne of heaven appeared too majestic and awe-inspiring to capture with human vocabulary,[18] except praise. Revelation 4:8b,

> Holy, holy, holy, is the Lord God almighty,
> who was and is and is to come!

Then into the court's startling glories and angelic praises walked the Lion of Judah, Revelation 5:5, also called the Lamb, 5:6; he is the resurrected Lord Jesus who upon the momentous and all-pervasive victory on the Cross—the primary Judgment—majestically approached the throne to receive from the One the power, wealth, wisdom, might, honor, glory, and blessing, attributes crucial to the judging and ruling offices. The Author indicated that upon the beaten beasts initially controlled by the Antichrist the Son of Man had impressed his permanent victory. Thus he revealed to the New Church in the end times, that is, to the saints of the Most High then, the abundant grace to sustain to covenant community even in the worst of the tribulations.

V

---

17. Revelation 19:20, "And the beast was . . . thrown alive into the lake of fire that burns with sulfur."

18. First Timothy 6:16; John 1:18a.

In his victory the "one like a son of man" had mercilessly decreed and executed the death-sentence also upon the fourth beast, the most ferocious of the lot. Daniel 7:13–14, in the full court,

> I saw in the night visions,
> and behold, with the clouds of heaven there came one like a son of man,
> and he came to the Ancient of Days and was presented before him.
> And to him was given dominion and glory and a kingdom,
> that all peoples, nations, and languages should serve him;
> his dominion is an everlasting dominion, which shall not pass away,
> and his kingdom one that shall not be destroyed.[19]

The "one like a son of man" owned all dominion, glory, and a kingdom prior to the victorious judgment;[20] after all, since earliest beginnings peoples, nations, and languages had but one obligation, to serve him only. From the first day of the Creation his everlasting dominion and eternal rule lay globally upon the earth. His victory over the beasts opened up the Kingdom more expansively and purposefully than had the first Lion of Judah,[21] King David. Hence, because of and after the conquest the beneficiaries lived on; Daniel 7:18, " . . . the saints of the Most High shall receive the kingdom and possess the kingdom forever, forever and ever." The "one like a son of man" under his rule forged freedom and safety pertinent to living in the Kingdom.

At the conclusion to the first dispensation the "one like a son of man"[22] revealed the wholly beneficial judgment over the scatological beasts, debauched monstrosities of anarchic violence. To the faithful remnant, that is, to the ongoing Church, the LORD God thus promised the glories of the Kingdom. Not the Ancient of Days, who remained on the throne, but the "one like a son of man" descended to accomplish the Judgment, upon

---

19. First Corinthians 15:27a, "For 'God has put all things in subjection under his feet.'" Ephesians 1:22, "And he put all things under his feet and gave him as head over all things to the church."

20. Tödt. *The Son of Man in the Synoptic Tradition*, 24, "Confining ourselves to the features of this Son of Man without taking account of the secondary interpretation of the vision in 7.15ff., we can only name, in addition to his marvelous advance with the clouds of heaven, the tokens of an everlasting universal ruler. To the Man is given by the Ancient of Days dominion, glory and kingdom for ever and ever."

21. Genesis 49:9.

22. Against the biblical grain: Taylor. *The Names of Jesus*, 26, "In Dan. vii 13 the phrase 'one like unto a son of man' describes a human figure who is brought to the Ancient of Days, and represents the Jewish community, 'the saints of the Most High', to whom are promised 'dominion, and glory, and a kingdom' (vii 14, 27)."

which "was given" the restored attributes of glory. For that triumph the "one like a son of man" moved purposely onto the road to the Incarnation, at that time and in that mystery to recreate the liberty of the Church.[23]

Daniel's vision concluding the first dispensation revealed powerfully also the historical terminus for the second dispensation, plus peering visionarily into the Parousia. Consider: as much as the four beasts had vented fatalistic ire in order to supplant the Kingdom in the first dispensation with idolatrously synthesized world orders, the one after the other failed. Similarly, in the second dispensation successive beasts moved against the New Testament revelation of the Kingdom, the last pan-imperialistically superior. The last of these beasts foreshadowed (still from Daniel's place) the rule of the Antichrist; that rule, Daniel foresaw, the "one like a son of man" also foredoomed and in its season quashed, indicating thereby the preservation of the Church and magnifying the exaltation of his judgeship.[24]

Through aging Daniel's ministry the LORD God illumined the end times. That which Daniel saw and troubled him involved pervasively the fourth irreversibly obscene monstrosity, which *thing* had consecutive lives: one at the end of the first dispensation and the other at the conclusion to the second. With such prophetic elasticity Daniel perceived that beast; transmogrified, it became the Antichrist in his scandalous reign, the satanic terror of the end times. The conclusion of the second dispensation the Author of Daniel's dreaming indicated by phrases as the opening of the books, Daniel 7:10–11/Revelation 20:12, and 8:19, "at the latter end of the indignation," as well as "the appointed time of the end." The vision

---

23. A common feature appears in Son-of-Man literature with respect to the Daniel 7 vision, the identification of the one like a son of man with the Christ.

Against the biblical grain: Dodd. *The Founder of Christianity*, 117–118, "The human figure of Daniel's vision has acquired a new identity. It is this historical Person in whom, as its 'inclusive representative,' the new Israel, the people of God, is to emerge from apparently irretrievable disaster—'raised to life with Christ,' as Paul was to express it." See Colossians 3:1.

Against the biblical grain: Tödt. *The Son of Man in the Synoptic Tradition*, 24, "Thus the image of the Man in the context of the description of the vision attains only a limited prominence. The interpretation of vv. 15ff. robs him 'who is like a man' completely of his individuality and puts 'the people of the saints of the Most High' in his place."

Such identification—"the one like a son of man"= "the people of the saints"—opens a blindness to the actuality of this passage, and also robs the Son of Man of preincarnate glories.

24. Toon. *Jesus Christ is Lord*, 36–37, re: Daniel 7:14, "... where the Son of Man is given 'authority, honour and royal power, so that the people of all nations, races and languages would serve him'. The kingdom of the ascended Messiah is both the community of disciples and the whole world."

of the fourth beast, hence, owned a second life; the second envisioned the satanic violence and the devilish destruction of all civilization worsening. In Daniel's double vision the complications for the closing of the second dispensation extended the fierceness of the fourth atrocity.

At the conclusion of the first dispensation stereotypical enemies within and without the covenant community on account of arrogant intolerance had built idolatrous barriers to hamper and hinder the Lord Jesus from completing his earliest prophecy, Genesis 3:14–15. Outside, the Romans had pushed Daniel's fourth-beast prophecy into the foreground. Within the Church the Pharisees with the Tradition of the Elders had bound the people of the covenant by means of the Oral Law.

Jesus' Son-of-Man Sayings

Within the Church the Pharisees/Sadducees by way of the Tradition of the Elders bound the believers with the Oral Law; they actually assisted the fourth monstrosity in troubling the covenant community to prevent the creation of the Gospel in its fulfilment.

Consequently, upon his commissioning, Matthew 3:13–17; Mark 1:9–11; Luke 3:21–22, and John 1:29–34, the Son of Man—judging/condemning/ruling/mediating—displaced the idolaters who blinded the Church to and withheld his people from the elementary grace of salvation; they as well concealed from Jesus' followers the luminous glories of the Parousia once swept into view by, for instance, Isaiah 65:17–25, among its myriad inner-relationships also the final Judgment.

Name and office, the Son of Man, as the others—the Christ, the Lord, the Messiah, the Savior, the Son of God, etc.—belongs to the gracious essence of Jesus' Person.[25] This office and name appeared unannounced and unqualified first in the Synoptics;[26] neither Matthew, nor Mark, nor Luke explained its meaning, which from its first usage indicated suffering for Jesus and followers. The three knew the Church they addressed intimately, also her familiarity with the Son-of-Man naming.[27] Matthew, *circa* AD

---

25. Pentecost. *The WORDS & WORKS of JESUS CHRIST,* 34, "From the days of Daniel, the title *Son of Man* was considered by the Jews to be a messianic title."

26. Similar to the Creation account: the LORD God spoke without identifying himself with an ontology or theogony; by speaking he identified himself, thereby demonstrating the actuality of his existence.

Each Gospel contains history, prophecy, wisdom, teaching, law-giving; etc.

27. Rosen. *Y'SHUA,* 35, "By the time, then, that Jesus arrived on the scene, it is likely that the title, 'Son of man' had accumulated a good deal of mystery around it . . . . He

63–66, Mark, *circa* AD 40–65, and Luke, *circa* AD 61–63, John, *circa* AD 90, worked with two foci: 1) to bring to remembrance for second and third generations the Son of Man's ministry in and for the Church, and 2) to lead under the Son-of-Man's revelation the covenant community further, prepared for centuries and millennia.

The Gospel authors in the typical Old Testament historical documentation chained together, the one to the other, the units of the records they bequeathed to the Church, creating account-to-account a continuous history. The early readers capably interpreted the significance of the Son of Man in each element as well as throughout the whole. Thus the Gospels, critical components of the founding identity of the New Testament, edified the covenant community then and since.[28]

Luke initiated the ready-to-hand Son-of-Man naming, 6:22. Matthew, 5:11, presaged the same without, however, the Son-of-Man name.[29] In the

---

offered no explanation for it, assuming that His hearers would understand."

28. The eighteenth-century Enlightenment troubled Biblical exegesis in a manner now foundational to liberal theology with a strange sort of ongoing revelation; in effect, developing church communities read back into and then rewrote the Gospels. Or even stranger, those early church communities collectively rewrote primarily the Gospels to suit theological trends in development. Borg. *Jesus*, 28, "The foundation is a way of seeing the gospels that has emerged since the Enlightenment. In a sentence, *the gospels are products of early Christian communities in the last third of the first century.*" This short sentence carries a freight of meaning. On its exegetical foundation not Matthew, Mark, Luke, and John, but early and diverse Christian communities collectively authored the Gospels to satisfy, or cement in place current theologies, a sort of ongoing revelation supportive of world conformity.

In the 1930s Rudolph Bultmann gave full voice to this exegetical theory, and others followed—Tödt, Taylor, Higgins (see below).

Better: Dodd. *The Founder of Christianity,* 21–22, "When allowance has been made for ... limiting factors—the chances of oral transmission, the effect of translation, the interest of teachers in making the sayings 'contemporary,' and simple human fallibility—it remains that the first three gospels offer a body of sayings on the whole so consistent, so coherent, and withal so distinctive in manner, style, and content, that no reasonable critic should doubt, whatever reservations he may have about individual sayings, that we find reflected here the thought of a single, unique teacher."

Brown. *Jesus God and Man,* 92, "The present writer believes strongly that there is a core of historical material in the fourth Gospel, but he also recognizes that this material has been rethought in the light of late fourth-century theology."

Brown. *The Virginal Conception & Bodily Resurrection of Jesus,* 44, "In Matthew and Luke we have the Christology moved back to Jesus' infancy in Mary's womb, for an angel proclaims that from the moment of his conception he was already the Messiah and the Son of God."

29. Funk. *Honest to Jesus,* 90–94, consistently and persistently preferred, rather than the Son-of-Man naming, a "son of Adam" identification, in this manner denying Jesus'

formative dimensions of wisdom literature Jesus revealed the animosity his judgeship evoked in the Pharisee/Sadducee dominated covenant community.[30]

Luke, 6:22–23, registered the consuming hatred of opponents resident in the Church; those Pharisees stoked up burning rivalry against Jesus and his disciples. To guide his own with wisdom, the pericope, "Blessed are you when people hate you and when they exclude you and revile you and spurn your name as evil, on account of the Son of Man! Rejoice in that day, and leap for joy, for behold, your reward is great in heaven; for so their fathers did to the prophets." Revolution refused to bow before reformation. Matthew, 5:11–12, placed this teaching early within the so-called Sermon on the Mount; at that still relatively irenic time of its composition Jesus perceived no occasion for the Son-of-Man naming. In Luke, however, by the Son-of-Man naming the Lord held the Pharisaic opposition to account.

Matthew and Luke announced again the Son-of-Man naming. In contrast to foxes and dens as well as birds and nests, the Son of Man had nowhere to lay his head, Matthew 8:18–22; Luke 9:57–62; rather than declaring the Lord's poverty, this saying intended to lay two converging centers of activity. 1) Thus he revealed that none followed him out of wish fulfilment—as a scribe, as a disciple, and as a third individual with vain hopes elected to do. As the Son of Man he commanded only those whom he chose to follow him—the Twelve in particular. In this manner he initiated the New Israel. 2) Thus he also expressed his judiciary disinterestedness; unbribable, nothing in heaven, on earth, or under the earth covetously diverted him from this goal, to recreate the citizens of the Kingdom. In fact, with this poignant homelessness Jesus declared that though he was in the world, he was not of the world; in other words, he had no prejudicial interests that threatened to turn him away from his sole task.[31]

---

divinity.

30. Kee. *Jesus in History*, 87, "In the present situation of conflict the followers of Jesus can expect rejection and persecution at the hands of those who consider themselves God's people. To 'cast out one's name as evil' is a Semitic expression that means to speak ill of someone. The calumny heaped on Jesus' disciples is not for their own sake but because they are publicly identified with the Son of Man (Luke 6:22). The use of the term 'Son of man' heightens the significance of the persecution and suffering that the followers of Jesus are passing through."

31. Against the biblical grain: Crossan. *Jesus*, 51, " . . . my point is that here 'the son of man' certainly does not mean the imminent or future agent of divine judgment. Jesus used the generic term 'son of man' to identify himself with those he was addressing, to emphasize that he shared with them a common destiny as *we* poor or destitute human beings."

Following the commandment he gave Moses, Exodus 23:1–3, 6–8, Jesus himself honored the objectivity of justice. His sole purpose constituted the coming of the Kingdom, his rule, in this manner to glorify the Father who glorified him. Among the people of the covenant, his own community of idolatrously consumed and divisive members, he with perfect righteousness and holiness revealed his judgeship expressive in that irrefragable office executed by the Son of Man.

For careful readers, disingenuous notes:

1. In the wider historical framework the crushing weight of Roman occupiers initially withstood the coming of the Kingdom; Daniel's fourth beast tolerated no opposition and therefore Pontius Pilate crucified the King of the Jews.
2. In the narrower historical framework the Jews led by the Pharisees and abetted by the Sadducees comprised Jesus' foremost enemies. That his own refused to accept him, John 1:11, came across as understated intransigence.
3. Within Israel first the Son of Man executed his divine justice.

V

When Pharisees with internal haranguing questioned Jesus' divinity and therewith his authority to forgive sins, he revealed his stainless credibility by healing a paralytic. Matthew 9:1–8; Mark 2:1–12; Luke 5:17–26. Matthew 9:6, "But that you may know that the Son of Man has authority on earth to forgive sins"—he then said to the paralytic—"Rise, pick up your bed and go home." In the Pharisaic manner leading men of the Tradition of the Elders sought to prevent Jesus' ministry among his own. He, in effect, judged them in error and thus exposed the grouping positioned on the dark side of the dividing-line. At the same time, on the light side of the dividing-line he pronounced the paralytic righteous. As the Son of Man,[32] Jesus carved separation in Israel.

Against the Biblical grain: Borg. *Jesus*, 145, "The implication is that itinerancy was not about homelessness, but about mission. He sought to reach as many of the peasant class in Galilee as possible."

32. Cullmann. *The Christology of the New Testament*, 158–159, "We see how the New Testament deepens the concept of the Son of Man as Judge: Jesus is both the incarnate man who is the representative Suffering Servant of God, and the future 'Man' who is the Judge."

Matthew, 10:23, revealed Jesus' warning to the Twelve of the persecution and mystery of suffering at the ready on the near horizon, as near as the first apostolic mission in Israel. "When they persecute you in one town, flee to the next, for truly, I say to you, you will not have gone through all the towns of Israel before the Son of Man comes." Thus Jesus prepared the Twelve first for Israel's deep animosity in the leading up to the First Judgment, the Crucifixion. Despite this hostility he still, sovereignly, declared his penetrative judgeship, therewith to hold the entire covenant community accountable for sinning against his teachings as well as him; for all who refused to listen to the apostles trespassed against him, thereby preventing the Church-in-recreation at the heart of the coming of the Kingdom.

Mark, 8:38, in close proximity to Jesus' initial crucifixion-and-resurrection prophecy recorded the Lord's condemnation upon all who, ashamed of him and his teaching, turned away from him and his unstinting ministry. In point of fact, "For whoever is ashamed of me and of my words in this adulterous and sinful generation, of him will the Son of Man also be ashamed when he comes in the glory of his Father with the holy angels." For or against him, this *either/or* defined the dividing-line firmly pressed down in the covenant community. Luke, astute historian, confronted that generation also with Jesus' teaching. For the Lord made the dividing-line visible in a warning against Pharisaic leaven; as tensions swept about the Twelve and through the multitudes, Jesus gave due caution. Luke 12:8–9, "And I tell you, everyone who acknowledges me before men, the Son of Man also will acknowledge before the angels of God, but the one who denies me before men will be denied before the angels of God. And everyone who speaks a word against the Son of Man will be forgiven, but the one who blasphemes against the Holy Spirit will not be forgiven." In Matthew's recording of this warning, 10:32–33, Jesus directly identified this judging authority as his, leaving the Son-of-Man naming out; in this cascade of events corrosive Pharisaic animosity flew about less drastically than the situations in which Mark and Luke chronicled its bitter hostility. "So everyone who acknowledges me before men, I also will acknowledge before my Father who is in heaven, but whoever denies me before men, I also will deny before my Father who is in heaven." According to Matthew, the Lord alerted the multitudes to the accumulations of tension along the dark side of the dividing-line. Hence, he repudiated all of the covenant community who broke away from his ministry. However, with intercessory actuality he promised to plead the cause of each and all steady and steadfast in the Faith, persevering.

Concerning Mark 8:38, Luke 12:8–9 on one side and Matthew 10:32–33 on the other, Jesus and the Son of Man are the same Person, only the situations differ (somewhat). Moreover, in the process of reforming the Kingdom and therein the Church Jesus judged the Twelve and the multitudes, running the dividing-line between believers and unbelievers.

Historian Luke, 9:26–27, 12:8–12, similar to Matt 10:32–33, after Peter's large-hearted confession of faith, Matthew 16:13-20; Mark 8:27-30, placed a pericope on servanthood near Jesus' first-of-three prophecies with respect to the Crucifixion and Resurrection; aware of worse persecution coming the Lord prepared the interdependent Twelve for eventual suffering. The road ahead came with distracting obstacles and bewildering opposition. In those wrenching shifts, though, the Lord Jesus placed his Son-of-Man name, with a measure of sarcasm laying open the fact of Israel's judges presiding over the Judge. At that time the disciples missed the impact of the saying.

V

Four observations, preliminary, of course:

One: Context too controls the Son-of-Man name. The more direct the Pharisaic intrusions upon him and his ministry the more likely Jesus spoke of himself (in the third person) as the Son of Man.

> 1) Matthew 10:32–33, "So everyone who acknowledges me before men, I also will acknowledge before my Father who is in heaven, but whoever denies me before men, I also will deny before my Father who is in heaven."
>
> 2) Mark 8:38, "For whoever is ashamed of me and of my words in this adulterous and sinful generation, of him will the Son of Man be ashamed when he comes in the glory of his Father with the holy angels."[33]
>
> 3) Luke 12:8–10, "And I tell you, everyone who acknowledges me before men, the Son of Man also will acknowledge before the angels of God, but the one who denies me before men will be denied before the angels of God. And everyone who speaks a word against

---

33. Against the Biblical grain: Tödt. *The Son of Man in the Synoptic Tradition*, 43, "In demanding this, Jesus utters an unsurpassable claim. No prophet in Israel ever claimed that men should confess him."

the Son of Man will be forgiven, but the one who blasphemes against the Holy Spirit will not be forgiven."

Comparing Matthew with Mark and Luke proves the above; hence, the "I" of Matthew equals Mark and Luke's "the Son of Man." Context is determinative.

Two: the Son-of-Man naming bore out Jesus' independent judiciary; as the Judge he stood apart, unbiased, from the covetousness of human nature evident in the disciples and Israel's religious leaders.

Three: intriguing is the fact that Jesus consistently with respect to the Son-of-Man's naming spoke of himself in the third person, almost as if he referred to one distinct from himself.[34]

Four: the Son-of-Man name occurred only in the four Gospels, except for Acts 7:56, Hebrew 2:6–8, and Revelation 1:13, 14:14. This widely acknowledged observation invites a question, To what end this limitation?

V

Matthew, 11:16–19, and Luke, 7:31–35, included a saying, which Mark bypassed, in response to another Pharisee attack on Jesus and his ministry. Matthew 11:18–19, " . . . John came neither eating nor drinking, and they say, 'He has a demon.' The Son of Man came eating and drinking, and they say, 'Look at him! A glutton and a drunkard, a friend of tax collectors and sinners!' Yet wisdom is justified by her deeds." By designating himself as the Son of Man the Lord and Savior clarified that the hatred of that childish generation had inevitable consequences; they who praised the Baptizer

---

34. Against the Biblical grain: Taylor. *The Names of Jesus,* 35, "For our present inquiry the importance of the title is its meaning for the person of Jesus. It is the name chosen by Him, in conscious preference, we must suppose, to the more colourless 'Christos' and the human and nationalistic title 'Son of David'. It expressed the idea of lordship, of rule over the Messianic community, and its associations are supernatural. Strange to the Gentile world, it embodies His conception of Messiahship, as the more familiar names could not do, and perhaps in particular the idea of a concealed Messiahship yet to be manifested in action."

Against the Biblical grain: Dodd. *The Founder of Christianity,* 112, "There are sayings so astonishingly bold that their very boldness might seem to justify the avoidance of direct statement in the first person."

Against the Biblical grain: Bultmann. *The Theology of the New Testament,* I, 9, "He does not proclaim himself as the Messiah, i.e., the king of the time of salvation, but he points ahead to the Son of man as another than himself."

and condemned the Son disbelieved the significance of both—John as last forerunner, he as Israel's primary Judge.

Pharisee attackers on the Twelve insisted on the Oral Law to structure Sabbath-keeping. Jesus, however, made the judgment, Matthew 12:8; Mark 2:28;[35] Luke 6:5, "The Son of Man is lord of the Sabbath." He had created the Sabbath; he recreated its future, Exodus 20:8–11. The Pharisees seduced by inner turmoils of covetousness had deformed the Seventh Day into a collection of dull works aimed at the production of self-righteousness. However, for the ongoing Church, Jesus, the Lord of all creation, reformed the Sabbath into the Sunday. Since this declaration of sovereignty none with impunity dared bungle the Fourth Commandment to squander (any part of) the day of rest for satisfactions alien to the Kingdom.

Next, by means of Luke 12:10 and Matthew 12:32 the Lord Jesus directly confronted his fault-finding enemies, Pharisees, who had moved with grim resolution against him. Matthew, "And whoever speaks a word against the Son of Man will be forgiven, but whoever speaks against the Holy Spirit will not be forgiven, either in this age or in the age to come." In Mark, 3:28–30, Jesus with a distinctive phraseology spoke protectively of "the children of man." However, as the bleakness of the conflict deepened, inevitably, the Lord recreating the Kingdom and the Jews losing privileged ground,[36] still the sizeable opposition refused to recant; they had, presumptively, better papers to the ownership of Israel than the Son of Man.

As Pharisees and scribes pressed Jesus for an additional sign to prove his messiahship, they in entrapment-mode envisioned his failure, then loss of credibility before the multitudes of Israel. The Lord responded with a prophetic warning, Luke 11:30; Matthew 12:40, "For just as Jonah was three days and three nights in the belly of the great fish, so will the Son of Man be three days and three nights in the heart of the earth." For those unbelievers Jesus judged that Jonah's sign sufficed. Solemnly he alerted these enemies to the perilous undertaking they had assumed and to the sound of the death knell in his refusal. With this early prophecy regarding his death and resurrection Jesus foretold all within hearing to register the condemnation of enemy opposition.

---

35. Fredriksen. *Jesus of Nazareth*, 2, "When Jesus speaks of himself as Son, he only does so obliquely, in the third person; and he calls himself the Son of Man (2:10)"

36. Against the Biblical grain: Kee. *Jesus in History*, 135, "His message of the coming Kingdom of God and the signs of its inbreaking, evident in his healings and exorcisms, called men to decision; the Son of Man would confirm that decision in the eschatological judgment (Mark 8:38)."

At interpreting for his immediate disciples the parable of the weeds in the field, Matthew 13:36–43, Jesus taught 1) "The one who sows the good seed is the Son of Man," and 2) "The Son of Man will send his angels, and they will gather out of his kingdom[37] all causes of sin and all law-breakers." Matthew thus kept alive in the Church's memory the moving melees of hostility that the Lord had aroused and that believers throughout the centuries, even millennia, faced. Matthew also transmitted to coming generations what Jesus' enemies had to absorb, the Judge's eternal damnation.

Near Matthew's physical center Jesus asked the Twelve the crucial question, 16:13, "Who do people say that the Son of Man is?" With variations Luke, 9:18, and Mark, 8:27, also placed this question strategically. The Lord called the men to speak from the center of the faith he was creating in them. In terms of placement Matthew situated the question outside immediate Pharisee territory, near Caesarea Philippi, amidst relaxed pressures. To the complexity of Jesus' Person—the Son of Man, the Son of God, the Christ—God the Father gave the Twelve the answer, the great confession of faith, which sounded forth from the faithful since. Through Mark and Luke the Author suspended the Son-of-Man naming; these authors addressed believers mostly out of the Gentiles and held the Savior up more as the Messiah, less as the Judge. Whereas Matthew countered Israel's unfaithfulness, Mark and Luke persuaded respective addressees to believe Jesus' messiahship.

Jesus by way of Matthew, 16:27–28, followed through upon the Twelve's basic confession of faith and opened the yet latent hardness in his divine justice. "For the Son of Man is going to come with his angels in the glory of his Father, and then he will repay each person according to what he has done. Truly, I say to you, there are some standing here who will not taste death until they see the Son of Man coming in his kingdom." Everyone who opposed the coming of the Kingdom forfeited also the life in the age to come.[38] On the other hand, all who followed Jesus in faith, serving in the Kingdom, gained life.

---

37. Against the Biblical grain: Kee, *Jesus in History*, 163, "The present age is designated by Matthew as the Kingdom of the Son of Man, during which time the church is composed of good and bad (13:41); it will end in the judgment (13:49; 25:31–46). The Age to Come will be the Kingdom of God or, as Matthew prefers, the Kingdom of the Father (13:43; 25:34)."

38. Hendriksen. *Matthew*, 658, "The glory of the Son of man is revealed also in this very fact, that he will be the Judge who will render to each man according to his deeds."

By means of Matthew 17:9 and Mark 9:9, 12, Jesus taught Peter, James, and John restraint;[39] upon his Transfiguration the Lord intended to keep the honor and the glory of his judgeship to these three disciples, until post-Resurrection times, that is, until after the First Judgment. Moreover, he added, to prepare for the Crucifixion: as the Baptizer had suffered at the hand of the authorities, Matthew 17:12p, "So also the Son of Man will certainly suffer at their hands." Even though the Twelve recognized Elijah in John the Baptizer, they utterly failed to comprehend Jesus' pain.

Jesus promised first the Twelve the authority of judgeship. Luke 22:28–30; Matthew 19:28, "Truly, I say to you, in the new world, when the Son of Man will sit on his glorious throne, you who have followed me will also sit on twelve thrones, judging the twelve tribes of Israel." With the Lord then they had to oversee earth-bound enemies—in the holiness and righteousness of divine justice. This hope too the Savior installed in the Twelve to overcome the uneasiness and hatred in the weeks ahead, until the Resurrection. The Apostles' judging service began on Pentecost Day, for during the Incarnation/Crucifixion/Resurrection/Ascension complex Jesus had recreated the Age to Come, the beginning of the second dispensation.

As pressures of the moment mounted among Jesus' disciples, Mark 10:35–45; Matthew 20:20–28, the upstart sons of Zebedee sought the upper hand among the Twelve; domination rather than service and suffering dazzled momentary hopes. To break James and John's covetousness Jesus declared his authority. He had the authority to move Israel's judges to cause him, the Son of Man, to suffer, and he elected the Twelve to follow in his suffering. In his suffering however he prophetically revealed the deepest compassion for his own. Matthew 20:28; Mark 10:45, "For even the Son of Man came not to be served but to serve, and to give his life as a ransom for many." The Judge knew and planned the guilt-atoning justice of the Cross which he handed down globally, beginning in the New Church, of which the Twelve the first members.

At concluding the parable of the widow and the recalcitrant judge Jesus asked, rhetorically Luke 18:8b, " . . . when the Son of Man comes, will he find faith on earth?" Reaching beyond the First Judgment to the Second he seeks and searches; amidst continuous, even deadly, social, political, and emotional upheavals the Lord expects the Church to reply.[40]

In Luke 19:10, Jesus unambiguously revealed his mission indispensable relative to the coming of the Kingdom, "For the Son of Man came to

---

39. Peter honored Jesus' command until the end of his life, 2 Peter 1:16–21.

40. At another time Jesus declared, Matthew 24:12, "And because lawlessness will be increased, the love of many will grow cold."

seek and to save the lost." Intended for congregations and believers drawn out of the Gentiles, Luke concentrated on Jesus' ministry of discipling a chief tax collector; as the Lord and Savior drew Matthew into his community of soon-to-be apostles he revealed a place for one despised in Israel among the Twelve. Here, again, the Son of Man, judging, demonstrated the work ethic in "Jesus," Matthew 1:21, which Luke too perpetuated. As the Judge, Jesus promised throughout the ages of the second dispensation to find all whom the Father appointed for salvation, that is, all who by grace consequently believed and lived the Faith. Separated from the general condemnation, the New Church only gained in glory, reflective in her magnificence.

In Jesus' announcement of the last Passover, Mark 14:1–2; Luke 22:7; John 13:1–20, Matthew alone, 26:2, recorded the Son-of-Man name. To his disciples, "You know that after two days the Passover is coming, and the Son of Man will be delivered up to be crucified." Potently, he thus identified the Judgment inherent in the Crucifixion, the atoning sacrifice, which constituted the dividing-line for innumerable generations past and future. Throughout the momentousness of this Passover Jesus prophesied with the symbol of the lamb in hand, Exodus 12:1–6, that he was the Lamb whose shed blood atoned for sinners. The Judge summoned then the second and third generations to stand still, remember, and be in awe, despite overbearing Jewish persecution, John 16:1–4, and Roman occupation, powerful rivals both. Thus his own believed the ransom he gave for all of the Faith, nominal converts excluded. This Passover, which Jesus celebrated with the fully attentive and introspective Twelve, signified its relevance for all generations hence of the covenant community. At the ending to the first dispensation and at the beginning of the age to come the Lord unveiled the mystery of the Incarnation perceived in the breaking of the bread and the drinking of the cup. Purposefully, the Son of Man approached the Cross of Golgotha.

As Jesus strode ahead, pausing only in the Garden of Gethsemane, Matthew 26:36–46; Mark 14:32–42; Luke 22:39–46, he again called forth his judging office. At the approach of Judas Iscariot with Roman soldiers and Temple servants, the Lord clearly identified this office to illustrate the grim irony of the situation, asking Peter, James, and John, Matthew 26:45; Mark 14:41, "Are you still sleeping and taking your rest? It is enough; the hour has come. The Son of Man is betrayed into the hands of sinners." The ominous stress on "sinners" awoke the still uncomprehending disciples to accumulations of hostility concentrating on Jesus.

V

In contrast to Peter's magnificent "You are the Christ" and "the Christ of God," Judas Iscariot stooped low and dredged up out of a pit of covetousness the audacity to betray the Son of Man. Luke 22:3–6, "... Satan entered into Judas called Iscariot, who was of the number of the twelve. He went away and conferred with the chief priests and officers how he might betray him to them. And they were glad, and agreed to give him money. So he consented and sought an opportunity to betray him to them in the absence of a crowd."[41] He connived with Israel's magistrates and sold them firsthand information with which to confine the Son of Man in captivity; the avarice of this duplicity made him a devil, John 6:70, irredeemable. Mercenary Judas nevertheless served a key function in Jesus' predetermined and ignominious murder.

Much appears of this Judas in the Gospels, competing for space with the other disciples, Peter specifically. The Iscariot, however, only broke open (a little) the darkness of obstinate perversity conceived in depths of depravity. Mark 14:21; Luke 22:22; Matthew 26:24, "The Son of Man goes as it is written of him, but woe to that man by whom the Son of Man is betrayed! It would have been better for that man if he had not been born." Jesus had commissioned him to discipleship. And Judas scheduled time and place for Jews and Romans to arrest *the* Judge.

In the stillness of Gethsemane the servants of the Sanhedrin and the soldiers of Pontius Pilate with swords and clubs seized Jesus, ready as a sheep led to the slaughter. As the enormity of the betrayal unfolded, John 18:1–11; Matthew 26:47–56; Luke 22:47–53; Mark 14:43–50, Jesus asked that damning question, Luke 22:48, "Judas, would you betray the Son of Man with a kiss?" Before the Judge, culpable Judas stumbled into his eternal damnation, the evidence sufficient.

Judas Iscariot through his collusion with the Sanhedrin (for thirty pieces of silver, Zechariah 11:12) lay bare Israel's heart, in its hatred prepared to do in the Son of Man, fearless of the consequences, ready to murder the one who questioned as well as condemned the religiosity they had spawned.

The Son of Man's Prophetic Sayings

Three times in different locales throughout the unerring journey to Jerusalem, which the Author recorded in the Synoptics, Je-sus in specific ways prophesied his suffering, death, and resurrection to prepare, initially, the

---

41. John 13:2, 21, 27; etc.

disciples for the First Judgment and grant, second, new generations insight into the history of the Atonement. For in the eschatology definitive of the conclusion to the first dispensation the Lord determined the time and the place of the Crucifixion-Resurrection revelation. Luke 9:51; Matthew 16:21; John 11:7; etc.

In the first instance:

Matthew 16:21, "From that time Jesus began to show his disciples that he must go to Jerusalem and suffer many things from the elders and chief priests and scribes, and be killed, and on the third day be raised."

Mark 8:31, "And he began to teach them that the Son of Man must suffer many things and be rejected by the elders and the chief priest and the scribes and be killed, and after three days rise again."

Luke 9:22, "The Son of Man must suffer many things and be rejected by the elders and chief priests and scribes, and be killed, and on the third day be raised."

Obviously, Jesus and the Son of Man, the Savior and the Judge, are one and the same Person. What galled the Twelve more than the third-person identification of the Son of Man was the Messiah's suffering. A suffering messiah? A hitherto unimaginable concept, despite Isaiah 52:13—53:12.

In the second instance:

Matthew 17:22–23, "As they were gathering in Galilee, Jesus said to them, 'The Son of Man is about to be delivered into the hands of men, and they will kill him, and he will be raised on the third day.' And they were greatly distressed."

Mark 9:31, "... for he was teaching his disciples, saying to them, 'The Son of Man is going to be delivered into the hands of men, and they will kill him. And when he is killed, after three days he will rise.'"

Luke 9:44, "Let these words sink into your ears: The Son of Man is about to be delivered into the hands of men."

Despite the force of the third-person, obviously Jesus meant himself, to carry a mystery further. That, and also the passive voice, for the Father too determined time and place.

In the third instance:

Matthew 20:17–19, "And as Jesus was going up to Jerusalem, he took the twelve disciples aside, and on the way he said to them, 'See, we are going up to Jerusalem. And the Son of Man will be delivered over to the chief priests and scribes, and they will condemn him to death and deliver him over to the Gentiles to be mocked and flogged and crucified, and he will be raised on the third day.'"

Mark 10:32–34, "And they were on the road, going up to Jerusalem, and Jesus was walking ahead of them. And they were amazed, and those who followed were afraid. And taking the twelve again, he began to tell them what was to happen to him, saying, 'See, we are going up to Jerusalem, and the Son of Man will be delivered over to the chief priests and scribes, and they will condemn him to death and deliver him over to the Gentiles. And they will mock him and spit on him, and flog him and kill him. And after three days he will rise.'"

Luke 18:31–34, "And taking the twelve, he said to them, 'See, we are going up to Jerusalem, and everything that is written about the Son of Man by the prophets will be accomplished. For he will be delivered over to the Gentiles and will be mocked and shamefully treated and spit upon. And after flogging him, they will kill him, and on the third day he will rise.' But they understood none of these things. This saying was hidden from them, and they did not grasp what was said."

Did the third-person development of the Son-of-Man naming[42] compel first the Twelve to focus more on the Person of Jesus and less on the aversion to his suffering and the Judgment?

Throughout these prophetic statements each time in and to the community of the Twelve,[43] Jesus, fully aware, declared in full knowledge what awaited him. With the omniscience of divinity he also prepared his humanity to bear the punishment for the guilt of the sinning his own committed.

---

42. Against the Biblical grain: Conzelmann. *Jesus,* 45, "If the entire Son-of-man concept is posited as theology of the early church (*Gemeindetheologie*), one still must explain the fact that the title occurs only on the lips of Jesus. Yet it is possible to do this. The negative finding, namely that this title is never used as an address to Jesus, corresponds to the negative finding with the early Christological formulas. Unlike 'Christ' and 'Son of God,' Son of man' is not a confessional title. Jesus was not *called upon* as the Son of man, but *awaited* as such. The juxtaposition of the groups of sayings reflects the three aspects of the early church's faith, which also found expression elsewhere: the church looks back upon the earthly existence of Jesus (group a); it acknowledges in the kerygma its faith in his resurrection (with which an interpretation of the passion is connected) (group b); and it looks forward to the parousia (group c). The synthesis came then in the existence of the church as such. It was only relatively late that the church also consciously produced a synthesis by combining the individual groups of sayings into a whole."

43. Brown, *Jesus God and Man,* 62, "John too has three predictions by Jesus that the Son of Man (or Jesus) must be crucified and raised up." John 3:14, 8:28, 12:32.

The Son of Man's Futurity Sayings

In the traumatic tribulations of the First Judgment, Jesus also revealed the conclusion to the end of time and history.

Matthew, Mark, Luke

He prophesied, Matthew 24:30, "Then will appear in heaven the sign of the Son of Man, and then all the tribes of the earth will mourn, and they will see the Son of Man coming on the clouds of heaven with power and great glory."[44] Mark, 13:26,[45] and Luke, 21:27, also carried this prophecy forward for the benefit of all new generations. In the eschatological discourses— Matthew 24, Mark 13, and Luke 21[46]—Jesus bared the ultimate discomfort of all who realized too late failures at real amendment.

Luke, for one, without reservations repeated Jesus' summons to watchfulness, 21:36, "But stay awake at all times, praying that you may have strength to escape all these things that are going to take place, and to stand before the Son of Man." Matthew, too, blunt, send warning ahead to drifting-in-the-Faith generations, 24:44, "Therefore you also must be ready, for the Son of Man is coming at an hour you do not expect." Mark ends this eschatological discourse with the simply formidable, "Stay awake." All faithful, that is, the living covenant community, have to appear before the Judge, to hear the awing declaration of grace originating in the First Judgment.

---

44. Against the Biblical grain. Tödt. *The Son of Man in the Synoptic Tradition*, 34, "The Author of the Gospel of Matthew, who is more intimately attached to Jewish apocalyptic literature, . . . adds an allusion to the negative side of the Son of Man's appearance. The passage from Zechariah which he quotes in Matt. 24.30 points indirectly but clearly to the seriousness of the judgement at the parousia. He does not actually describe the Son of Man acting as a judge, but he definitely states that all the tribes of the earth will mourn when the sign of the Son of Man appears in heaven."

45. Against the Biblical grain: McGrath. *Christian Theology*, 278, "References by Jesus to 'the Son of Man coming in the clouds with great power and glory' (Mark 13:26) are thus, according to Bultmann, to be understood to refer to a figure *other than* Jesus. Bultmann suggested that the early church subsequently merged 'Jesus' and "son of Man,' understanding them to be one and the same. The early church thus invented the application of the term to Jesus."

46. Brown. *Jesus God and Man*, 75, "The eschatological discourse in Mk 13, Mt 24–25, and Lk 21 lists the signs that will precede the coming of the Son of Man, e.g., false-Messiahs, persecution, war, and cosmic cataclysms. While these chapters open with the question of the destruction of the Temple, they discuss both the punishment of Jerusalem and the Parousia; and it is very difficult to interpret what the apocalyptic signs were originally meant to precede."

Steadily, indeed, patiently, the Lord Jesus prepared his followers for the suddenness and the awesomeness of the Parousia. Matthew 24:27, "For as the lightning comes from the east and shines as far as the west, so will be the coming of the Son of Man." Luke 17:24, "For as the lightning flashes and lights up the sky from one side to the other, so will the Son of Man be in his day."[47] The command to preparedness reverberates through the living congregations for the unexpected hour to arrive. As the Deluge overtook Noah's generation, though warned by the herald of righteousness, 2 Peter 2:5; Genesis 7:4, and as deadening sulfur and fire rained upon Sodom and Gomorrah, though warned, 2 Peter 2:6; Genesis 19:14, thus the Parousia will utterly surprise the world.[48] Matthew 24:37–39,

> As were the days of Noah, so will be the coming of the Son of Man. For as in those days before the flood they were eating and drinking, marrying and giving in marriage, until the day when Noah entered the ark, and they were unaware until the flood came and swept them all away, so will be the coming of the Son of Man.

Luke presented the same more emphatically, to ensure that the believers out of the Gentiles shed every sort of unpreparedness. Luke 17:22–30,

> And he said to the disciples, 'The days are coming when you will desire to see one of the days of the Son of Man, and you will not see it. And they will say to you, "Look, there!" or "Look, here!" Do not go out or follow them. For as the lightning flashes and lights up the sky from one side to the other, so will the Son of Man be in his day. But first he must suffer many things and be rejected by this generation. Just as it was in the days of Noah, so will it be in the days of the Son of Man. They were eating and drinking and marrying and being given in marriage, until the day when Noah entered the ark, and the flood came and destroyed them all. Likewise, just as it was in the days of Lot—they were eating and drinking, buying and selling, planting and building, but on the day when Lot went out from Sodom, fire and sulfur rained down from heaven and

---

47. Against the Biblical grain: Dodd. *The Founder of Christianity*, 114, "Of course it is imaginative symbolism; but what does it symbolize? It occurs in association with language about the Last Judgment and the End of the World, which apparently are conceived (at least in some passages) to coincide with the coming of the Son of Man. We cannot but recognize here traits of the 'apocalyptic' hopes and speculations which, with a long ancestry behind them, revived in strength during the feverish years that preceded the fall of Jerusalem." See: 116.

48. Kee. *Jesus in History*, 82, "The appearance of the Son of Man, God's eschatological judge, will be as instantaneous and as public as a flash of lightning; it will not be a hidden event, as some Jewish sectaries expected or claimed with their 'Lo, here!'"

destroyed them all—so will it be on the day when the Son of Man is revealed.

Whether Matthew or Luke, such will be the Son of Man's appearing, glorious and fearful beyond measure. The command to the Church to prepare stands until times cease. In his appearing the Son of Man will be instantaneous, also public, as a flash of lightning surprising the night sky in the circumference; all idolatrously/ideologically locked away into complacency and occupied with mammonism will self-righteously ignore the command. Yet Jesus persisted, Matthew 24:44, " . . . you also must be ready, for the Son of Man is coming at an hour you do not expect."[49] In the Parousia[50] the punitive condemnation that fell on Noah's generation and on Lot's Sodomites will reform history eternally. The sudden coming of the Day will astonish most the damnably unprepared.[51]

As Jesus transformed the covenant community to prepare for the Parousia, so he reinforced second and third generations to stand at the ready. Matthew 25:31, "When the Son of Man comes in his glory, and all the angels with him, then he will sit on his glorious throne." At this prophecy even believers trembled, Matthew 16:27, "For the Son of Man is going to come with his angels in the glory of his Father, and then he will repay each person according to what he has done." Jesus allowed none to disengage from the Judgments,[52] not the First, not the Last.

---

49. Tödt. *The Son of Man in the Synoptic Tradition*, 50, "As uttered by Jesus, this saying is apparently not only meant to caution against the coming world-judgement in general; otherwise there would have been no need to mention Noah's behaviour in particular. The meaning is that the present generation, though living before the end, does not watch the signs of the times (cf. Luke 12.54-56 and par.; Mark 13.29f.) in the way Noah did. Hence the same will happen to this generation as happened to mankind in Noah's time; it will perish unsuspectingly."

50. The Parousia in translation often loses its glory. Matthew 24:3, the disciples to Jesus, "Tell us, when will these things be, and what will be the sign of your [*parousia*] and of the close of the age." Matthew 24:27, "For as the lightning comes from the east and shines as far as the west so will be the [*parousia*] of the Son of Man."

Against the biblical grain: Bultmann. *The Theology of the New Testament*, I, 29, " . . . the synoptic tradition contains no sayings in which Jesus says he will sometime (or soon) return. (Neither was the word *parousia*, which denotes the 'coming' of the Son of Man, ever understood in the earliest period of Christianity as 'return,' but correctly as 'arrival, advent.'"

51. Borg. *Jesus*, 255, "In the gospels, the sayings about the coming of the 'Son of Man' in the near future also seem clearly to refer to the second coming of Jesus."

52. Tödt. *The Son of Man in the Synoptic Tradition*, 226, "In the Gospel of Matthew, too, the Son of Man is seen to have especially the task of carrying out the office of the Judge of the world."

Before the Sanhedrin,[53] as Israel's leading judiciary fabricated a charge for Jesus' condemnation, he asserted, Matthew 26:64; Mark 14:62; Luke 22:69, "But from now on the Son of Man shall be seated at the right hand of the power of God." This prophetic saying, of course, reflected Daniel 7:13–14,[54] the one like the son of man approaching the Ancient of Days. Though Israel's judges presumed legal domination over the Judge and consigned him to the Roman death, Jesus prophesied that in the Parousia they belatedly will see him, the presiding Judge seated at the right hand of the Father, and hand down with finality the judgment revealed on Golgotha. In and with the First Judgment Jesus promised to meet those venal and venomous judges again in the Second Judgment, then with merciless specificity. The Synoptics affirmed the glory of the Son of Man at the right hand of the Father.[55]

Jesus, Lord God Almighty, governed the heavens and the earth with respect to the Parousia; in the glory of the end he shall vindicate his own and condemn the reprobates forever.

John

In the Fourth Gospel the Author/author combination fortified the Faith by calling second and third generations to remember that which was necessary for the ongoing Church, especially the multi-faceted glory of the Son of Man in his ministry. As such, each believing generation had to hold the

---

53. Against the Biblical grain: Tödt. *The Son of Man in the Synoptic Tradition*, 37, "The allusion to the coming Son of Man places the scene before the Sanhedrin in a definite light which illuminates the absurd arrogance of the earthly judges who wish to judge the one who confesses that he is the Christ and the Son of God and will be vindicated as such at the coming of the Son of Man."

54. Against the Biblical grain: Borg. *Jesus,* 264, "The symmetry is almost too good to be factual—Jesus was condemned for what amounts to an early Christian confession of faith. Jesus is the Messiah, the Son of God, who will come again on the clouds of heaven."

55. Tödt. *The Son of Man in the Synoptic Tradition,* 39, "In this scene a definite correlation of the designations Christ, Son of God and Son of Man is established by placing them as close together as possible. The designation Christ applies to the present; it will be confirmed by the parousia of the Son of Man."

Against the Biblical grain: Higgins. *Jesus and the Son of Man,* 19–20, "In fact, it seems most probable that Jesus neither referred to the Son of man *as an objective existent being* distinct from himself, nor therefore identified himself with such a figure. Nevertheless, I believe that he did see some kind of connection between himself and the Son of man *concept*—an interpretation which is more credible than any other known to me, and which removes the psychological difficulties to which reference has been made."

Faith in heart and in mind to move ahead, despite enemy diversions and socially/politically massaged upheavals. John, Spirit-moved, displayed Jesus' transcendence to a degree greater than the Synoptics, as the One who came from above. Moreover, John accentuated stronger the Son/Father bond. Both these identifications, the Son's transcendence and the Father/Son bond, ran strong in the Fourth Gospel.

At the same time, paradoxically, Jesus throughout the Fourth Gospel also called to mind his servant-status, the glory of the Servant prophetically alive in accomplishing Isa 52:13—53:12.[56] This immanence appears in the repeated assertions that the Father sent the Son to whom he then delegated the Second Judgment also.

Jesus' ministry brought about the First Judgment, John 12:31, "Now is the judgment of this world; now will the ruler of this world be cast out."

1–2

In several instances Jesus asserted the Son-of-Man name to reveal that he, and he alone, drew to him all whom the Father granted him for the New Church and the coming of the Kingdom.

At his ministry's beginning—according to John—Jesus declared to disbelieving Nathanael (alias Bartholomew), John 1:51, "Truly, truly, I say to you, you will see heaven opened, and the angels of God ascending and descending on the Son of Man."[57] Thus the Lord judged the man, one without guile, now included with the Twelve, even promised him to see "greater things" throughout the coming years, more so in the Parousia. Henceforth commissioned Nathanael, and Philip too, had to walk with Jesus, Golgotha-bound.

---

56. Toon. *Jesus Christ is Lord*, 28, "Whether we are right—in terms of Old Testament theology—to identify the Messiah-King, who is 'Son of God', with the Suffering Servant of Isaiah (42: 1ff., 49: 1ff., 50: 4ff., 52:13–53:12) is not easy to answer for scholars are not in agreement. It is possible that in Isaiah's thought the Servant was the whole Israel or a righteous remnant of the people. However, Jesus of Nazareth certainly appears to have identified himself as fulfilling to some extent the role of the Servant who suffers and is vindicated finally by God."

57. Against the Biblical grain: Bultmann. *The Theology of the New Testament*, II, 37, "... out of Jewish and earliest Christian tradition comes, finally, the title '*Son of Man*'... Though John mostly understands it in the sense of the Gnostic myth as a designation for the pre-existent one who became man and must be exalted again (1:51; 3:13f.; 12:23, 34; 13:31 and elsewhere), he nevertheless is referring to the Jewish and earliest Christian meaning in letting Jesus' office as judge of the world be founded upon his being Son of Man (5:27, unless this sentence is a redactional gloss)."

Slow-moving into the Faith, Nicodemus at first refused to believe the reality of the second birth. Therefore Jesus said to him, John 3:13–15, "No one has ascended into heaven except he who descended from heaven, the Son of Man. And as Moses lifted up the serpent in the wilderness, so must the Son of Man be lifted up, that whoever believes in him may have eternal life." As the Lord taught regeneration, a teaching too majestic and transcendent ever to occur to a finite being, he imposed this truth from above. Jesus, confronted by a unbelieving and nay-saying ruler of the Jews, thus called forth his judgeship and imparted to the man the grace of salvation. For Nicodemus believed the lifted-up Son of Man and, regenerated, attested to this fundamental of the Faith, John 19:39.

When Jesus heard that Pharisees had cast out of the local synagogue the man he had healed, he found him. This miracle highly actualized his authority over Jewish leadership and the multitudes burdened by faithlessness. In the short conversation encapsulated as John 9:35–38, the Lord most patiently revealed himself in his judgeship. "Jesus heard that they had cast him out, and having found him he said, 'Do you believe in the Son of Man?' He answered, 'And who is he, sir, that I may believe in him?' Jesus said to him, 'You have seen him, and it is he who is speaking to you.' He said, 'Lord, I believe,' and he worshiped him." In the face of the malice the man once blind and Jesus with him experienced from the Jews, the Son-of-Man name was in place, to strengthen the man in the justice the Lord exercised. This same justice he planned for the Twelve as well as all of the New Church, the whole of which condemned the Jews and, longer-range, also the Romans. In shepherding the man through the confrontation, which the Jews caused, the Lord revealed (once more) the significance of the Son-of-Man name. John 9:39, "For judgment I came into this world, that those who do not see may see, and those who see may become blind." This paradox came into daylight as another expression of the dividing-line. As Israel's judges illicitly moved to crucify the Judge, which he and the Father had planned for the salvation of the New Church, the murderous despots remained in the Old Church, eternally baffled and bypassed.

Frequently, as in the Synoptics, so throughout John, Jesus addressed the Crucifixion the fact of life. When Greeks, or proselytes, synagogue adherents out of the Gentiles, through the assistance of Philip and Andrew sought to see him, the Savior spoke of the immediate Gospel center, 12:23, "The hour has come for the Son of Man to be glorified." In this instance, not enemies but potential converts sought him out. Hence, with this antecedent to the Gentile mission the Lord pointed to ministry beyond Israel's demographics. Or, because of the Son-of-Man name, did Jesus recognize an animosity in these proselytes?

It remains important: Jesus alone selected those companions whom the Father had appointed. The multitudes followed him for reasons other than the coming of the Kingdom.

2–2

Jesus in John revealed also Son-of-Man namings as the Synoptics, to call the Pharisees and the Sadducees to account.

John 5:27 clarified directly Jesus' rulership in the court of life and death; the Father "... has given him authority to execute judgment, because he is the Son of Man." Within the brevity of John 5:25–27, the Son of God, the Son, and the Son of Man, that is, Jesus, stated the multifarious tasks he carried out, always and only serving through the Father-given authority.

In the "I am the Bread" presentation, Jesus commanded the multitude eager to see and eat the multiplication of loaves and fishes, 6:27a, "Do not labor for the food that perishes, but for the food that endures to eternal life, which the Son of Man will give you." As the preeminent Judge, Jesus separated food with temporary and temporal value from nourishment for eternal life. This latter food the Judge commanded Israel to eat, rather than the starvation diet known as the Oral Law. The Judge not only separated the believers from the unbelievers, he also granted the life-giving food, which determined placement in the First Judgment, and the Second.

Disbelief in Israel with respect to Jesus' ministry ran rampant, John 6:36; therefore he asked rhetorically, 6:62, "Then what if you were to see the Son of Man ascending to where he was before?" He, the Messiah, proclaimed the Gospel destructive of the Tradition of the Elders as well as the Jewish brand of self-righteousness. When, however, Jesus specified the Gospel—6:56, "Whoever feeds on my flesh and drinks my blood abides in me, and I in him"—many of the covenant drew back, murmuring, 6:66. Miracles, yes. Reformation of the heart? Yet the Lord's word granted the Spirit and the life, as opposed to the death inherent in the Oral Law.

John recorded the explosive tensions of hatred expressive of Jewish animosity. Jesus responded with a declarative, 8:28, "When you have lifted up the Son of Man, then you will know that I am he, and that I do nothing on my own authority, but speak just as the Father taught me." Totally in the care of the Father, the Lord walked also through this murderous clamor,

Cross-bound. To know him as the Judge in the horror of Golgotha[58] and afterward was too late for Israel's self-appointed judges.

At one point, the Father addressed the Son publicly. The unbelieving crowd, listening, interpreted the words as thunder or angel speech. In the swelling shiftlessness of such darkness Jesus again invoked his judging office. In response, according to John 12:34, for the first time others than Jesus expressed the Son-of-Man name.[59] "So the crowd answered him, 'We have heard from the Law that the Christ remains forever. How can you say that the Son of Man must be lifted up? Who is this Son of Man?'" Those Israelites recognized a unity between the Christ and the Son of Man, yet with obvious hostility called the Son-of-Man name into question, which enmity gave the reason for its usage on this occasion. That Old-Church crowd, ill-defined and resistant to the Savior's ministry, vindictively questioned his integrity as well as authority, for they sensed his divinity, a to them presumed equality with the God in whom they believed, an impossibility in Jewish monotheism. However, as the Light, Jesus warned unbelieving Israel against the darkness of the Tradition of the Elders.

Once more John recorded the majestic name that more than the others set Jesus apart. Lord, Savior, Messiah, Rabbi/Teacher, etc., drew the people to him. The Son-of-Man name alerted crowds and individuals to beckoning eternities far beyond human control as well as grasp. For an individual: at table for the Passover Jesus dismissed venom-laden Judas Iscariot with finality from his presence and when the Iscariot had departed declared with solemn dignity, John 13:31, "Now is the Son of Man glorified, and God is glorified in him." From this identifiably high point in his ministry he addressed the Twelve (temporarily eleven men), in a sense already accessing, gloriously confident, the finality of the Resurrection and the Ascension.

Hereafter, Jesus walking to the Cross no more identified himself as the Son of Man;[60] nevertheless, his kingship, inclusive its office of judging, dominated throughout the Fourth Gospel. With royal dominion, he governed the much-awaited history leading up the Cross, the Crucifixion by which he judged first Israel, simultaneously also the world of people as a whole.

---

58. Luke 23:39–43 related the one exception, a criminal crucified with Jesus.

59. See Acts 7:56 for the other.

60. Against the Biblical grain: Neill. *The Interpretation of the New Testament*, 165, in reference to theological developments in the early Church, " . . . to a very large extent the Son of Man has been forgotten, and remains in the Gospels as a hieroglyph, the true significance of which has been forgotten; the future belongs to the *Kyrios,* who is present in the act of worship.

John, as the Synoptics, glorified Jesus' Son-of-Man office; despite difference in presentation, the four maintained the unity of the Gospel. The consistency with respect to the Son-of-Man naming identified the Judge, Jesus, unquestionably.

V

Again, for what purpose and to what end did Jesus relative to the Son-of-Man office resolve to identify himself in the third person, as if he and the Son of man constituted separate and distinctive beings?

1. More than any other name, the Son-of-Man name set him apart, a necessary otherness for judgeship.
2. As the Judge he with righteousness and holiness revealed the standard of justice consistent with this office; no covetousness attached itself to or hid itself in his Person.
3. When enemies attacked him or (one of) the Twelve he warned with the Son-of-Man naming.
4. Predominantly in the Gospels occurs the Son-of-Man naming; as in Ezekiel, this name enforced the judgment first upon Israel. That Judgment completed, the name had served its purpose.[61]

Acts-Revelation

Four more times Author recorded the Son-of-Man name in the Scriptures, its majesty in judgeship forever secure.

Stephen, dying a martyr, full of the Holy Spirit declared, Acts 7:56, "Behold, I see the heavens opened, and the Son of Man standing at the right hand of God." Standing.[62] Intercessorily? As the exalted Judge Jesus

---

61. Neill. *The Interpretation of the New Testament*, 283, "After the Resurrection the title is no longer used. For this it would seem that there is a perfectly sound historical reason; what follows the Resurrection is testimony *about* Jesus, not the testimony *of* Jesus."

This reasoning is flat, though it may be true. Jesus as the Son of Man accomplished the Judgment and therefore this title was no longer required.

62. Normatively Israel's judges sat during the execution of office: Exodus 18:13; Isaiah 6:1; Matthew 26:64; Mark 14:62; Luke 22:69; Hebrews 10:12; Revelation 11:16, 14:14, and presumably also in Revelation 1:13.

perceived the sinfulness also of this murder in the name of Israel's God and held, condemning, the killers accountable.[63]

In Hebrews 2:6-8 the author recited Psalm 8:4-6, bringing and holding the placement of that Old Testament royal profession of faith in the New Testament Church.

> What is man, that you are mindful of him,
> or the son of man, that you care for him?
> You made him a little lower than the angels;
> you have crowned him with glory and honor,
> putting everything in subjection under his feet.

This recitation placed the regal function of judging pertinently not in the hands of everyman, certainly not. David as Israel's monarch had reflected—with awe—on the authority given him by way of the office, one consistent with image bearing and dominion.[64] The LORD God had crowned the man to execute this office; much more, and now supremely, the Father glorified the Son of Man, " . . . you have crowned him with glory and honor, putting everything in subjection under his feet." Empathically: as the LORD God put all in Israel under David's authority, thus the Father placed the earth, indeed, the universe under the Son's judgeship. The Spirit-driven Christological interpretation of Psalm 8 in Hebrews magnifies the Trinity.

To John, Revelation 1:13, 14:14, Jesus appeared like a son of man enveloped in majesty and crowned with dominion. In the first instance, seated in judgment, the sharp two-edged sword, the word issuing from his mouth, held attention. Moreover he carried the keys of Death and Hades. The sword symbolized his judging prowess, omniscient, and the keys represented his predestinarian powers, omnipotent. In the second instance, with no less majesty, Jesus' capably handled sharp sickle further signified his judging authority. Both visions unmistakably call forth Daniel 7:13-14, the "one like a son of man" who approached the Ancient of Days. Whereas in the Gospels Jesus stood forth physically approachable as the Son of Man, in the visions of Daniel and John his glory and majesty revealed awesomeness too great for languages of men.

---

63. Along with John 12:34, this is the second time that someone other than Jesus spoke the Son-of-Man name.

64. Pentecost. *The WORDS & WORKS of JESUS CHRIST*, 372, "By divine appointment (Gen. 1:26) creation was subjected to the authority of man, and that authority would be exercised by the Son of Man (Ps. 8:4-8.). Now as the Son of Man Jesus was exercising authority over creation."

Conclusion

In the Gospels the Son of Man revealed the totality and the finality of his judging office; he called Israel and the peoples of this world to appear before him. In consequence, representatives of Israel and Rome encircled the Cross, each to receive according to predestinarian design. They of the Faith—believing and living the Gospel—he called to his right hand. They against the Faith—disbelieving and denying the Gospel—the Judge of all the earth dismissed to the darkness on his left.

Before and after the Synoptics the Scriptures revealed the judging office inherent in the Son-of-Man name.

For now, the first Judgment is past.

The second Judgment reveals the power, wisdom, might, honor, glory, and blessing of the first.

BIBLIOGRAPHY

Borg, Marcus J. *Jesus: Uncovering the Life, Teachings, and Relevance of a Religious Revolutionary.* New York: HarperCollins, 1989.

Brown, Raymond E. *Jesus God and Man: Modern Biblical Reflections.* London-Dublin, 1968.

———. *The Virginal Conception & Bodily Resurrection of Jesus.* New York: Paulist, 1973.

Bultmann, Rudolf. Tr. Kendrick Grobel. *Theology of the New Testament, I&II.* New York: Charles Scribner's, 1951, 1955.

Conzelmann, Hans. Tr. J. Raymond Lord. *Jesus.* Philadelphia: Fortress, 1973.

Crossan, John Dominic. *Jesus: A Revolutionary Biography.* HarperSanFrancisco, 1994.

Cullmann, Oscar. *The New Testament Library: The Christology of the New Testament.* Philadelphia: Westminster, 1959, 1963.

Dodd, C.H. *The Founder of Christianity.* London: Colliers-Macmillan, 1970.

Fredriksen, Paula. *Jesus of Nazareth, King of the Jews: A Jewish Life and the Emergence of Christianity.* New York: Alfred A. Knopf, 1999.

Funk, Robert W. *Honest to Jesus: Jesus For a New Millennium.* HarperSanFrancisco: 1996.

Hendriksen, William. *New Testament Commentary: The Gospel of Mark.* Grand Rapids: Baker Book, 1975.

———. *New Testament Commentary: Exposition of the Gospel According to Matthew.* Grand Rapids: Baker 1973.

———. *New Testament Commentary: The Gospel of Luke.* Grand Rapids: Baker, 1978.

Higgins, A.J.B. *Jesus and the Son of Man.* London: Lutterworth, 1964.

Kee, Howard Clark. *Jesus in History: An Approach to the Study of the Gospels.* New York: Harcourt, Brace & World, 1970.

McGrath, Alister E. *Christian Theology: An Introduction.* Oxford: Blackwell, 1994.

McKenna, Megan. *Parables: The Arrows of God.* Maryknoll, New York: Orbis, 2006.

Neill, Stephen. *The Interpretation of the New Testament 1861–1961.* New York: Oxford University Press, 1962.

Pentecost, J. Dwight. *The WORDS & WORKS of JESUS CHRIST: A Study of the Life of Christ*. Grand Rapids: Zondervan, 1891.

Rosen, Moishe. *Y'SHUA: The Jewish Way to Say Jesus*. Chicago: Moody, 1982.

Spykman, Gordon J. *Reformational Theology: A New Paradigm for Doing Dogmatics*. Grand Rapids: Eerdmans, 1992.

Taylor, Vincent. *The Names of Jesus*. London: Macmillan, 1962.

Tödt, H.E. Tr. Dorothea M. Barton. *The Son of Man in the Synoptic Tradition*. London: SCM, 1965.

Toon, Peter. *Jesus Christ Is Lord*. Valley Forge: Judson, 1978.

MANY SON-OF-GOD NAMINGS

A RICH AND MEANINGFUL history identifying sons of God moves through the Scriptures. At times this naming identifies people and angels. Most profoundly the weight of this identification concentrates on Jesus Christ, the Son of God relative to his work of salvation and God the Son relative to his divinity; with respect to the Son-of-God and God-the-Son namings, these the Author placed within the trinitarian unity of the Divinity. In the revelation from Genesis through the Apocalypse attention falls first on the sons of God and second concentration on Christ Jesus. Thus, then, the structure of this composition:

> The Sons of God
> The Son of God, and
> God the Son.

These headings demonstrate the essence of this scriptural theme in its rich and meaningful identity.

THE SONS OF GOD

In the Old Testament the Author revealed many sons of God, inclusive then daughters too. These instances of naming illustrated the intimate covenant bond between the Creator, the Christ and his people. Also, each naming marked the humanness of covenant inclusion for responsibility before the LORD God, the Christ. Thus he began with Adam's identification, "the son of God," Luke 3:38, upon whom he with Eve placed dominion over the earth.[1]

---

1. Genesis 1:28, "And God blessed them. And God said to them, 'Be fruitful and multiply and fill the earth and subdue it and have dominion over the fish of the sea and over the birds of the heavens and over every living thing that moves on the earth.'" Living things eventually also included the subtle serpent.

Moreover, the Scriptures' Author identified sons as well as daughters of God creatively in Israel's distinctive circumstances. Out of the ordinary, however, at one point he included angels. Primarily, the sons-of-God naming concentrated on the men and women populating the covenant community, those whom the Christ—generation upon generation—gathered as his. For these men as well as women the LORD God throughout the ordering of time created Israel—Old Testament and New—and intended that his people as one acknowledge the identification of sons and daughters only because of grace, glorious in its unmerited mercy.

1–2

At an undisclosed point in the history of Job's earlier life the LORD brought the sons of God, archangels, together in council, Satan among them. Studiously, in these councils the LORD distanced the Adversary from the lively worship of glorious messengers, Job 1:6–12. Later, 2:1, the LORD again brought these sons of God and Satan together in order to remind the latter of the range within which he had license to trouble Job. Toward the conclusion of this wisdom literature, 38:7, the Author remembered the angels in the days of creation, in which work Job had not participated, " . . . when the morning stars sang together and all the sons of God shouted in joy." The intimacy of the LORD God and these earliest witnesses to creation disclosed the power of this sons-of-God naming.

V

One negative identification of the sons of God the Author disclosed in the time frame prior to the Flood. Genesis 6:2, " . . . the sons of God saw that the daughters of man were attractive. And they took as their wives any they chose." Those sons of God, the descendants of Seth and, hence the covenant community, purposefully and disobediently crossed over the dividing-line and through "mixed marriages" blended in with the descendants of Cain, a process of world conformity. Cain whom the LORD had dismissed from the covenant community initiated the first evidence of the anti-covenant community, the community with which the sons of Seth identified themselves. This occurred at the time Nephilim lived; these mighty ones who regarded neither God nor man reigned as lawless rulers. In the age of these rebellious Nephilim, and afterwards, Genesis 6:4, " . . . the sons of God came into the daughters of man and they bore children to them. These were the mighty men who were of old, the men of renown." The blending of the two communities produced even more rebellious offspring.[2] Only on account of the covenant membership did the Christ acknowledge these people.

More to the point, the LORD God called the numerous many of Israel by this illustrious name. Exodus 4:22–23, Moses to Pharaoh, "Thus says the LORD, Israel is my firstborn son, and I say to you, 'Let my son go that he may serve me.'"[3] Hence the LORD included all Israel, the men and also the women, in the firstborn community. This sonship reappeared as a comparative in Moses' history of Israel's journeying, Deuteronomy 1:31, "... in the wilderness where you have seen how the LORD your God carried you, as a man carries his son, all the way that you went until you came to this place." Deuteronomy 8:5, another comparative, "Know then in your heart that, as a man disciplines his son, the LORD your God disciplines you." Yahweh thus treated Israel as his offspring.[4]

Excursus

Throughout the Scriptures the LORD God's expressive fatherhood served as the protective against the follies of idolatrous ambition.

2. The Nephilim in Numbers 13:33 were men renowned in rebellion against the LORD God, similarly those in 2 Samuel 21:15–22, men bold in the intimidation of Israel. See: Goliath—1 Samuel 17:1–58; 2 Samuel 21-19.

3. An explanation of this father-son bond. Joshua called Achan, "My son," without a paternal claim to fatherhood, Joshua 7:19. Rather, Israel's leader took a protective stance over against the thief, as yet willing the man to acknowledge his sin and repent. Boaz in the patriarchal manner called Ruth, "my daughter," though absent every such blood connection, Ruth 2:8, 3:10–11; the man thereby shielded the young woman against abuse. David anticipated a father-son sharing between Nabal and himself, 1 Samuel 25:8. Elisha called after Elijah. "My father, my father! The chariots of Israel and its horsemen!" Second Kings 2:12. Elisha knew his predecessor in the prophetic office as the guardian of Northern Israel. Job defined himself as the father of the needy and the protector even of strangers, Job 29:16. The father-son, or father-daughter, metaphor extended beyond procreation, not to a secondary meaning, but to one of the main responsibilities of fatherhood, protection of mother and children.

4. Synonymously with sonship the LORD God variously also spoke of Israel as his children:

Deuteronomy 32:6b, "Is he not your father who created you, who made you and established you?"

Hosea 1:10a, "Yet the number of the children of Israel shall be like the sand of the sea, which cannot be measured or numbered."

Hosea 11:1, "When Israel was a child, I loved him, and out of Egypt I called my son."

Hosea 13:13, "The pangs of childbirth come for him, but he is an unwise son, for at the right time he does not present himself at the opening of the womb."

This generous father-analogy in comprehensive ways enriched the biblical history marking similarities and dissimilarities between the Christ and, specifically, covenant fathers. From the beginning fathers procreated and then safeguarded progeny, parentage attentive to protection; procreative efforts were momentary, while protectivity lasted for decades. Similarly, upon creating his people by way of conversion the Christ revealed his paternal care through consistent protectivity.

V

At specific times, then, for shielding[5] Israel the LORD revealed the protectivity inherent in fatherhood. According to Deuteronomy 14:1, Moses in the name of the Christ recognized Israel nationally as the "sons of the LORD your God," therewith to strengthen and also to guard the travelling nation against the infernal horrors of idolatry. Accordingly, reflective Moses asked in a rhetorical manner, "Is he not your father, who created you, who made you, and who established you?" Israel served the Christ as the historical bedding for the Incarnation.

Similarly, drawing out 2 Samuel 7:14a's light, the LORD loved David paternally. "I will be to him a father, and he shall be to me a son." By means of this fatherliness he promised to withhold David from iniquity in the way of sanctification.

Further, the author of Psalm 2, explicitly 2:7b, revealed the glory of David's analogical sonship, " . . . you are my [s]on;[6] today I have begotten you." The creative fiat of begetting lasted by a moment, whereas the paternal defense lasted decades. In effect the LORD promised to secure the second[7] monarch against his own sinning and from the unchained license of idolatrous forces. Towards the end of his reign, David eyeing the high priority of the Temple construction, magnified the LORD God. First Chronicles 29:10b, "Blessed are you, O LORD, the God of Israel our father, forever and ever." Through David, a type of the Christ, the Preincarnate Lord protected his promises to Israel/Jacob in order to arrive at the Incarnation. For the Temple construction the LORD had created Israel and through the

---

5. Genesis 15:1b, "Fear not, Abram, I am your shield; your reward shall be very great."

6. The ESV capitalization of "son" removes the prophetic typology not only from the text, also from the psalm. Only after the Incarnation did the Author interpret the Psalmist's "son" as the" Son."

7. The third, counting Ish-bosheth, 2 Samuel 2:8–11.

Jacob-naming revealed his perseverance to come to the point of the Old Testament dispensation. Therefore the Christ jealously and consistently fortified David against human enemies, 1 Samuel 16:1–13; 2 Samuel 2:1–4. Before and after the man's coronation the LORD consistently safeguarded him.

Psalm 68:5 further revealed high praise for the Christ, "Father of the fatherless and protector of widows is God in his holy habitation." Of course, he had not procreated those orphans and widows, but through fatherhood activities certainly shielded the vulnerable in Israel.

Ethan the Ezrahite promised that a Davidide prayed before an imminent crisis. Psalm 89:26–27,

> He shall cry to me, "You are my Father, my God,
> and the Rock of my salvation."

And the LORD's reply?

> And I will make him the firstborn,
> the highest of the kings of the earth.

This monarchial *Father*-cry called for protection against superior enemy forces physically advancing. The Christ revealed his faithfulness to mitigate and/or turn away the savagery of enmitous hordes—never idle fears.

V

Throughout the Proverbs, starting at 1:8, the son-naming identified teacher-student bonds and cut to the purpose of biblical wisdom literature, the erasure of covetousness.

V

The messianic pronouncement of Isaiah 9:1–7 included among Yahweh's names also "Eternal Father," who promised in the national anxieties prior to the Assyrian invasion to protect and care for his children. The "Eternal Father" as the other names disclosed the lofty glory and the laudable authority of the pre-incarnate Son. He declared his eternally valid protection against the evils of empire and the pretensions of nations imperiling Israel.

Isaiah 43:6–7 revealed in another basic communication the authority of the pre-incarnate Son, thereby further preparing Israel's hope during the Exile.

> I will say to the north, Give up, and to the south, Do not withhold;
> brings my sons from afar and my daughters from the end of the earth,
> everyone who is called by my name,
> whom I created for my glory,
> whom I formed and made.

The Lord thus extended maximal security to his sons and daughters even if they for rebellious living had doubly earned this exile, captivity, or slavery; all the authorities of the earth, mere men, had to emancipate those who were the LORD's. Out of procreative jealousy and as the providential God he cared for his own, because of the covenantal promises.

Isaiah 63:16 exuded protectivity for Israel, the covenant nation, its roots within the patriarchy; the covenant promises to Abraham, Isaac, and Jacob retained eternal validity.

> For you are our Father,
> though Abraham does not know us,
> and Israel does not acknowledge us;
> you, O LORD, are our Father,
> our Redeemer from of old is your name.

With deep-rooted love the God of Israel oversaw from generation to generation the historical wellbeing of Abraham's seed.

At times Israel, contrary to its rebelliousness, even responded faithfully. Isaiah 64:8,

> But now, O LORD, you are our Father;
> we are the clay, and you are our potter;
> we are all the work of your hand.

At least toward the conclusion of this prophetic work Isaiah held out a twinkling hope for covenant faithfulness on the part of the sons (and daughters) of God.

V

Jeremiah carried the father-son analogy deep into Israel's heart to bring about conversion in and among the sons and daughters of God. Jeremiah 3:4–5c,

> Have you not just now called to me,
> "My father, you are the friend of my youth—
> will he be angry forever, will he be indignant to the end?"

More pertinent, through Jeremiah's prophetics the LORD God revealed an end to his patience. His people worshiped idols and then dared call upon his name? Step by step, the Father, the pre-incarnate Son, prepared Israel for the justice of the Exile. For the covenant community to bow before idols and still also call upon the Father for protection? In the toxicity of faithlessness the LORD challenged Israel prophetically. Jeremiah 3:19,

> I said
> How I would set you among my sons,
> and give you a pleasant land,
> a heritage most beautiful of all nations.
> And I thought you would call me, My Father,
> and would not turn from following me.

Rocklike in unbelief, rather than reliance upon the Father, Israel's sons and daughters communally groveled before idols for *purchasing* life, food, and space. Consistently, generation upon generation, even as Northern Israel, Jeremiah 31:9c, " . . . I am a father to Israel, and Ephraim is my firstborn." Naming the parallelism between Israel and Ephraim, his *firstborn*, took nothing away from Judah's primogeniture; only the LORD signified the covenant origins of the Ten Tribes, which they rejected. Jeremiah 31:20.

V

In dependence upon the Messiah's fatherhood fathers too protected respective progeny, in part therewith to remember covenant roots. In a powerful way the LORD summoned Israel to remember these origins. Psalm 78:1–4; Deuteronomy 32:7,

> Remember the days of old;
> consider the years of many generations;
> ask your father, and he will show you,
> your elders, and they will tell you.

Fathers had to instruct children in Israel's malleability to sin. Deuteronomy 32:17, "They sacrificed to demons that were no gods, to gods they had never known, to new gods that had come recently, whom your fathers had never dreaded." With such instruction in head and heart fathers led sons and daughters into waiting tomorrows.

V

Paul to the Synagogue at Antioch in Pisidia declared Jesus' Sonship, therewith expressly his divinity. Acts 13:32–33, to Gentiles, "And we bring you the good news that what God promised to the fathers, this he has fulfilled to us their children by raising Jesus, as also it is written in the second Psalm,

> 'You are my Son,
> today I have begotten you.'"

The father-reference applied originally to Abraham, Isaac, and Jacob, but also to the Israel at Mt. Sinai. Paul addressing recently converted Gentiles revealed fulfilment of the prophecy emanating out of Psalm 2 to show that the generation that had heard the Incarnation announcement and suffered the Crucifixion judgment gave way to the entry of Gentiles into salvation.

Explicitly, relative to Psalm 2, in the first dispensation, Yahweh, the Lord Jesus with pre-incarnation authority enthroned David. In and with the New Testament dispensation God the Father, thus the Apostle, selected the second psalm to declare the awesomeness of the Resurrection-Ascension glory; this Jesus in his divinity and humanity, the Father placed at this right hand to rule heaven and earth—to the consternation of unbelievers and for the hope of the believers. Now the sonship is of a different magnitude, not between the Lord and a man, but between God the Father and the Son of God. This transformation memorizes the vast difference between the two dispensation for the benefit of Gentiles. Similarly in Hebrews 1:5, "For to which of the angels did God ever say,

> 'You are my Son,
> today I have begotten you'?

Or again,

> 'I will be to him a father,
> and he shall be to me a son'?"

Jesus as the Firstborn inherited and owns all according to the law of primogeniture,[8] inclusive angelic forces, to say nothing more of the kings and the empires of the earth. Thus the sonship strong in Psalm 2 underwent an awesome transformation, the Father declaring the Son of God the Lord of all creation.

---

8. Genesis 21:10, 27:27–29.

MANY SON-OF-GOD NAMINGS

V

Throughout the seventy years of the Exile, Jeremiah 25:11, 29:10; Daniel 9:2, the LORD God prepared a remnant as the sole covenant community for resettlement in and about Jerusalem. To that community Malachi addressed questions, which he also answered, 2:10, "Have we not all one Father? Has not one God created us? Why then are we faithless to one another, profaning the covenant of our fathers?" Hollowing out love of neighbor, the part of the Summary of the Law that makes the love of God apparent, still stifled Israel's hope on the doorstep to the second dispensation.

Summarily, then, throughout the Old Testament Scriptures the LORD God revealed many sons and daughters, each instance illustrative of the intimate covenant bond between himself and Israel. Each revelation marked out his fatherhood. It bears repeating that the sons-of-God naming identifies the people of the covenant.

2–2

At times New Testament writers referred to believers as "children of God," as in John 1:12. In this mode of address too the Bible's Author in continuance with the Old Testament documented the sons-of-God naming specific to all who believed the Person of the Christ. This *little-children* language never appeared as a diminutive of personhood, patronizing, but as evidence of the Apostle's pastoral care.

Paul equally wrote freely to the children/sons of God. Romans 8:14, "For all who are led by the Spirit of God are (sons – Gr.) of God." Romans 8:16–17, "The Spirit himself bears witness with our spirit that we are children of God, and if children, then heirs—heirs of God and fellow heirs with Christ, provided we suffer with him in order that we may also be glorified with him." Romans 8:19–23. More emphatically, Romans 9:8, " . . . it is not the children of the flesh who are the children of God, but the children of the promise are counted as offspring." So, too, Galatians 3:26, "... for in Christ Jesus you are all sons of God, through faith." So, too, Galatians 4:28, "Now you, brothers, like Isaac, are children of promise." Thus the Apostle, always within the covenant bond, identified believers as sons (and daughters) of God.

Hebrews' author also worked with this reliable family analogy. Hebrews 2:14–15, "Since therefore the children share in flesh and blood, he himself likewise partook of the same things, that through death he might destroy the one who has the power of death, that is, the devil, and deliver all those who through fear of death were subject to lifelong slavery." The family analogy intensified the bond.

The elderly Apostle John favored addressing believers as "little children." First John 2:1, 12, 13, 18, 3:1a, 10; 2 John 1, 13; etc. Paul, in places too found this naming expressive of his apostolic heart, 1 Corinthians 4:14; Galatians 4:19. Both men suffered intensely and much for the sake of the Gospel; aging and approaching death they looked at the Church manifested primarily in Asia Minor as children with much to learn and experience in the name of the Christ.

Sons and daughters of God circumscribed the believers; they acknowledged Jesus who on the Cross agonized in his human nature under the burdens of guilt his people earned sinning. Due to his victory over death all his knew and obeyed his lordship. Hence, sons and daughters represented the remarkable covenant name and therewith ennobled the Church.

V

Sons/children of God from the beginning to the end are people remarkable for the grace of salvation that motivates the work of the Church and the Kingdom. By such naming Jesus identifies all his.

THE ONLY SON OF GOD

Incomparable differences separated the sons and daughters of God from the Son of God. This distinction centered in Jesus' divine as well as human natures—without penetrating into the ineffable glory of the impenetrable Trinity. The Son-of-God naming therefore revealed his Person in relation to the Atonement. Hence, Son of God consistently equals Savior.

Not only John 3:16[9] revealed Jesus as the only Son; this uniqueness the Holy Spirit first created in and through the Incarnation, as recorded in Luke's Gospel. Archangel Gabriel to Mary, 1:31–33,

> ... behold, you will conceive in your womb and bear a son, and you shall call his name Jesus. He will be great and will be called the Son of the Most High God. And the Lord God will give him the

---

9. John 3:16 is clear in its pronouncement regarding the "only Son," the "only" specifically interpreting *monogeny*. Older translations intended the Greek to say, "only begotten," which fitted in the theology of eternal generation, but disturbed Luke 1:35, the fact that the Spirit *sired* the Son. At the same time, this *monogeny* forcefully stressed the unique bond between the Father and the Son of God.

throne of his father David,[10] and he will reign over the house of Jacob forever, and of his kingdom there will be no end.

In response to this awe-inspiring announcement Mary asked, "How will this be, since I am a virgin?" And the archangel's answer?

> The Holy Spirit will come upon you,
> and the power of the Most High will overshadow you;
> therefore the child to be born will be called holy—
> the Son of God.[11]

The Incarnation constituted the first revelation of the Son of God; this naming Peter associated with the Messiah, the Christ, Matthew 16:16.

8–1

Within the trinitarian structure of this revelation, 1) the fact stands out that God the Holy Spirit *fathered* God the Son, and 2) the fact that the naming, the Son of God, encapsulated Jesus' two natures, the divine and the human. Also, 3) here for the first time, against every assertion of the Son's eternal generation[12] the historicity of the Son of God appears. Thus, Mark, 1:1, began, "The beginning of the gospel of Jesus Christ, the Son of God." This naming recognized Jesus' saviorhood in its historical setting

Only commencing with the Gospels appears the trinitarian distinction between the Son of God, God the Father, and God the Spirit. Contrary to superficial readings and other follies of eisegesis the Scriptures reveal no hierarchy in the Trinity, as if the Father surpasses the Son of God in authority and glory. Nor are the Father and the Son-of-God more glorious and authoritative than the Holy Spirit. The Church throughout the ages confessed the equality of the trinitarian Persons by way of the Athanasian Creed. Discernibly, the Father protected the Son of God's humanity throughout the vortex of the hellish agony on the way to and in the Crucifixion.

8–2

---

10. This connection to King David revealed Jesus as a Davidide, *the* Davidide, 2 Samuel 7:12; Acts 2:30–31.

11. Paul's singular assertion of the Incarnation, Galatians 4:4, "But when the fullness of time had come, God sent forth his Son, born of woman, born under . . . law, so that we might receive adoption as sons."

12. Specifically in the Nicaeno-Constantinopolitan and the Athanasian Creeds.

As the New Testament Church throughout the Roman Empire settled into Spirit-moved congregational formatting, her members confronted the rationalism of the Gentiles, at first in the spirit of Plato, Neoplatonism or Gnosticism. Students of the Bible, fluent in the language of the Gentiles, struggled with that Greek philosophy, which encouraged penetration into the mysteries of the gods, hence also to understand the unknowability of Jesus' two natures in the one Person.

Over the early centuries of the Church various *understandings* of the Son of God maximized or minimized the secret of the two natures in Jesus' Person.

One. To maximize the distance between the humanity and the divinity of Jesus, Apollinarius denied the fullness of the Incarnation: Jesus possessed a human body as well as soul, with an added divine spirit; without a human spirit Jesus' humanity missed an active ingredient of humanness. Also maximizing the distance between the two natures, Nestorius posited the Son of God with two separate and distinct centers of consciousness. Greek mindedness to penetrate and understand the Person of Jesus taught the Church to avoid such rationalistic errors.

Two. Minimizing the divine-human distinction, Gnostics lessened the separation; adherents of such sects believed his divinity and rejected his humanity. Docetism thereby insisted that Jesus had only the appearance of a human body. Ebionites taught that God adopted Jesus, adoptionism, and at his baptism bestowed divinity upon him, by which he also established his own fatherhood. Arius found that Jesus was the first and greatest of God's creatures, but not divine. Eutychus had the Son of God in one person and one nature, the divine subsuming the human, a composite neither human nor divine—monophysitism. One Sergius of Constantinople wanted a Son of God fully divine as well as fully human, however with a divine will only—monothelitism.

In the seventeenth century yet Neo-Scholasticism sought to penetrate rationalistically the Incarnation, promulgating the theory of eternal generation as expressed in the Nicene Creed (the historic Nicaeno-Constantinopolitan) and the Athanasian. According to this Arian idea the Father created the Son from eternity to eternity, God of God, which creation before creation may have made sense to rationalistic spirits, but which diminished the astonishing fact that the Word became flesh. Moreover, such eternal generation presupposed a work of creation *long before* the creator initiated the history of Genesis.

As well, the theory of eternal generation inserted into the Trinity's ontological unity a hierarchy, the Father over the Son, to which Scriptures gave no trace of support. Distinctions between the persons appeared only after the Creation, more sharply at the Incarnation.

In deep and profound ways through Greek rationalism early thinkers attempted to breach and comprehend Jesus' Person, even the bond between the divine and the human. At the same time because trinitarian confusions compounded this centuries-long Christological wrangling to know the impossible, maximizing or minimizing the two natures in the one Person carried unfaithfulness into the Church, causing ideological sects and streams carrying leaders with followers into condemnation.

8–3

The Church believed the mystery inherent in Jesus' divine and human natures; the Holy Spirit called not through insufferable Greek flowerings of rationalism, but through faith to believe the Son of God. All of the Church then trusted the perspicuity of the Scriptures, specifically now passages as Luke 1:32–33, 35; Matthew 1:20–21; Galatians 4:4; and even Revelation 12:1–6.

By means of Gabriel's announcements to Mary and to Joseph the Author of the Scriptures named the Son of God Jesus for the first time; that is, in the trinitarian unity the overshadowing Spirit sired the Son of God, the bonding of his divinity from all eternity—equal to the Father's and the Spirit's—and of his humanity through Mary, woman.[13] The Child thus procreated Matthew 1:20 corroborated. To Joseph then, " . . . do not fear to take Mary as your wife, for what is conceived in her is from the Holy Spirit." Two natures inhabited and comprised the Person of the Son of God, a bonding mentally incomprehensible, beyond the profoundest cogitations of the mind. Thus the matchless Son of God entered into the history of the Church as her Lord and Savior, the Christ, or the Word become flesh. Early Christological controversies failed to break the mystery of his uniqueness; he is beyond every examination and penetration, subtle or audacious, the bond between the human and divine natures inviolable.

In and with the Incarnation the Author of the Scriptures revealed the profound distinctions between the Father and the Son of God. After the Church gave birth to the Son of God, Revelation 12:1–6, the actual Father-Son bond enlivened the Faith in ways impossible prior to Gabriel's revelation. In that unveiling the Son of God for the work of salvation in the

---

13. The Incarnation and Mary's participation therein, giving the Son of God an actual human body and soul escalated pharisaical opposition even more; they were conditioned to expect nothing good from women.

Church depended upon the Father, which dependency Jesus' human nature required. However the unique bonding of the two natures in the one Person established Jesus' inimitable signature for the work of salvation.

8–4

Throughout the Gospels God the Father in the trinitarian bond acknowledged the Son of God as his, not through procreation nor through adoption, but for working together with the Spirit to gain the salvation of the Church and the coming of the Kingdom.

At Jesus' baptism the Father addressed the many gathered about John the Baptizer by the Jordan. Matthew 3:17, "This is my beloved Son, with whom I am well pleased." Mark 1:11, "You are my beloved Son; with you I am well pleased." Luke 3:22b, "You are my Son; with you I am well pleased." As the Father recognized the Son of God as his and as the Spirit in the form of dove descended upon Jesus, the Father in that trinitarian revelation addressed many, primarily for the benefit of Jesus at the start of his ministry, confirming the omnipotence and the omniscience shared in the Father-Son of God bond on the way to the Crucifixion. John, the Apostle, too perceived the significance of this baptism. John 1:29–34,

> The next day [the Baptizer] saw Jesus coming toward him, and said, "Behold, the Lamb of God, who takes away the sin of the world! This is he of whom I said, 'After me comes a man who ranks before me, because he was before me.' I myself did not know him, but for this purpose I came baptizing with water, that he might be revealed to Israel."
>
> And John bore witness: "I saw the Spirit descend from heaven like a dove, and it remained on him. I myself did not know him, but he who sent me to baptize with water said to me, 'He on whom you see the Spirit descend and remain, this is he who baptizes with the Holy Spirit. And I have seen and borne witness that this is the Son of God.'"

By that baptismal ceremony centered in and about the Jordan the Father-Son of God bond, or the Son of God-Father bond, appeared in its earliest profundity. This revelation evidenced that the Father did not generate the Son but that he reached out to protect and sustain the Son of God in his humanity, first in this way: the Father too held all accountable who damaged the Son of God's in any way, either in his Person or in his work.

During the Transfiguration, then, the Father spoke mainly to Peter, James, and John. Matthew 17:5b, "'This is my beloved Son, with whom I am well pleased." Mark 9:7b, "This is my beloved Son; listen to him." Luke 9:35b, "This is my Son, my chosen One; listen to him!" These words the Father directed at the leaders of the Twelve, and thus to the Church, which Peter indicated by recounting the event, 2 Peter 1:16–21. Nevertheless, the Father's directive encompassed the Son of God too, placing him central in the believing covenant community.

John, the Apostle, similarly recounted this protectivity, 12:28, first Jesus to the Father, "'Father, glorify your name.' Then a voice came from heaven, 'I have glorified it, and I will glorify it again.'" A crowd of Israelites following the Messiah heard the voice without comprehension; its message, however, was clear: as Jewish enmity enclosed about the Son of God the Father's warning to the Church, Israel, sounded most clearly.

8–5

Throughout the Synoptics early in Jesus' ministry the Father and the Son of God reaffirmed the trinitarian bonding in this manner, fulfilling Hosea 11:1/Matthew 2:13–15, "Out of Egypt I called my son." Whereas the LORD himself had called Israel his firstborn, Exodus 4:22–23, now the Father summoned the Son of God to Canaan, all the while shielding him, specifically his human nature, against Herodian tyranny.

At one point the Son of God thanked the Father for clarity in predestination, Matthew 11:25–30/Luke 10:22, quoting the latter, "All things have been handed over to me by my Father, and no one knows who the Son is except the Father, or who the Father is except the Son and anyone to whom the Son chooses to reveal him." Also at laying the dividing-line the Son of God left no doubt with respect to the unity in working with the Father.

Peter's confession on behalf of the Twelve, which confession Jesus had created and then elicited, centered the unity between the trinitarian Persons, Matthew 16:16; Mark 8:29; Luke 9:20, quoting Matthew's version, "You are the Christ, the Son of the living God." Because the Father with the Son of God initiated this indisputable confession, both the Son of God and the Father cooperated in and through the Twelve to create this founding statement for the now eschatologically hastening New Testament Church.

At the trial the high priest in his capacity as office bearer commanded Jesus to acknowledge his origin. Monotheistic Caiaphas to Jesus, Mark 14:61; Luke 22:70; Matthew 26:63, "I adjure you by the living God, tell us if you are the Christ, the Son of God." Even though the high priest appealed to the Jewish god, Jesus gave the affirmative answer, most pointedly, "You have said so." Then the Sanhedrin accused him of blasphemy. As both the Father and the Son of God had repeatedly over three years publicly affirmed Jesus' Sonship, once more at the trial the Lord and Savior confirmed the obvious. Thus publicly and juridically Israel denounced her Savior.

Not only in the Sanhedrin but also about Golgotha the Son of God's avowal of divinity led to blasphemy; his monotheistic enemies out of the covenant community struggled for the last word. Matthew 27:40, 43, "He trusts in God; let God deliver him now, if he desires him for he said, 'I am the Son of God.'" The god of the Sanhedrin and of the blasphemers at Golgotha was not God the Father, the Father of Jesus. That god was the devil who slyly had inserted himself at the place from which he could do the most damage. He had no son and had wanted nothing of Jesus except his submission, Matthew 4:9; Luke 4:7.

In Jesus' dying and death, a Roman centurion, a man inured to the sufferings of crucifixions, declared, Mark 15:39; Matthew 27:54p, "Truly this was the [s]on of God!"[14] Whether or not the centurion and the troops under him, no doubt idolaters, appreciated anything in Jesus' Person, at least from a distance these executioners sensed the awesomeness of this crucifixion, in contrast to flagrantly unbelieving Jews, covenant people.

Once more, in Matthew, 28:19, the Author in Jesus' summons to the Twelve affirmed his Sonship, "Go therefore and make disciples of all nations, baptizing them in the name of the Father and of the Son and of the Holy Spirit." Hence, throughout the Synoptics the Author confirmed Jesus' origins, the divine and the human.

V

John, too, from his place among the Twelve in numerous ways revealed the Son of God. The Apostle recognized Jesus as the [only-begotten] Son, 1:14, 18,[15] 3:16 (Son = Son of God), which Sonship commenced in and with the Incarnation. John wrote with awe at the grace of the Incarnation and the actual Church believed that the Word had become flesh.

This Sonship inspired the Baptizer, John 1:34, to exclaim, "And I have seen and have borne witness that this is the Son of God." Nathanael similarly witnessed, 1:49, " . . . you are the Son of God!" Israel's Savior.

The Apostle severally revealed the Father's love. God the Son in his humanity depended upon the Father for protection. Throughout that dependence Jesus revealed salvation, John 3:17, "For God did not send his Son

---

14. More likely he, a pagan, referred to an unspecified denizen out of the Roman pantheon.

15. The ESV translated "the Son" as "the only God."

into the world to condemn the world, but in order that the world might be saved through him." Hence, since the world in this context equaled Israel, Jesus came to save his own. For this purpose the Lord laid the dividing-line, John 3:18, "Whoever believes in him is not condemned, but whoever does not believe is condemned already, because he has not believed in the name of the only Son of God." John 3:36, "Whoever believes in the Son has eternal life; whoever does not obey the Son shall not see life, but the wrath of God remains on him." John 17:2. The difference between grace and wrath comprised the divine judgment centered on the Cross. As the Son of God has life in himself, John 5:26, to grant life in the name of the Father he will resurrect his own from the dead, John 5:21–22, in order that the dead also hear him. John 5:25,[16] "Truly, truly, I say to you, an hour is coming, and is now here, when the dead will hear the voice of the Son of God, and those who hear will live." Thereby, beginning in this life Jesus established freedom, John 8:36, "So if the Son sets you free, you will be free indeed." That is, free from the shackles of Pharisaism, free from the legalism of the Oral Law, free for believing and serving Jesus Christ. In the lively dependence upon the Father's love Jesus as the Son of God, Savior, engaged in ministry on both sides of the dividing-line.

Deliberately Jesus affirmed his origins, John 10:36, "I am the Son of God." All heard him, John 5:23, that all honor and glorify him. Thus for the Sanhedrin to deny him in his Person, that blasphemy reflected the darkness of unbelief moving into condemnation, first for the Jews. John 19:7, the Jews to Pontius Pilate, "We have a law, and according to that law he ought to die because he has made himself the Son of God." That condemnatory sentence culpably denied the purpose for which the Word became flesh, John 20:31, " . . . that you may believe that Jesus is the Christ, the Son of God, and that by believing you may have life in his name."

V

The Synoptics and John, however different, nevertheless with one voice honored the Son of God, Savior—before the Father and in the Church—for the grace of his ministry.

8–6

Everywhere in his ministry, though concealing the totality of his omnipotence and omniscience, Jesus demonstrated evidence of his standing

---

16. This Jesus affirmed in Lazarus's resurrection, John 11:4, 27.

authority. He spoke and miracles happened—healings, exorcisms, and resurrections. Throughout in material ways and without ever calling upon the Father he proved the glory of his ministry. Upon stilling a storm, the disciples asked, Matthew 8:27, "What sort of man is this, that even winds and sea obey him?" Always Jesus reflected the limitations of his humanity. Many times he verified the splendors of his divinity.

However, on specified occasions, when the burden of salvation pressed upon his human nature, Jesus called upon God the Father for sustaining strengths.

8-7

To recreate the Kingdom (of heaven, Matthew; of God, Luke) the Son of God entered the world, that is, Israel, to reconstruct his rule. On the way Jesus had also to defeat Rome with its Hellenistic religiosities, plus its control over the Sanhedrin, Israel's then ruling body. The militaristic clout of these two political entities hindered the coming of the Kingdom considering specifically that these two belonged to the rulers, the authorities, the cosmic powers over this present darkness, and the spiritual forces of evil in the heavenly places. Within the macro-political sphere the Son began to reclaim the Kingdom.

To stop Jesus in his ministry, Matthew 4:8; Luke 4:5–6, " . . . the devil took him to a very high mountain, and showed him all the kingdoms of the world in a moment of time, and said to him, 'To you I will give all this authority and their glory, for it has been delivered to me, and I give it to whom I will. If you, then, will worship me, it will all be yours.'" These kingdoms, inclusive Rome and Israel, Satan offered for a bartering opportunity. For a momentary act of obeisance, for a mere genuflection, Jesus needed only to bow to the Devil to receive all the kingdoms of the earth without even a passing pang of suffering—all the earth, for that matter, the entire universe for a brief act of homage. For Satan allegedly owned all these rulers, authorities, cosmic powers, and spiritual forces of evil. As his, he considered himself free to give all to whomever. The devil knew full well that he had to prevent Jesus in his mission.

As the Son of God walked towards the pit of cruelty, once more his humanity cried out for the strength to persevere. In dark Gethsemane, that ancient olive grove, Jesus' cry of anguish broke out from his human nature—"My Father, if it be possible, let this cup pass from me: nevertheless, not as I will, but as thou wilt." "My Father, if this cannot pass unless I drink it, thy will be done." And once more this cascading anguish squeezed from the Son of God's humanity the agony of the coming pain.

Throughout Israelite territory Caesar's appointees also knew full well the danger to Rome that Jesus represented. To prevent the rise of *the* King, Herod the Great, 72–4 BC, infamously covetous, murdered the young boys of Bethlehem. Matthew 2:16–18. To prevent the followers of John the Baptizer from insurrection against Roman authority Herod Antipas, 4 BC–AD 39, tetrarch, imprisoned the Lord's last Old Testament prophet; under the guise of pleasing the wife of his brother Philip, this Herod removed John from his prophetic office, Matthew 14:1–12; Mark 6:14–29; Luke 9:7–9. To prevent Jesus from journeying direction Jerusalem some Pharisees warned him of Herod Antipas' homicidal malice, thus to divert Jesus as a coward from his course, Luke 13:32. To prevent Jesus from his righteous dominion Pontius Pilate tried him on treason. To Jesus, "Are you the King of the Jews?" Only the answer interested Caesar's man in Jerusalem, John 18:33; Luke 23:3; Mark 15:2; Matthew 27:11. He found Jesus' reply treasonous and condemned him to death by crucifixion, even though his superior, Herod Antipas had found no fault in the Savior, Luke 23:6–12. The point: of the Roman authorities Pontius Pilate recognized in Jesus a threat to the Caesar's domination; therefore the governor surrendered Jesus to the Jews and the Cross, John 19:16.

All the while in the confrontation with the political powers the Son of God without calling upon the Father moved quietly in his divinity and humanity against the forces of darkness suppressing Israel, from which base he recreated the Kingdom, eventually also to throw the weight of his dominion against Rome. He came to reclaim his own from those who allegedly owned the world. In his Person with teachings and miracles the Lord called fraudulent claimants to account.

Romans and Jews, jealously protecting spheres of power with unscrupulous political authority, condemned Jesus to death in order to remove an irritant. Long before this illegitimate condemnation Satan had overpowered Adam and shut the LORD God out of the earth, if not the universe, in leaving him with little more than a garden east of Eden. Once more in the Sanhedrin and Pontius Pilate's Roman court of law the Adversary revealed the limits of his reach, *almost* defeating the Son of God, leaving him but a cross. As the rulers, the authorities, the cosmic powers over this present darkness, and the spiritual forces of evil in the heavenly places—revolting against the legitimate King, pressing about and against him—indicated on Golgotha that the entire world order contracted in revolutionary solidarity to slay the Son of God, Matthew 21:33–46; Mark 12:1–12; Luke 20:9–19.

This biblical teaching, so the parable of the wicked tenants, Matthew 21:33–46, put Israel as well as Rome on notice and on the defensive.

8–8

To recreate the Kingdom, the Son of God entered Israel and from out of the midst of the covenant nation called forth a new people, beginning with the Twelve. To gain these men and others he challenged the Pharisees who through the synagogues *owned* Israel, its citizens. Under the microreligious sphere of Canaan—as distant from the Roman Empire—the Son of God initiated the ministry of creating many, to the astonishment of Nicodemus, *born-again* beings, men and women, sons and daughters too, Matthew 1:21; Mark 1:15; Luke 1:68–75; John 3:3. In the approach to the place of recreation, Golgotha, the Son of God knowing the Father's wrath gathering over all Israel appealed out of his flesh and in his human nature to the Father. Matthew 26:36–46; Mark 14:32–42; Luke 22:39–46; John 18:1. Throughout these horrors of torment, the Father's justice pressing down upon him, Jesus' divinity strengthened his humanity, that nature which had never sinned, now for the salvation of many had to pay the price of disobedience, thus to make atonement for malefactors walking into the fate of untold thousands

By means of the Flood, Lot's death, Egypt's destruction, etc., the weight of the divine wrath crushed unbelievers in death. In every covenant reformation throughout the First Dispensation from Adam, Genesis 3:14–19, over Noah, Abraham, Moses, and David to himself; upon the Incarnation Jesus promised the covenantal life, food, and space for his people that he acquired in the fullness of time on Golgotha. In the last dispensation, wherein the Son of God assumed the place of a servant, Philippians 2:1–11, he in the Crucifixion embodied for his own the full brunt of divine fury; the grace of the Atonement lived only for whom the Christ gathered as his own. The self-righteous Pharisees, Sadducees, Romans, Hellenists, etc., unbelievers all, he bypassed.

Atonement the LORD God had made requisite since the beginning, from Genesis 3:1–7 onward, to and including Revelation 22:15, every sinner to bear the full wrath of God. Throughout the dispensations the Son of God, Yahweh, revealed death in condemnation and life in salvation.

GOD THE SON

Apostle John in bitter controversies with the Jews[17] accentuated Jesus' divinity in the God-the-Son naming. With desperate intensity reflected in the Fourth Gospel the god of the Jews refused Jesus the victory of the Resurrection and the Ascension by coaxing the Church back into Judaism. Hence, such absorption into the religiosity of the synagogue as yet defeated the Christ. Therefore the Jews attacked God the Son[18] first for healing invalids on Sabbaths, a work according to the Oral Law reserved for the other six days of the week. To this verbal assault Jesus replied, John 5:17, "My Father is working until now, and I am working."[19] When Jesus equaled himself to the Father by determining the worth of Sabbath laboring he added fuel to the fire in opposing the Jewish god.

Rejection of Jesus' preexistent divinity came from the Devil deeply ensconced within the Jewish heart, his safest lurking place; to destroy him Jesus had to terminate the covenant people. As the god of the Jews,[20] John 8:44, Satan had twisted the leaders of the covenant nation into most aggressive proxies with whom to achieve his will, driving the heads of the Church into murderous paroxysms.[21]

Upon the Incarnation the Satan drove Herod the Great into a self-consuming fit of jealousy severe enough to kill Bethlehem's boys. Through a temptation he challenged Jesus to throw him from the Temple's pinnacle

---

17. Brown. *The Gospel According to John (i–xii)*, lxxi, "The polemic attitude of the Fourth Gospel toward Judaism is seen in the use of the term 'the Jews,' which occurs seventy times in John as compared with five or six occurrences in each Synoptic Gospel."

The Jews amalgamated as remnants of the Pharisees and Sadducees; they collectively represented the primary forces of attack against God the Son.

Morris. *Studies In the Fourth Gospel*, 284, "The manner of referring to 'the Jews' points to a time when they had become confirmed enemies of the church."

18. Morris. *Studies in the Fourth Gospel*, 50, "It was because He was the Son that He acted as He did on the sabbath. Therefore the Jews saw in His attitude to the sabbath not merely the breaking of one of the commandments, but blasphemy, and that of the most serious kind: 'making himself equal with God.'"

19. Bultmann. *The Gospel of John*, 244, "The Jews rightly understand that Jesus makes himself equal to God in these words, and so for their ears it is an insane blasphemy."

20. In the Synoptics he is called Beelzebul, Matthew 10:25b, 12:24; Mark 3:22; Luke 11:14–15, 18–19.

21. Bultmann. *The Gospel of John*, 244–245, "One thing, however, they do not understand, namely that Jesus's Sonship, and his claim to be equal to God and to work like God, only make sense in that Jesus, as the Son and as the one who works like the Father, *reveals* God, and that precisely because he is the Revealer he must make the claim which sounds so blasphemous to their ears."

onto rocks below, Matthew 4:5–6; Luke 4:9–11. In his ultimate attempt to kill God the Son physically he persuaded the merciless Jewish heads of the people to cry out, "Crucify him!" Matthew 27:23b; Mark 15:13–14; Luke 23:21; John 19:15. Israel's *father* swayed the Jewish heart to execute the God the Son; in this deicide they therefore committed themselves to the Devil's desires. He was a murderer from the beginning, Abel the first victim, and at the historic point of the Crucifixion only Jesus blocked his way to rule over all creation. This crucifixion had to trump all homicides. Or else the Devil faced eternity in the darkness of the Pit and the heat of all hell fires. Thus through pre-Crucifixion Jewish harassments he exposed measures of desperation, which peaked in the "Crucify him" cries.

Jesus on the way to the Cross revealed his equality in divinity with the eternal Father, both working on and judging the works of the Sabbaths. This rulership over Sabbath regulations toppled the Jewish Oral Law off its prominence and undermined the foundation of the Tradition of the Elders,[22] which left Judaism floundering in its sins and the Devil cringing in the damning light of the Gospel. At this time the *father* of Israel through the heads of the people pronounced condemnation upon the Judge of all judges less for his healing works and more for his divinity, John 5:18. John 3:35. For the revelation of Jesus' divinity recorded as John 5:19–23 bared the crux of Jewish hatred.

> Truly, truly, I say to you, the Son can do nothing of his own accord, but only what he sees the Father doing.[23] For whatever the Father does, that the Son does likewise. For the Father loves the Son and shows him all that he himself is doing. And greater works than these will he show him, for that you may marvel. For as the Father raises the dead and gives them life, so also the Son gives life to whom he will. The Father judges no one, but has given all judgment to the Son, that all may honor the Son, just as they honor the Father. Whoever does not honor the Son does not honor the Father who sent him. Truly, truly, I say to you, whoever hears my

---

22. Hoogsteen. *The Tradition of the Elders*, 117, "This evolutionary shift demonstrated a highly controversial paradigmatic alteration, much more involved than an absent-minded domestication of the Tradition of the Elders."

23. Brown. *The Gospel According to John (i–xii)*, 218, " . . . a Johannine passage like vs. 19 ultimately led Christian theologians to an understanding that the Father and the Son possess one nature, one principle of operation."
Morris. *Studies In the Fourth Gospel*, 152–153, "This expression of subordination . . . comes from Jesus Himself rather than the Evangelist." As much as biblical students favor a subordinating interpretation, more is at stake. See below.

word and believes him who sent me has eternal life. He does not come into judgment, but has passed from death to life.

As Jesus also declared his Son-of-Man judgment over Israel and over the Devil, the Crucifixion approached at him as the point of no return; not unexpectedly the controversy over authority erupted once more when Jesus declared that he and the Father are one, John 10:30, to which the Jews responded, John 10:33, "It is not for a good work that we are going to stone you but for blasphemy, because you, being a man, make yourself God." In the Fourth Gospel Jewish unbelief burned and raged, for the Devil perceived his end[24] unless he could claw the New Church back into Judaism and after all conquer God the Son. Under no circumstance were they ready to release the covenant nation, the Church, from the clutches of the Devil.[25]

V

Since his mysterious origination the Devil had nothing to do with the truth. As the father of lies—"Did God say?"—he spoke according to his own character. Also as the main instigator of deceit he convinced the Church at the end of the Old Testament dispensation and the beginning of the New to deny Jesus' divinity and therewith the relevance, much more the necessity of the Atonement. On the way to Golgotha he had engaged the Jewish nation, except for God the Son, to deny God the Son's divinity and make him thus susceptible as any man to human weaknesses. Out of this conviction he still, in desperation after the Ascension and Pentecost chose to wreak defeat upon the nascent New Church; the Old Church was the continuing ascendency of the Oral Law and the Tradition of the Elders, for which purpose the Sanhedrin arrested, scourged, and killed Apostles, plus persecuted the emerging Christians, Acts 5:17–41, 11:1–3; Galatians 3:1–6; etc. By destroying the Church the Devil had the last opportunity. In the process of this opportunity the Lord Jesus now out of the fullness of majestic divinity turned the Jews away into rabbinic Judaism, never again directly threatening to the Christian Church.

---

24. In the Synoptics this hatred broke out in the Jewish challenge to Jesus' authority recorded as Matthew 21:23–27; Mark 11:27–33; Luke 20:1–8.

25. Bultmann. *The Gospel of John*, 246, "The relationship between the dispute over the Sabbath and Jesus' reference to his work as Judge is now plain: the constancy predicated of the divine activity is also predicable of Jesus' activity, precisely because the work of the Revealer is the work of the Judge."

Conclusions

Throughout the Fourth Gospel more than elsewhere in the New Testament documents John repeatedly asserted God the Father's involvement; he *sent* the Son thereby to mock the Devil. The Father's *sending* is less subordinationist and more disruptive concentration attacking the Jewish heart. It is important to remember that God the Son assumed his humanity willingly, which took away any negativity in the subordination. John 1:14, 18, 3:16–17, 35–36, 5:26, 44, 8:36, 17:1, 3, 21, 23, 25. This sending came not in the Origenist spontaneous generation and must less in Arius' creation in eternity; the Devil, the Jewish god, under no circumstances as an archangel could sent a son into Israel to create an atoning death. His people were going down with him, forever. But God the Father sent the God the Son with his divinity and humanity to reveal in and to Israel that he supported as well as protected Jesus for the ultimacy of the Incarnation, the Crucifixion, and the Resurrection. Henceforth denial of Jesus' divinity displayed agreement with eternal damnation. First John 2:22.

V

Except for Romans 8:32; Philippians 2:6; and perhaps Hebrew 1:5, 5:5, most references to Jesus' timelessness with respect to his divinity the Author concentrated in the Fourth Gospel.

Now, throughout the New Testament the authors as one distinguished between the sons of God, the Son of God, and God the Son to glorify the Lord and Savior.

BIBLIOGRAPHY

Brown, Raymond E. *The Anchor Bible: The Gospel According to John (i–xii)*, 29A. Garden City: Doubleday & Company, 1966.

Bultmann, R. Ed. G.R. Beasley-Murray Trs. R.W.N. Hoare and J.K. Riches. *The Gospel of John: A Commentary*. Philadelphia: Westminster, 1964/1971.

Hoogsteen, T. *The Tradition of the Elders: The Way of the Oral Law*. Eugene, OR: Wipf & Stock, 2014.

Morris, Leon. *Studies In the Fourth Gospel*. Grand Rapids: Eerdmans, 1969.

LEFT, LEFT, LEFT

Two gates straddle the way, the one broad and massive. None bypasses either to enter into the future. Through the massively large and ornate gate stride confident masses purposefully moving to a *left, left, left* cadence. The huge swinging doors in this gate stand perpetually open, held so by crowds pushing day and night through and beyond.

The nondescript narrow gate to the right, marked by a small cross, opens only occasionally, at recognizing a quiet knock.

Both gates are accessible, only the left much more so; it glistens with welcoming electronic energies.

Onto the road from all directions of this civilization majorities march to an overpowering *left, left, left* cadence into the larger and more accommodating gate.

INTO THE GATES

The gate drawing human traffic to the left funnels attention, plastered as it is with numerous gaudy symbols of the people—a much battered Star of David, a hammer-and-sickle, a large coppery eagle, an always stunned looking beaver, a blood-red swastika, a multi-colored flag—along with wild and loud swelling music that calls forth rebellion. The peoples with the *left, left, left* stride head for the greater gate, eyes ablaze with the splendors of the future.

For the multitudes nearing the gates leaders of the past posted electronic arrows consistently and persistently flashing *left, left, left*, driving the masses on the way to follow the frontrunners. Drones overhead shout a *move, move, move* tempo that allows no rest; invigorated arms and legs swing with determination.

Often the intense *left, left, left* rhythm hides commandeering leaders who shout *right, right, right* to social conservatives, Neanderthals, archconservatives, Nazis, Fascists, and retrogrades while pointing to outdated neon signs with arrows that haphazardly also point left. The *right, right, right* marchers unconsciously follow the only viable direction of this civilization. They ignore the jibing and mocking of the *left, left, left* hordes. Unable to resist socialization pressures they conform to the majority; in the larger masses they mix and match into smaller countercultures of the new world—retrogrades with retrogrades, Neo-Fascists with Neo-Fascists, Neo-Nazis with Neo-Nazis, archconservatives with archconservatives, Neanderthals with Neanderthals, and socons with socons, joined by socialized Muslims with Muslims, enculturated Hindus with Hindus, assimilated Somalians with Somalians—out of the conviction that misery loves company. For all the *right, right, right* bravado of the *right, right, right* peoples they too show the revolutionary colors of muted reds, yellows, blacks, blues, oranges, purples, and greens, all the while singing *right, right, right* with a firm determination that matches the *left, left, left* beat.

On into the great and garish gate the crowding *right, right, right* walkers blend in with the *left, left, left* crowds, eyes glowing with the perceived beauties of the new world. The enlarging masses of libertines, libertarians, socialists, communists, feminists, liberals, communitarians, environmentalists, indigenous, humanists, humanitarians, LBGTs, and free thinkers swallow up the *right, right, right* countercultures to form immense masses streaming into the great and people friendly gate. They sing the powerful tunes of the peoples, the voices often blending into an uncontrollable roar; as they leave old worlds behind they belt out chest-expanding songs—*Free America. Hey Jude, Power to the People, the International, Horst Wessel, Movin' in the wind, Turn, turn, turn, Inner City Blues, I fought the law, My way, the Marseillaise*—and spend the wealth of the nations on the garments of the age, body-clinging covetousness, entitlement, greed, religiosity, blasphemy, anti-authoritarianism, and lust. In the new world the clothing makes the man, and the woman.

Gleaming and glowing with hopes and ambitions the *left, left, left* and the *right, right, right* marchers increase the pace to a half-shuffle, the faster to enter into glory. Many in a hurry to get through the main gate overtake others, impatient with the slower moving. Some even seek a detour through the little gate at the right, which remains locked, the doorkeeper unmoved by imperious banging.

At times when the intermingling *left, left, left* and *right, right, right* throngs pause to draw breath, peer ahead, and gain a second wind other sounds rise above the noises of the masses, psalm singing. As entire congregations step along, at the approach to the great and dazzling gate they irresistibly edge away, to the little gate, and knock.

Thus the entire Westernized world, no stragglers permitted, moves into the gates. They who tramp through the gate on the left discover blood surging and dreams beckoning, the slightly downwards slope easing the strains of the march.

PAST THE GATES

In response to the knocking the small door opens. Sometimes entire congregations, sometimes part congregations, sometimes individuals find the *left, left, left* way blocked and moving forwards means to go through the narrow gate. Sometimes the pastor of a congregation moves with the *left, left, left* determination through the great gate, loudly singing common-cause songs of unchained license. It happens that a congregation blends into the *left, left, left* cadence and a pastor alone knocks at the unremarkable door. Some who go through the little gate glance back or look at the popular way into the future; they hesitate in clouds of doubt. Then they persevere, down steep inclines and up sharp gradients, step by step entering the eternal way of life, freed from mass cultures and countercultures on the broad way. Amidst the rocks, turns, valleys, and beside pitfalls they wend forwards, the vibrating pulse of *left, left, left* and *right, right, right* no longer as temptingly misleading arms and legs. Taunts and jeers shouted from the broad way strike with less repugnance. After a time on the narrow path the *left, left, left* and *right, right, right* cadences fall away and the *tramp, tramp, tramp* of determination impinges with less spiteful pain. To the *grace, grace, grace* of the walk on the way congregations find each other and form continuous lines moving forwards. Individuals join in, filling the place vacated by those unable and unwilling to break with the *left, left, left* rhythms; unmerited mercy pushes away the once dominating appeal of the broad way. Only, the way into deep valleys, over steep hills, around bottomless swamps, and across sandy deserts have become slippery with cast off sins.

As the congregations united in faith and life move forwards great psalms create the new cadence; at time the awesome *hallel* songs inspire hope as the contours of the eternal city gain in outline.

> Jerusalem—built as a city that is bound firmly together,
> to which the tribes go up, the tribes of the LORD,
> as was decreed for Israel, to give thanks to the name of the LORD.

That destination holds the people, sometimes two abreast, over rocks and around precipices—climbing, descending, falling—the strong helping the weak, the wealthy the poor, the young the elderly, the lovable the unlovables. A father, arm around a mother carrying a newborn and guarding others, moves with the line. A couple, lost in early bliss, stops to help a scooter-seated grandmother up and around a steep corner. In one of the forests, under massive oaks away from the burning sun, others find opportunity to rest, in Christ-mindedness preparing for more ruggedness on the way ahead.

V

On the broad downslope formations of like-minded bond into convulsive masses, individual sensitivities surrendering to group-think. Kaleidoscopic colorings of oranges, reds, yellows, greens, and blues merge into doomsday grey, forecasting treacherous powers of evil, greed, gloom, jealousy, cowardice, decay, aggression, domination, distrust, lust, deceit, and death.

From the great road some deign to glare down on the other way and sneer at careworn who shed scads of self-righteousness, shreds of conceit, piles of distrust, heaps of domination, pools of lust, loads of prejudice, oodles of greed, and tons of covetousness. Those on the broad way wrinkle noses at those struggling on the narrow way, taunting and jeering, then return to chasing the future in the new world.

On the great incline the *left, left, left* and *right, right, right* tramping merges into the plodding *stomp, stomp, stomp* of get-out-of-my-way self-indulgence; all vie for control of the road, right of way, and ownership of the future, jostling, pushing, and climbing over the backs of the weaker for pride of place. All demand priority for gods that are no gods and for religiosities that know no light. They see the future and they are the future.

Far, far down the great road of the peoples racketing sounds of shooting erupts over and over, punctuated by heavy artillery and vicious bombing as populations under mushroom clouds clear the way into new-world dreams. Sounds of war and howlings of agony crumpling in eternal fires mark that end.

CONFESSIONAL STUDIES

OVER THREE ESSAYS, FIRST, I reflect on commitment to my core beliefs, second, I critique two of the Forms of Unity, and, three, because of the critique I created a statement of faith that structures the way of sanctification.

1–3

CORE BELIEFS:

THE THREE FORMS OF UNITY

Between birth and death all pass from one to the other. Normally, on the way to death maturing in belief or hardening in unbelief takes place. Such growth in the one or the other typically happens in and through conscious-decision making, its processes and temporary results only reflectively apprehended. Thus from the vantage point of today the unfolding of the past enlightens the future. Now, in a listening disposition I *hear* many of yesterday's decision still speaking. As I then advance into my core beliefs this meditative work generates gratitude to the Lord Jesus for what appears as typical evidence of his mercifully distributed grace in its day-to-day meaning.

V

The conscious start of my core beliefs began in the Aylmer, Ontario, Christian Reformed Church. Her office bearers, signatories to the Form of Subscription, promised the Head of the Church and the congregation to uphold and interpret the Scriptures as the Word of God according to *the* 1561 *Confession of Faith, the* 1563 *Heidelberg Catechism, and the* 1618–1619 *Canons of Dort,* the latter explanations and clarifications of points of doctrine associated with predestination. These explanations and clarifications became necessary due to the rise of seventeenth-century Arminianism, the Protestant variation of Roman Catholic Semi-Pelagianism. Moreover, those office bearers year after year affirmed the promise to lead the congregation in the interpretation and application of the Bible according to these historic Forms of Unity. The Confession and the Catechism, both laden with perseverance pertinent to the congenial heart of the sixteenth-century Reformation, carried that historic event into every present since. As a conscious and conscientious member of the congregation I too became directly involved in the orthodoxy of the Forms of Unity, reading and interpreting the Word of God according to these statements of faith.

Here is a representative taste of the Catechism:

Q/A 32
Why are you called a Christian?
Because I am a member of Christ by faith and thus share in his anointing,
so that I may
as prophet confess his name,
as priest present myself a living sacrifice of thankfulness to him,
and as king fight with a free and good conscience against and the devil in
this life,
and hereafter reign with him eternally over all creatures.

The depth and the assurance of the Forms of Unity penetrated the Aylmer congregation as a whole and members individually in different ways:

Per the Church Order

For the heart of the Sunday afternoon services and at the insistence of the Consistory, congregational ministers selected consecutive Lord's Days from the Catechism as preaching texts, each a summary of a specific and crucial doctrine. The fifty-two Lord's Days of the Catechism, one each Sunday, demonstrated again and again to the congregation that each doctrine advances a faithful summary of a biblical theme. By way of the Catechism the congregation heard and received in an orderly fashion the teachings of the Word, the whole a faithful shepherding of the members.

Per the preaching.

Sundays, specifically afternoons, with the congregation I listened to the catechetical preaching, which over the years gained hold. At first, however, with the congregation I listened, unaware of the origin, history, and even purpose of the three Forms, particularly the Heidelberger. Also, without much interest I listened because my parents insisted I attend and pay attention. Often I did not listen, my youthful mind roaming in the elsewhere and the faraway.

Per catechetical instruction.

As sacramental commitment, parents vowed to instruct children in the Faith. Following through upon this promise in congregations such as the Aylmer Church the office bearers, usually the minister of the congregation, taught teenagers first the contents of the Heidelberg Catechism; the Heidelberger came very much into the foreground during these weekly catechism classes, the instruction moving from Lord's Day to Lord's Day to know the Bible as the Word of God. I cannot remember much diligence in the way of learning. For a time when the Consistory of the Aylmer Church sought another minister an elder took on the responsibility. Because of scheduling, the catechism class that year followed immediately after the morning service. The elder, caught up in an old tradition, expected that we memorize the questions and answers; he asked the question and called upon consecutive students to recite the answer. The man, elderly, failed to exercise control over the class. To bring some order into the class he asked a fellow elder to come in and help maintain a listening and cooperative attitude. This second elder stationed himself in the corner behind my chair and I forgot about him, busy with some other catechumens. Came my turn and the answer flipped off my tongue, *Ik heb het glad vergeten.* In other words, the answer had completed slipped away. The elder behind me reminded me of his presence with a hearty slap up the side of the head. The class as a whole quieted somewhat. Year after year I attended this instruction, little aware of the importance of this teaching process, even unaware that my life in Christ as well as that of classmates depended upon the questions and answers shaping our future.

Per Young Peoples.

In the weekly Young People's Society meetings the three Forms found less energy; the leaders tended to raise other themes—predestination, Arminianism, ecclesiology, common grace, presumptive regeneration; etc.—as debates and argumentations carried over from origins in the Old Country. When the older members disappeared into marriage commitments they left the Society and the younger had to grapple with much the same questions, slowly becoming aware that we had to do it in another environment unfamiliar with great issues of the past.

Per Profession-of-Faith instruction.

In the profession-of-faith class, the minister/teacher opened up the other two statements of faith, the Confession of Faith and the Canons of Dort. Of this instruction too I remember little, if not less than from the earlier catechetical instruction. It was a process pertinent to coming of age. Late each summer or early fall the minister called those desirous to make public profession of faith to come together on a weekly basis during the winter months. Members who considered themselves mature enough to take on the responsibilities of congregational membership formed the class for that year. At the end, during an interview with the Consistory, the elders asked pertinent, actually probing questions, even engaged in conversation, to know the heart of each applicant. Because of a consistorial decision I gained the freedom to enter the communicant fellowship of the Aylmer Church through public profession of faith.

I remember a night living in the Avon, Ontario area, that I kneeled in bed and acknowledged my salvation and life in Christ Jesus.

Now to this public profession of faith. At the administration of the baptismal sacrament parents answer several questions at the heart of which the promise to raise respective children in the Reformed faith, the Faith. At the public profession of faith itself applicants to communicant membership answer the same questions as parents had, but now for themselves, believing the great doctrines of the Scriptures and taking on in the congregation the commitments and responsibilities of adulthood. One of the responsibilities? To ensure that the preaching conformed to the Scriptures as summarized in the Forms of Unity. Instruction in the three Forms had prepared us for this duty. At the same time each applicant promised to continue in the study of the Scriptures read through the eyes of the three Forms. This commitment to grow in the knowledge of the Word as well as living membership in the congregation to the glory of God somehow settled in. But not much showed that Sunday of that Public Confession of Faith.

I do remember that public profession-of-faith service, a glorious May morning. In number twenty or so, we sat in front pews. I sat in the second row on the outside, near an exit, which stood open to encourage air circulation in the overcrowded sanctuary. During the sermon as I looked out at the green of grass and blue of sky the temptation to walk away hit hard. Why not fade away in the glories of the day? Why did I stay seated and promise commitment to the ceaseless struggles of membership in the congregation?

Later, that morning at home, my parents gave a small, black KJV inscribed with the following: *Dear Ted. This bible is given to you in remembrance of your confession of faith on May* 28, 1961. Then follow written out also in my mother's hand the words of Ps 118:14-17. At that time even a small KJV must have cost them, considering the penury at home.

Per theological training

My wife and I were more or less committed that I enter the legal profession. However. One evening while deeply absorbed in preparing for the Grade Thirteen second-semester examinations, out of a clear blue sky the conviction hit: into the ministry of the Word. From that moment on the Lord Jesus prepared the way into ministry.

Throughout the seven years at Calvin College and Seminary the three Forms, as I remember, received little prominence, if any, and instruction in catechetical preaching as much, other than on summer assignments in Salt Lake City, Utah, and Walnut Creek, California. Yet Sundays, on preaching assignments, we faced the responsibility. Perhaps, unless avoidable. As I reflect on Calvin Seminary and the three years with preaching consent, few were the catechetical sermons, unless a Consistory insisted. During this time I was unaware of the anti-confessionalism dragging us along, down.

What I do remember with respect to the three Forms, vividly, was an elective in the last year: two seminarians under Dr. F. Klooster's leadership working through the wonders and intricacies of the Questions and Answers at a measured pace. Why this elective? Because it fitted in the course schedule? Probably I sensed the need relative to preparation for the ministry. Several times per week throughout that course with Dr. Klooster, Dennis Boogerd and I reached deep and wide into the treasure that is the Catechism.

Two relevant memories:

During the summer assignment in Walnut Creek, California the Billy Graham Golden Gate Crusade took place. The pastor of the Walnut Creek Christian Reformed Church, Henry Visscher, signed on as a captain and volunteered my services as a sergeant, he and I with many others to be on the ground in the San Francisco stadium to talk and pray with *converts*. The entire Arminian exercise of the Crusade—yes, I talked and prayed with a few of the converts—left me extremely uncomfortable for confessional/theological reasons. To this day, when remembering my however inconsequential participation I still ask the Lord Jesus to forgive my involvement.

While attending Calvin College and Seminary I found full-time employment at an acute-care mental institution, Kent Oaks Hospital. Even though the days shifts were more instructive, afternoon shifts more interactive with patients, I preferred the night shifts. When Cecil VanDalfsen, a Christian Reformed minister from Holland, Michigan, and I worked together we had in the quiet of the night time to talk about ministry, faith, thankfulness.

V

All the while the Spirit-induced faith, believing Christ Jesus as my Lord and Savior, grew in terms of commitment to glorify him and the Father in living. Over the years since the power of the doctrine by grace (alone) captivated more persistently and irrepressibly.

V

In the summer of 1973, the annual Synod of the Christian Reformed Church declared with many others also my candidacy for the ministry of the Word in the denomination. Soon I provisionally accepted the call from the Blyth Christian Reformed Church, Blyth, Ontario. That acceptance set in motion the central agenda item for the meeting of Classis Huron of the Christian Reformed Church early that September; at this classical meeting in Blyth, Ontario, which drew many members of the Blyth Church, area clergy governed the examination, which by and large moved smoothly to the expected conclusion, until one of the colleagues-to-be asked for an evaluation of a conservative organization, I think it was the Reformed Fellowship, which protested the rising liberalism in the Christian Reformed Church. As a typical Calvin Seminary graduate I shot out—rather spontaneously—such qualifiers as unreformed, unbiblical, and a few others. Up jumped red-in-the-face Dr. L. Praamsma, a member of the Reformed Fellowship and one of the next examiners. "Young man! I demand an explanation!" Through my mind raced the thought, "That blew the examination." Many of the colleagues-to-be, I noted, grinned, smiled, or laughed approvingly at the qualifiers. Apparently, during an intermission these colleagues-to-be humored Dr. Praamsma's wrath, and also his part in the examination process came to an amiable conclusion. Yes, there was also a probing examination into my familiarity with and commitment to the three Forms.

I find separatist organizations and movements in the Church reprehensible, several of which then operative in the Christian Reformed Church to overturn, or at least stem the denomination's slide into liberalism. Since that time I made one exception, supporting the Christian Reformed Alliance that developed into the United Reformed Churches. Why did I not stay with the Alliance and enter the ministry of the United Reformed Churches? I saw too many problems carried over from the Christian Reformed Church—agitation for an evolutionistic interpretation of Genesis, agitation for women-in-office, agitation for allowing children to attend the Lord's Supper celebrations, and agitation for an underlying Evangelicalism/Arminianism as the answer to liberalism.

V

The classical examination took place on a Wednesday. The ordination/installation as minister of the Word occurred that Friday evening.

The first Sunday morning as the minister of the Blyth Church ran well. That afternoon I presented the second sermon of the day; as conclusion to this sermon I read the Questions and Answers of Lord's Day One, an appropriate conclusion, considering the contents of the preaching. This was a different way of dealing with the Catechism, not even in the spirit of the Church Order to which I had committed myself. Pressure came immediately, gentle and considerate, insisting I take each Lord's Day consecutively and more seriously. I asked for one change. After due consultation with the Consistory we agreed that for the first time through the Catechism I consider each question and answer separately and successively. One hundred and twenty-nine. That took a while. My purpose? By this variant of catechetical preaching I had opportunity to think the Catechism through in the context of the congregation.

At the weekly catechetical instruction I taught the Heidelberger to different age groups. In the profession-of-faith classes each year I dealt with the Confession and the Canons, convinced that communicant members ought to have a working knowledge of the three Forms, something of their histories, and the sense of each in the Church, in short, not begin as I had, inattentive. Therefore, I taught students year by year with sensitive attention to and respect for the three Forms, indeed, the immensity of these Statements of Faith in the history and the life of the Church. Over the years, each sermon series on the Catechism, from Lord's Day One to Fifty-two, became more intense and each year catechetical instruction more relevant. In the passion of ministry the three Forms gained more of my heart, for which in part I thank the Blyth Church of that time.

V

At this point I find a general explanation necessary; at least it came up in my mind as such. Growing up in the Netherlands and then in Canada the history of the Reformation intrigued; I read age-related history books and historical novels. Were hero-worship permissible, those people who experienced the Spanish Inquisition came the closest. Also, I found over the years an identification with the 1834 *Afscheiding*, which way of believing and living the founders of the in 1857 established Christian Reformed Church in North America prolonged.

The *Afscheiding* as historical development faded away in the nineteenth and twentieth centuries, pushed under by liberal movements in theology and ecclesiology. Yet I find the *kleijne luijden* who peopled the *Afscheiding* more representative of Christianity than other ostensibly reformed movements, a light in the darkness. The other reformative movement of the nineteenth century, the 1886 *Doleantie*, with Abraham Kuyper leading, was more rational than heart-moving. Nevertheless, both the *Afscheiding* and the *Doleantie* gave new life to the sixteenth-century Reformation, allegiance to which strengthened my heart convictions.

V

In the fall of 1978, with the permission of the Council of the Blyth Christian Reformed Church and Classis Huron of the Christian Reformed Church, I solicited a Letter of Call in the Netherlands, from within the *Gereformeerde Kerken*, a sister denomination to the Christian Reformed Church. For what purposes? In part to further academic studies. In part to experience the liberalism of the *Gereformeerde Kerken in Nederland* before it engulfed the Christian Reformed Church. For a Sunday evening service in the *Haaksbergse Gereformeerde Kerk*, I selected Lord's Day One as preaching text. Fearful of my limited Dutch, I chose this familiar Lord's Day and planned to flourish my orthodoxy. When I reached for the Catechism from a shelf in the pulpit area no such book lay to hand. It meant that the Catechism was no longer preached or ministers brought their own. However, one of the members present withdrew a small psalm book from her purse and we proceeded apace. It seemed that catechetical preaching proved my *backwardness* more than my orthodoxy, if orthodoxy mattered at all. With a Letter of Call in my left inside pocket from a dual charge, the *Haaksbergse* and *Needse Gereformeerde Kerken,* the hours for the journey home flew away.

Once installed, 1979, I preached the Catechism as much as possible. Also, I taught the three Forms in catechetical and profession-of-faith classes, thus true to ordination vows, the Form of Subscription as well.

Throughout 1979–1983 the three Forms served as a lifeline—1) from my heart to the Christian Reformed Church in Canada, of and in which I remained a minister of the Word, 2) from my heart to the ordination promises spoken out before God and congregation in 1973, and 3) from my heart to the Reformation, a bonding with those who had suffered and died for the Faith. All the while intense pressures to conform to the mounting theological liberalism pained.

\/

The four years in *Neede* and *Haaksbergen* were difficult, tiring—serving two congregations (each different on the conservative/liberal continuum), seeking to understand the culture, updating outdated Dutch, and pursuing a study program in a very liberal environment, theologically. Without the heart commitment to the three Forms, God-given, what may have happened? In reflection, I still shudder. Holding to the three Forms was a strength, a perseverance, granted by the Spirit of the Son and of the Father.

After three years in the Netherlands the Council of the Blyth Christian Reformed Church unilaterally cut the agreement—we had agreed on a five-year span—compelling me to come back within the year, or else. That left me scrambling to do the work of ministry in two congregations, finish a study program, and seek a call to one of the congregations of the Christian Reformed Church.

\/

In due time within the twelve-month time limit I finished the course of study and accepted the Letter of Call from the First Christian Reformed Church, Brantford, Ontario. A Letter of Call from the Ottawa, Ontario,

Christian Reformed Church seemed less significant in terms of congregational needs.

In the First Christian Reformed Church, Brantford, Ontario, 1983–89, I found resistance to catechetical preaching an old problem, that and the inroads of intrusive Evangelism, part of which rising women-in-office tensions. Congregational opposition to the Forms of Unity and, hence, catechetical preaching, a denomination-wide phenomenon, made adherence to the ordination promises and the Form of Subscription daunting, especially in comparison with the years in the Blyth Church.

To relieve tensions I preached a series on the 1561 Confession of Faith and also on the 1984 version of *Our World Belongs to God*, a semi-confessional document peculiar to the Christian Reformed Church. However, resistance to catechetical preaching had settled in deep, the Evangelical revulsion to all confessional statements of faith a principle matter. I found again that I lacked the sort of elasticity of soul and of commitment that allows for quietly ignoring or neglecting solemn promises, and easily drift into congregational preferences, such as anti-confessionalism, a form of encultured Protestantism, lukewarm.

Whereas the Catechism and even the Confession are eminently preachable, the Canons differ in this respect; the Heads of Doctrine are only teachable, in classroom situations, within the give-and-take of discussion.

By and large, throughout the years at First Brantford I found the theological and doctrinal foundation of the three Forms strong enough to withstand pressures of Evangelicalism and Liberalism, which speaks well for the Confession of Faith, the Heidelberg Catechism, and the Canons of Dort.

V

In the years serving in the Brantford First Church two problems came up that bothered me in the Blyth years and also during the four years in the Netherland: indifferent church attendance Sunday afternoons and/or evenings. The Evangelically persuaded failed to share in the Sunday rest to prepare for the week ahead and had a different take on First Day gratitude.

The second involved the 1988 Billy Graham Golden Horseshoe Crusade, which drew enthusiastic attention from area Christian Reformed Churches.

Out of the Blyth years I remember two local crusades, in the first of which I felt *pressured* to participate. My part? The Scripture reading, Luke 15:11–31. In the second crusade spread over three meetings I refused to play a part, precisely because of commitment to the Forms of Unity. Crusades in

North America come out the Evangelical heart and focus on Arminianism, a faith roundly condemned in and by the Canons of Dort. I sat in on one of these meetings, finding the situation awkward. The sponsoring area clergy with whom I had some contact through the ministerial association sat up front, behind the evangelist, and I sat in the back of the auditorium. At the same time this commitment made clear the void between the area clergy and myself.

In response to the Golden Horseshoe Crusade (at least one Consistory in the Hamilton, Ontario area cancelled the evening service to allow the members to attend the Crusade), I prepared a *gravamen,* an official protest, which I presented to the Consistory of the Brantford Church; after a discussion the Consistory refused to undersign the protest. That provided freedom to present the protest over my own name to the Classis Hamilton of the Christian Reformed Church. This caused a minor disturbance. The Classis after a debate voted to reject the *gravamen*. How those men dared to betray commitments to the Form of Subscription and the Forms of Unity!?! The *gravamen* caused more tension in the congregation. Many almost worshiped Billy Graham who once in the sixties found the Christian Reformed Church a sleeping giant. That recognition of an immigrant denomination earned him a massive following.

The tensions in the congregation reached a point during the summer of 1988 that at a Consistory meeting a silence fell between us, the elders unable to deal with the impasse. This developed into a year-long leave of absence.

After the year I asked for a twelve-month extension, which the Consistory granted. During this time I worked as a security guard.

V

When a door opened for a call from a Canadian Reformed Church, it came as a God-sent, freedom to exercise the ordination vows. After several exploratory conversations with committees from area Canadian Reformed Churches who agreed that no such agitations as in the Christian Reformed Church hindered the ministry of Canadian Reformed Churches, plus the assertion that ministers preached the Catechism regularly and with great congregational recognition, I accepted the Letter of Call from one of these congregations, the then Rockway Canadian Reformed Church. However, also in this congregation I sensed resistance to catechetical preaching. Again, as in First Brantford, an underground upwelling of anti-confessionalism moved about. Yet in the catechetical teaching and in the profession-of-faith classes I found listening intense and response affirmative of the worth of the three Forms, also then of my commitment to these statements of faith. Eventually, the ministry in this congregation ran aground on a combination of anti-confessionalism and Evangelicalism.

Canadian Reformed ministers of the Word, to escape dual pressures of anti-confessionalism and Evangelicalism, during Sunday afternoon worship services still read the catechetical Lord's Days consecutively, but, apparently with the approval of the Consistories, referred to these as *confessional readings* and then preached on a biblical text associated with the pertinent Lord's Day. This is a novelty with respect to the Church Order regulation governing the usage of the Catechism.

The ministry in the Rockway Canadian Reformed Church was short, partly because of Evangelical anti-confessionalism.

V

In part of *Covenant Essays: One*, 2016, I researched and illustrated the anti-confessionalism in the Christian Reformed Church along with the same in the Canadian/American Reformed Churches. From the strengths of the founding fathers in 1857 and again of the immigrants in the early 1950s, anti-confessional sentiments wore down commitments to the three Forms, enculturation stronger.

The Forms of Unity encapsulate the Reformed faith. But a revolutionary spirit brought about Protestantism, a polyglot of mediating theologies, ideologies, and idolatries. In the course of readings with respect to *Covenant Essays: One* I came in touch again with the pantheizing of Hegel and James, as well as the agnosticism of Kant to find once more in those giants of the past the growth of old gods in harmony with human experience, the divine attributes humanized. In this expansion of polytheism Schleiermacher's deity continues with the world and is known only experientially, which furthered the movement to anthropology, anthropolizing. Protestantism became more an anthropology than a theology.

V

After 1995 I consciously reentered religious currents of the age—the Enlightenment/Liberalism, atheism, deism, evolutionism, humanism, Barth and Brunner's dialectics, Bultmann's demythologizing and existentializing, Tillich's Ground of Being, etc.—each and all typically anti-Reformative in character, also anti-confessional. Moreover, I found Lutheran and

Presbyterian writings with respect to statements of faith merely informative, Abraham Kuyper's teachings of sphere-sovereignty, presupposed regeneration, and common grace idealistic, and Dispensationalism presumptive, if not grandiose in attempts to monopolize Protestantism. All in all, the twentieth-century's endless roll of complexities and confusions exemplified Westernism's crumbling foundations, broken moorings, and mystified eschatological hopes, the whole lacking the fear of the Lord.

Each and together the Forms of Unity summarize the Faith, to stand strong against the vainglorious idolatries/ideologies of the age, also in the twenty-first century, thus, in the time-honored name of the Lord to overcome even the worst of the furies of unbelief. As one, these biblically based and structured statements of faith provide the solid base to confront coming heresies/apostasies, also such as Buddhism, Hinduism, and Mohammedanism. Despite multicultural and pluralistic protections, politically as well as socially, these fabrications of man fade before the globality of the three Forms to serve and glorify the Lord Jesus, and the Father, always in the Spirit, one God.

Over the centuries the foundational Forms of Unity served to hold and to strengthen the Faith. Consider, these statements of faith forge a straight line from the sixteenth-century Reformation into the present; the three have suffered from neglect and hatred—whatever the level of anti-confessionalism—and still run from the past through the present into the future. Rather than succumb to drifts into Evangelicalism and anti-confessionalism, I have grown over decades to love and to promote the three Forms.

Each of the three Forms created in the Reformation century summarized the essentials of the Scriptures for the Faith. These statements of faith stand strong against the idolatries and the ideologies typical of the spirits of each age.

V

Tension and resistance in the Rockway Canadian Reformed Church came to a head in 1995 in the form of dismissal from the office of minister in that congregation. In response Conrad VanAndel and I issued a charge of apostasy based on assertions in what became known as App C that with the strengths of *moral oughts* forbad teaching/preaching of the covenant promises and the doctrine of election, typical Evangelical/Arminian features. When the major assemblies—classes, regional synods, and general synods—accepted App C as a reformed document this led to deposition from the ministry and eventually excommunication.

This is where matters now stand, more than twenty -five years later.

Before moving from Welland, Ontario to Brantford in 2005 we still attended the then Rockway Canadian Reformed Church, however sporadically. Now we regularly attend the Ancaster Canadian Reformed Church. Beginning on Mondays we hear the call to worship issuing from the congregation and the Lord Jesus, the Head of the Church, also provides us with necessary seating.

For some years my wife and I found work with cleaning services, at one time to make sufficient hours we worked for three companies. Later Jayne returned to nursing work and I to guard duties. In this time I turned to writing, first with a friend and Jayne we published *The Journal of Reformation*, which consisted of papers stapled together. It lasted maybe two years; we did not have the money or the expertise to make it last. Later I worked out some essays and began with books. These books, I noticed last year, have a theme: each one opens up a forgotten or ignored teaching destructive with respect to the Person of Jesus Christ; each one also now opens perspective for the future of the Church.

2–3

CORE CRITIQUES: THE 1561 CONFESSION AND THE 1563 CATECHISM

The Confession and the Catechism, after more than five centuries, own impressive strengths. After a period of intense striving against Roman Catholic Semi-Pelagianism and then Protestant Arminianism the Forms of Unity stabilize *salvation* according to the Confession and *comfort* according to the Catechism. Rather than the pretentious self-righteousness in Semi-Pelagianism and in Arminianism the Church rested in the grace of Jesus Christ.

V

In addition to the Confession of Faith and the Heidelberg Catechism the 1618-19 Canons of Dort unambiguously and uniquely undergird the Confession of Faith and the Heidelberg Catechism. The first believers who with the Canons confessed the eternity of divine love faithfully confronted Semi-Pelagianism and Arminianism; these idolatrous forces presumed to know a foundation for the Faith within individuals according to something perversely called the freedom of the will, an arrogance that based believing Jesus Christ as Lord and Savior on a personal decision. In contrast to the flimsy foolishness of Semi-Pelagianism and Arminianism, the Canons prove the source of the Faith, Christ Jesus, Matthew 11:25–30; Luke 10:21–22, eschewing every manifestation of works-righteousness. Due to the nature of the Canons these are little subject to any critique.

The Canons created at the conclusion of the Reformation century display remarkable longevity. Its Heads of Doctrine will exist as along as Arminians and Semi-Pelagians dare oppose the Scriptures as well as deny the foundation of salvation and of comfort. Since all called by the Christ grapple with and strive against Arminian spirits the five/four Heads of Doctrine have a future, carrying the strength and the validity of the Canons far beyond the present.

V

Leaving the Canons for further observations aside, the following compares strengths and weaknesses of the Confession of Faith and the Heidelberg Catechism.

First, a shortlisting of strengths:

The *salvation*-themed Confession and the *comfort*-themed Heidelberger build up believers in faith commitment. The remnant, which the Head of the Church initially withdrew from Roman Catholicism and shaped as the Reformation, rejoiced in the unmerited grace of salvation and the comfort of belonging to Christ Jesus.

Both statements express era-sensitivity: trusting the *salvation* and the *comfort* confessed in both statements Christ-believers in the sixteenth century withstood fierce persecution.

The Confession and the Catechism own intensive and extensive orientation in the Scriptures. The Bible moved and shaped both statements. Everywhere, also in each apparatus, the scriptural foundation appears throughout for the Articles and the Questions/Answers.

The Church through the Confession and the Catechism faithfully acknowledges the Trinity—the Trinity in Unity and Unity in Trinity, one God in three Persons, Art. 8 and L/D 8. Atheists, agnostics, and other antitrinitarians find no voice in these statements of faith.

In both statements of faith the Church asserts the doctrine of predestination, election as well as reprobation, knowing therein the awe at and the sovereignty of the three Persons, one God. Art. 16 in this respect is more extensive than Q/As 20 and 54. Yet in the salvation of the one and the comfort of the other, the two speak univocally.

In the Confession and the Catechism the Person of the Lord Jesus—divine and human—is the Christ, Savior; in his life and death he revealed the grace of substitutionary atonement to redeem a people as powerfully demonstrated in the sixteenth-century Reformation. In his life, death, and resurrection he recreated the Church and the Kingdom, by grace. From the Incarnation through the Ascension, with the Cross and the Resurrection central, the Lord Jesus reestablished his dominion within and among his people. After the momentous hour of the Ascension, from the seat of sovereignty he recreated his universal rule, beginning in Europe, Acts 16:6–10; as the Lord he initiated the historical movement to the Eschaton.

Conforming intimately to the Scriptures, the Confession and the Catechism present the sacraments, the Commandments, and the Prayer most persuasively.

Particularly for the children of the Church, for maturing in the Faith, in the Catechism parents ask the right questions and give the right answers, which apply to newcomers in every congregation as well. Catechumens and converts to the Faith with great benefit take the Q/As to heart.

Both statements of faith are eminently preachable in the topical manner, since each article and question/answer summarizes a biblical teaching.

Now, out of the learned love for the Confession and the Catechism, as these statements of faith configure believing and living, believers find that each witnesses from the hiddenness of predestination to redemptive freedom in Christ Jesus who with the Father and in the Holy Spirit prophetically revealed the present in the past for the future.

Second, a shortlisting of weaknesses:

The aging of the Confession and the Catechism shows. The persecutory miseries in which both saw the light of day disappeared centuries ago, and have faded from the Church's memory. Roman Catholicism's Inquisition, pyres, indulgences, scholastic schools, monastic walls, and oppression of Christians few even know as historical facts; in other words, the religious/historical/political climate in which the Lord Jesus birthed the Reformation intrigues less and less. Without that bloody background the vanguard Confession and Catechism lost much verve; they who continuously uphold these two statements of faith must do so out of loyalty to historic documents adjusted to time and imagination. No longer are believers persecuted and/or murdered for the Faith on account of anti-papalism, Bible-reading, and freedom of worship, at least not in Westernized lands. In the twenty-first century no one sees and smells the blood of martyrs spilled for the name of the Lord Jesus Christ.

The Reformed/Lutheran conflict of the sixteenth century—central to which the *extra Calvinisticum* and Luther's consubstantiation—as resolved in L/Ds 46–48—no longer disrupts; the once powerful gravitas in Lutheran/Reformed ecumenicity broke down. The whole of this struggle disintegrated in the mists the Enlightenment and later secularism. Idolatrous movements as such shoved the pain of that schism aside for more tolerable, more engaging questions.

Following the Apostles Creed, an imbalance with respect to the Trinity also damages the credibility of the Confession and the Catechism. (The Confession in its structure follows the Creed; L/Ds 7–23 reflect the Creed's high worthiness in the Catechism.) In these statements of faith God the Father dominates at the expense of the Son and the Holy Spirit; though the three are equal in holiness, authority, and majesty, per the Athanasian, this inconsistency church members carried over from out of Roman Catholicism. In turn, unable to extrapolate the dominance of the Father from its theology the Reformation still attributed the greater workings of divinity to God the Father, leaving but salvation to the Son of God and ecclesiology to the Holy Spirit. This anomaly in trinitarian works skews the Faith to this day. Neither the Confession or the Catechism equated the Three of the Trinity in revelatory glory. In a hierarchical fashion the Father dominates in both statements of faith. Not so in the Scriptures, for the Son, the Father, and the Spirit involve(d) themselves in every aspect of creation, salvation, and sanctification.

Also the doctrine of the Son's *eternal generation* stands strong in the Confession, Art. 10, and in the Catechism, Q/A 33, despite lacking biblical warrant, resting only on mindless repetition, if not also pursuing a monotheistic tendency, the Son and the Spirit less authoritative than the Father. This teaching, of dubious origin, spun into existence a *begetting* before the *ex nihilo* creation of Genesis and limited the awe at the radical newness of the Incarnation. Perhaps *eternal generation* satisfied a rationalistic need to comprehend an incomprehensible; at the same time, it seeks to penetrate that which is impenetrable. Only, in the facticity of the creation the Son and the Spirit also participate. Only, with the facticity of Bethlehem, the enfleshment, did the Spirit generate the Son, bonding the divine and the human in the Person of Jesus, Luke 1:35; Matthew 1:20. Only, in the facticity of sanctification do the Spirit, the Son, and the Father participate. Whatever the source and the perpetuation of this *eternal generation*, it finds no scriptural basis, hence is eisegetically misleading.

Without dismissing Art. 37 and L/Ds 17, 19, 22, the Confession and the Catechism are static, lacking in eschatological vision, The *salvation* of the Confession and the *comfort* of the Catechism strengthened believers in the cold darkness of penitentiary cells, in the irrevocable condemnations handed down by Roman Catholic tribunals, and in the murderous fires of persecution, certainly. Still, even though both the Confession and the Catechism *proved* the orthodoxy of the Reformation in its beginning, each remained a human work born in the heat and the toil of persecution and in the fear of immediate arrest, both aroused more of Rome's wrath and revenge. The *salvation* and the *comfort* apply primarily to that period; to know one's *salvation* and *comfort* made suffering and death for the sake of the Christ a victory procession. At that time from the moment of confessing the lordship of Jesus Christ and salvation in him, thereby turning one's back to the mighty men of popery and the worth of membership in Roman Catholicism, often persecution followed. Nonetheless, as such, both *salvation* and *comfort* give off a staticity, even an individualism, neither of which conveys a strong eschatological awareness. Both salvation and comfort had to serve in the then and there of that historical moment.

The Confession and the Catechism lack awareness of the Bible's covenant structure. Covenantal references with respect to the sacraments, Art. 34, Q/As 74, 77, 82 do little more than to stress the importance of baptism and Lord's Supper, without, however, explaining the promises and obligations involved. The covenant applies only minimally to the *salvation* of the Confession and the *comfort* of the Catechism.

In the Confession through three lengthy Articles, 33–35, and in the Catechism through six extensive Lord's Days, 25–30, the two statements of faith reflect the meaning as well as the purpose of the sacraments. At the same time, each Article and Lord's Day offers deep evisceration of Roman Catholic teachings with respect to baptism and the Mass. Not submission to papal hierarchy created the assurance of salvation and the source of comfort, but believing the Word, redemption in Christ Jesus through the work the Spirit. However, the lengths of these Articles and Lord's Days overshadow the significance of the more important obligation of preaching. The length of the space accorded to the sacraments implies that these eclipse the word, as in Roman Catholicism.

In fact, the bulkiness of the Articles and Questions/Answers *persuades* subscribers into a sacramentalism not unlike the effect of the seven sacraments enforced by popes, all partake or else. The weight with respect to the sacraments in the Confession and the Catechism instigates superstitious awe at the elements, particularly of the bread and the cup. This overweight of the sacraments may have served to overcome the sixteenth-century popish imposition of the mass and such for the actuality of the Faith. At this time, moving further into the twenty-first century, the Church must put more heft on the preaching. The preaching creates and strengthens faith, sacraments—properly observed—strengthen faith. Yet many will avoid the preaching Sunday mornings and afternoons/evening, and then fearfully never miss partaking of the elements. The superstitious partaking of the elements display the severe abyss between the preaching and the sacraments. To overcome the misconception that the two statements of faith, much of the material now associated with the sacraments ought to be spread over the larger parts of the Confession and the Catechism.

The Confession and the Catechism, because of aging, reflect no awareness of the monstrous and deadening ideologies/idolatries of the present—evolutionism, Arianism, Gnosticism, Modernism, and Postmodernism, not even of the *discomforts* of secularism. In the Church such ideologies/idolatries turn into heresies and apostasies, each treasonous with respect to the Faith, destructive with respect to the Person of Jesus Christ, and damaging with respect the great and living doctrines of the Word.

Finishing Thoughts:

For the strengths of the Reformation the selection of *salvation* and *comfort* as the leading themes reflect pastoral genius. *Salvation* as confessed in the Thirty-seven Articles and the *comfort* as declared in the Heidelberger stabilized and strengthened believers. Salvation is in Jesus Christ, not in Roman Catholicism. *Comfort* existed in belonging to Jesus Christ, not membership in the Roman Catholic Church. For Rome membership equaled salvation and comfort; with respect to *comfort,* reliance on the Roman hierarchy offered a sense of security. Belonging to Christ Jesus, however, produced comfort in life and in death. Selection of these thematic words cut away all works-righteousness for founding redemption.

Nevertheless, despite the remarkable plenitudes of the Confession and the Catechism, both are more at home in the sixteenth century than in the twenty-first, the latter already a wreckage of ideological and idolatrous currents seeking to halt the eschatologically oriented present. Both statements of faith lack the powers required to conquer the illusion of progress in secular worlds.

3–3

COVENANT ESSAYS: TWO

CORE HOLINESS:[1]
THE SANCTITY CODE

1

As the Church eases into conformity with the world she slavishly appropriates teachings and lifestyles from idolizing cultures. Through adapting to this world, hypocrisy articulates the descent.[2]

To reverse this descent into darkness Jesus, the Head of the Church, always in every generation reforms a remnant. Since her origin Jesus separates and distinguishes the Church from the world; she is the beginning of the new creation.[3]

The Church is holy, a people set apart. Isaiah 51:1; Jeremiah 6:16a. Christ transforms her members into his likeness, as manifested by God the Father.[4] Therefore, in deteriorating faithfulness, the Lord Jesus reforms his people, sanctifying and cleansing his congregations of hypocrisy. The Lord and Savior decreed for all eternity that his people hasten to glorify him and the Father in the Spirit.[5]

JUSTIFICATION BY FAITH

The Shattered Righteousness

2

Since the Church is holy, a people separated to glorify him in his trinitarian sanctity, Jesus summons even hypocrites in the membership onto the way of sanctification.[6] Now, from out of the beauty of holiness Jesus' call penetrates throughout the Church.

1. Critiquing the Confession of Faith and the Heidelberg Catechism inspired the effort to do better along a theme crucially necessary for the Church, sanctification.

2. Judges 2:1–5; Isaiah 44:6–8; Hosea 6:4–6; Matthew 6:5, 7:5, 23:28; Luke 12:1; 1 Peter 2:1.

3. Matthew 19:28.

4. Deuteronomy 7:6–11, 12:29–31; Romans 8:10; 1 Corinthians 3:16–17; Colossians 1:13–14; Titus 2:11–14; Hebrews 3:6; James 3:9.

5. Psalms 115:1, 135:19–21; Romans 11:33–36; Revelation 4:11, 5:9–19, 15:3–4.

6. John 15:19, 17:14; 1 Peter 2:9–19; Revelation 21:2.

> You shall be holy;
> for I the LORD your God am holy.[7]

Again:

> You shall be holy, for I am holy.[8]

To reinforce holiness the Lord Jesus' summons permeates the Church, regenerating hearts, souls, minds, and strengths, all eventually to stand before him, the glorious Judge.

Everywhere in congregations, marriages/families, and schools believers listen and comply in employment, social media, technology, citizenship, transportation, business, and recreation. Jesus' holiness command requires immediate answer. Hence this urgent imperative compels all at the crossroads of life onto the narrow way, Matthew 7:13–14; Luke 13:24, to live and serve eternally.[9]

3

Barriers to holiness rise up from within human hearts as prison bars that defy sanctification and prevent the Lord and Savior from owning the Church.[10] Originating out of covetousness, Gen 3:1–7, the sin of the beginning excites revolutionary behaviors that prevent the coming of the Kingdom. These compulsions represent bars of self-righteousness, locking sinners into eternities of darkness.[11]

Sinners with self-justification rationalize every evil, herewith pushing blindly into the hellish future.[12]

4

On the Seventh Day Adam barred the advance of the glories of the first eschaton; he left Genesis 1:28 incomplete. As the head of the created order

---

7. Leviticus 11:44–45, 19:2, 20:26, 22:31–33; Joshua 24:19; Isaiah 6:3, 57:15.

8. Matthew 5:8; 1 Peter 1:16.

9. Deuteronomy 30:19–20; Joshua 24:14–15; Hebrews 13:44.

10. Matthew 15:19; Mark 7:21–22; Romans 1:18–32; Galatians 5:19–23; 1 Timothy 1:8–11; Titus 1:10–11.

11. Psalms 73:4–9, 74:22–23, 83:1–8; Ecclesiastes 3:16–22; Isaiah 59:1–8; Malachi 3:5; Matthew 16:11b, 22:13; Luke 13:10–17; 2 Corinthians 12:20; Galatians 3:23–29, 5:19–21.

12. Matthew 8:12, 13:42, 50, 18:9b, 22:13; Luke 13:28; Revelation 20:15.

the man chronically desecrated the original righteousness constituent of his created being, the woman with him too. As one the two lost the very goodness inherent in the creation.[13]

Created in holiness to will and to do righteousness, the two radically ruined the original goodness for all human beings. Genesis 1:31, 3:8-13. In the falling away Adam and Eve called forth the Adamic sin, covetousness, the power of the flesh, henceforth the Serpent's main assault weapon against the Christ.[14]

Falling for the Devil's bargain, Eve and Adam called into existence all horrors of self-justification, the meaning and purpose of life henceforth locked into idolatries. Now every generation of Adam's sons and daughters entered existence broken, sealed behind prison bars, committed to the Adamic sinning wherein intent on self-righteous strengths to excuse transgression.[15]

The Recreated Righteousness

5

With majestic holiness the Trinity pierces the hardiest blockades, cleansing and reforming a chosen people.[16]

With majesty the Son reveals his holy omnipotence.[17] Believers respond forthwith to the Lord Jesus' consecratory command.

> Glory in his holy name;
> Let the hearts of those who seek the LORD rejoice![18]

---

13. Genesis 3:1-7; Romans 5:12-14; 1 Corinthians 15:21-22; 1 Timothy 2:13-14.

14. Psalms 73:26, 119:120; Isaiah 40:6; Romans 7:4-6, 7:7-12, 8:3-8, 8:12-13; Galatians 5:16-17, 5:19-21, 6:7-10; Ephesians 2:11-12; 1 Peter 2:11-12.

15. Psalms 14:1-4, 53:1-5, 89:46-48; Ecclesiastes 9:13-16; Isaiah 1:4, 8:14-15, 30:8-14, 31:1-5, 47:8-9, 59:9-15; Jeremiah 17:9-10; Ezekiel 20:32; Amos 4:1-3, 6:1-3; Luke 12:54-56, 16:44-45; Romans 8:7-8; Ephesians 5:3-14; 2 Timothy 3:1-9; James 4:1-10.

16. Deuteronomy 7:6-11; Ephesians 1:3-10; 2 Peter 1:10.

17. Exodus 3:5, 24:15-18; Leviticus 9:23-24, 10:3; Deuteronomy 5:22-27, 6:20-25; Joshua 24:19; 1 Samuel 2:2; 1 Kings 8:10-13, 19:9-18; Psalm 85:4-7; Isaiah 5:24-25, 6:1-5, 43:3a, 55:5; Matthew 17:1-6; Mark 9:2-8; John 6:69; Acts 9:3-9.

18. First Chronicles 16:10, 16:28-34.

With equal majesty the Father through the Son reveals his holy omnipotence.[19] Believers respond with gratitude to the Father's acceptance of the Son's salvific ministry.

With equivalent majesty the Spirit of the Father and of the Son reveals his holy omnipotence.[20]

V

As one the Son, the Father, and the Spirit, future-minded, draw the elect into the transcending holiness of the Faith. Second Peter 1:3–11. Through Jesus' ministry the Three in One accomplished the recreation of righteousness, a people transformed for the eternity of service.

6

The one God reveals his holiness in righteousness.
In holiness the Son wills and does righteousness. [21]
In holiness the Father wills and does righteousness.[22]
In holiness the Spirit wills and does righteousness.[23]

Righteousness is integral to the Trinity. In trinitarian unity the Three reveal the consecratory power now at work in the Church. From out of the glory of the divine holiness the Lord Jesus created justification, its imputation by fiat* only. This imputation of the righteous judgment recreated a people to will and to do all works of rectitude. Within the Church the Christ compels his to believe justification by faith, the sole exit out of the discredited entanglements of hypocrisy.[24] The Judge of all the earth revealed on Golgotha the unmerited favor of the great judgment:

> You are righteous, for all eternity!

---

19. John 17:11; 1 Timothy 6:15–16; James 1:16–18; Revelation 4:3, 4:8, 21:22–23.

20. Isaiah 63:10; Acts 10:44–45, 11:23–24, 15:8–9; 1 Peter 1:10–12; Revelation 3:1.

21. Genesis 1:1–31; Exodus 20:1–17; Psalms 22:3–5, 33:4–5, 36:5–6, 50:6, 85:10, 89:14, 103:6–14, 118:19, 119:137; Isaiah 11:5; 45:21, 23, 59:17; Jeremiah 23:6, 33:15; John 6:37–40, 7:16–18, 8:29; Romans 5:17; Galatians 3:10–14; Colossians 2:6; Hebrews 1:1–4, 4:11–13; James 4:13–17; 1 John 2:1–2.

22. John 17:25; Acts 17:29–31; Romans 1:17, 3:21–22; 1 Corinthians 1:30; Colossians 1:24–29; 1 Timothy 6:14–16; 1 Peter 1:3–5, 17; 1 John 3:1–3; Revelation 4:1–11.

23. Acts 5:1–11; Romans 8:2, 8:11, 8:14, 15:19–21; 1 Corinthians 2:10; 1 Peter 1:10–12.

24. Genesis 15:6; Habakkuk 2:4b; Romans 1:16–17, 3:21–26, 27–1, 5:1–5.

Thus he with the actuality of grace handed down the sentence of justification. This is the almighty fiat from the Cross, the first and great Judgment.[25] Here, in the Church—and here only—is the access to holiness.

Jesus' imputation of grace the sovereign Father accepts and the sovereign Spirit implements. Now Christians believe the Gospel's covenant promises: of life,[26] of food,[27] and of space.[28] With the holiness of grace the Christ broke into the confines of idolatry, imputing that which his own never earned. Through sinning believers forfeit life, food, and space. Forgiveness of sin restores the legitimacy of living the covenant promises.[29] In the newness of believing the Gospel the stability of the covenant reforms the continuity of the Church.

---

*A command or act of the will without apparent effort.
A dictate or sentence at the bar of justice.
"Let it be done!"

SANCTIFICATION IN FAITH

The Recreated Holiness

7

The Christ prepared himself to reveal the teaching of justification. Thereto he structured the history of the world out of prophetic Genesis 3:14–19, the first dispensation of which inscripturated as the Old Testament.

---

25. Psalms 32:1–2, 33:4–5; John 3:18–21; Romans 4:7–8, 4:23–25, 5:15–17, 5:18–21, 6:15–19, 8:1–8; 2 Corinthians 4:6; Galatians 3:6–9; Ephesians 2:1–2; Hebrews 13:12.

26. Exodus 3:7–12, 12:1–20; Isaiah 40:1–2, 52:3; John 1:29, 3:36, 14:8–11, 17:24; Romans 10:10.

27. Exodus 3:17, 16:13, 15; Psalm 11:5; Matthew 14:13–21, 15:32–39; Mark 6:35–44, 8:1–10; John 6:1–14; 1 Corinthians 11:23–26.

28. Genesis 45:6–11; Exodus 3:7–10; Numbers 33:50–56; Deuteronomy 1:8, 6:10–15; Psalm 111:6; Romans 4:13.

29. Exodus 15:13; Psalm 70:4; John 12:44–50; Romans 3:21–26, 11:5; Galatians 3:23–29; Hebrews 4:14–16.

Justification re-initiates human holiness. In faith all believers put on the Christ, Galatians 3:27, and have the Christ in them.[30]

All with Christ Jesus in the heart, all with the youthful intensity of Isaiah 40:27–31, and all with childlike trust ever more believe the narrative of Jesus' Person and ministry.[31]. Trusting with indelible intensity the narrative of the Christ's Person and ministry—Genesis-Revelation—all find that daily he pours more holiness into new wineskins.[32] Thus from within begins and matures the new life, the new creation from inside each believer.[33]

The following light now is true, whatever the hypocrisies in the Church:

THE CHRIST IS THE ALPHA AND OMECGA,
THE BEGINNING AND THE END,[34]
IMMEASURABLE IN MAJESTY, OMNIPOTENCE, AND HOLINESS.[35]

In this light he sanctifies the Church and by this light congregations and believers measure consecration.

8

To achieve the Incarnation the Christ selected Abraham's descendants.[36] En route, throughout the first dispensation he foretold in and to the Old Church his coming in the flesh.[37]

---

30. John 17:23; Romans 8:10, 14:8; Galatians 2:20; Colossians 3:3–4, and live in Christ, 1 Corinthians 6:17; 2 Corinthians 3:3.

31. Psalms 73:26, 85:10–13; Isaiah 55:6–9; Luke 1:1–4; 2 Corinthians 4:6.

32. Matthew 9:16–17; Luke 5:36–39.

33. John 6:40, 15:1–11, 17:17; Romans 6:4, 8, 10, 7:22, 8:16; 2 Corinthians 4:16; Ephesians 3:16, 4:22–24; Colossians 3:10.

34. Isaiah 41:4, 44:6, 18:12; Revelation 1:8, 21:6, 22:13.

35. Psalm 145:13–20; Isaiah 57:15; Matthew 7:24–27; 1 Corinthians 1:18–25; 2 Peter 3:18; Revelation 3:15–19.

36. Deuteronomy 7:6–11, 12:29–31; I Chronicles 16:14–18; Matthew 1:1; Romans 4:17; Galatians 3:6–9, 29; James 2:21.

37. Genesis 3:14–15, 22:1–19; Deuteronomy 18:15–22; 2 Samuel 7:12–13; Psalm 132:11–12; Isaiah 7:14/Matthew 1:23; Isaiah 9:2–7, 11:1–3, 10, 28:16–17, 42:1–4/Matthew 12:18–21; Isaiah 52:13—53:12, 61:1–4/Luke 4:18–19; Jeremiah 23:6, 31:31–34; Ezekiel 1:26–28, 36:22–32; Hosea 11:1; Micah 5:2; Zechariah 2:6–10, 6:9–14, 9:9/Luke 19:38; Malachi 3:2b–4.

In the majesty of holiness* the LORD God—omnipotent and omniscient—with the Father and in the Spirit prepared Mary and his Israelite body.[38]

From within the tumult of the nations and empires he continuously broke open the way, majestically, for the salvation of the Church and the coming of the Kingdom.[39]

---

*Of the transferable attributes: holiness, righteousness, love, mercy, goodness, and grace, even veracity, spirituality, truthfulness, wisdom, knowledge, and sovereignty.

Of the nontransferable attributes: transcendence, divinity, immutability, infinity, eternity, omnipotence, omniscience, and trinitarian unity.

9

In the linear ascent of Old Testament history, the Preincarnate, by grace, initiated covenantal righteousness. Beginning with Abram (and Sarai), Genesis 12:1, he recreated in his own the will and the ability to believe the great teachings of the Scriptures, each always with respect to holiness.[40]

The Christ, with the Father and in the Spirit, created a movable horizon. On this horizon he appointed days of judgment, dread unimaginable, each a day of the Lord.[41] On those days he cleansed the covenant community of all reprobates, as well as gave the lie to false prophets.[42]

---

38. Isaiah 7:14; Matthew 1:18-23; Luke 1:26-35, 41-45; John 1:14; Galatians 4:4-5; Hebrews 10:5-7.

39. Psalms 65:5-8, 89:9, 93:3-4, 98:7-9; Isaiah 9:1-2/Matthew 4:15-17; Isaiah 34:1-4, 45:9-13, 51:15; Daniel 7:1-7; Luke 1:14-17, 67-79, 2:29-35, 21:25-28; John 8:23; Acts 4:23-31/Psalm 2:1-11; Revelation 18:1-24.

40. Genesis 15:6/Romans 4:5b; Joshua 24:16-22; Psalm 32:1-2; Isaiah 51:1-2; Habakkuk 2:4b/Rom 1:17; I Corinthians 3:16-17; Galatians 3:6; 1 Thessalonians 2:1-4; 1 Peter 2:4-5.

41. Isaiah 2:2-5, 2:20-22, 13:9-16, 30:27-28, 42:5-9, 51:4-6, 60:8-14, 65:17-25, 66:22-23; Joel 1:15, 2:1-2, 11, 31, 3:14; Amos 5:18-20, 8:1-3, 9-10; Micah 4:1-5; Zephaniah 1:7-9, 14-16; Malachi 3:1-4, 4:1-3; Matthew 24:1-51; Mark 13:1-37; Luke 12:49-53, 17:22-37, 21:5-36; Acts 2:19-21; 1 Corinthians 1:8; 1 Thessalonians 5:2; 1 Peter 4:7-11; 2 Peter 3:8-19; Revelation 19:11-16.

42. First Kings 18:20-29, 22:1-28; 2 Kings 3:13; Jeremiah 5:10-13, 5:30-31, 14:13-16, 28:1-4; Ezekiel 13:1-7; Micah 2:6-11, 3:5-8; Matthew 24:11, 24; Mark 13:22; Acts 20:29-30; 1 Corinthians 4:5; 2 Timothy 3:1-11; 2 Peter 2:1-3, 3:1-7; 1 John 2:26-27; 2

10

On the day of the Lord, at the natal hour, the incarnate Christ came forth, humble and homeless, glorious and regnant.[43]

He is sinless from conception on.[44]

Through the power of the Holy Spirit, God the Son assumed flesh, a humanly incomprehensible accomplishment.[45] For the Incarnation Day, the Spirit qualified him and the Father sent him.[46] The Son, God and man, willed this awe-inspiring event: dwelling among his own, to the horror of the nations.[47]

The immensity of the Incarnation astonishes still rising covenant generations: God on earth among his people in the Church.[48]

In respective Gospels, Matthew, Mark, Luke, and John centered on Jesus in his redemptive work for the recreation of holiness in his people.

11

With the Baptizer, Jesus began his ministry.[49] God the Son—in the Jordan and under the waters of baptism—assumed the burden of the Oral Law,* Israel's dominating sin, wherewith they of the covenant community coveted self-righteousness.[50]

V

John 7; Jude 4.

43. Matthew 2:1–2; Luke 2:1–7, 2:8–15; John 6:29; Galatians 4:4; Philippians 2:5–7; Revelation 12:1–6.

44. Hebrews 4:15, 7:26, 9:14; 1 Peter 2:22; 1 John 3:5.

45. Matthew 1:18–25; Luke 1:26–35; John 1:14; Philippians 2:5–11; Hebrews 2:9, 2:14–18; Revelation 12:1–6.

46. John 1:1–5, 3:31–36, 5:37–38, 17:25; Acts 13:33.

47. Psalm 2:1–2; Matthew 2:1–23; Acts 4:23–31; Revelation 12:1–6, 12:12.

48. Matthew 1:22–23; 2 Corinthians 8:9; Philippians 2:6–7.

49. Malachi 3:1–4, 4:5–6; Matthew 3:1–17, 11:11–15, 17:9–13; Mark 1:1–11; Luke 3:1–22; John 1:6–8,15, 3:22–30, 5:33–36.

50. Matthew 15:1–9, 23:1–36; Mark 7:1–8; Luke 11:37–44; Galatians 3:13; Philippians 3:2b–3.

The dark god possessed the Church, full of promising ways to self-justification.[51] Since the dawn the Satan promised to gratify the flesh. Flesh through covetousness wants satisfaction by sinning.[52]

V

Jesus in his first public work revealed the Trinity: the Father and the Spirit vowed to protect the Son in his humanity.[53] Thus Christ Jesus, with sovereign divinity supporting his humanity and with the Father's omnipotence, entered upon the way to Golgotha for the grace of imputed justification.[54]

The Incarnate made his humanity repeatedly visible:
Anger
Mark 3:5
Disgust
Mark 8:12
Distress
John 12:27
Affection
Mark 9:36
Sorrow
John 11:35
Sympathy
Hebrews 4:15
Weariness
John 4:6

---

*The Oral Law consisted of the legal tradition the Jews invented after the Exile. This other law served Pharisees/Sadducees to gain an impossible self-righteousness.

---

51. Genesis 3:1–7; Job 1:6–12; Isaiah 14:12–21; Ezekiel 28:11–19; Zechariah 3:1–5; John 8:38, 44, 13:27; Acts 16:16–18; 2 Corinthians 11:12–15; Ephesians 6:10–17; 1 Peter 5:6–11; 1 John 3:4–10; Revelation 12:13–17.

52. Genesis 3:1–7; Romans 8:5–8; Galatians 5:11–17; Philippians 3:3.

53. Matthew 3:13–17; Mark 1:9–11; Luke 3:21–22, 4:18–19; John 1:18, 29–34, 12:27–33; James 4:7b.

54. Matthew 16:13–20, 17:1–8; Mark 8:27–33; Luke 9:18–22, 28–36; John 6:68–69, 7:41, 12:29–34; 2 Peter 1:16–24.

12

While purposefully journeying toward Jerusalem, Jesus foretold to the Twelve the fact of the Crucifixion.[55] Consequently, in a ministry of inconceivable suffering, he walked—according to Mark—from Galilee into Jerusalem, planning the trials and the verdicts.[56]

V

To his suffering in Gethsemane he added Judas Iscariot's betrayal.[57] Peter also increased Jesus' suffering by denying him.[58]

V

This was the Son of Man's hour; for this he had come into Israel, to be the Sin-bearer and accomplish the Atonement.[59] At the appointed hour, the Judge's judges accused him of blasphemy.[60] Worsening, the Roman government condemned him on a contrived charge of treason. He came to claim his rightful place in the Kingdom, prepared to remove imposters as the Caesars.[61] The courts committed him—the Christ—to the Roman death for sedition. Then he walked to Golgotha to become sin.[62]

For this he had come: to atone for the guilt of sinning, his life a ransom for many.[63]

---

55. Isaiah 52:13—53:12; Matthew 16:21-23, 26:2; Mark 9:30-32; Luke 18:31-34; John 12:33.

56. 1) Matthew 26:57-68; Mark 14:53-65; Luke 22:66-71; John 18:12-14, 19-24, 18:28—19:16.
2) Matthew 27:11-26; Mark 15:1-20; Luke 23:1-5, 23:6-12, 23:13-24.

57. Psalm 41:9/John 13:18, Psalm 55:12-15; Matthew 26:14-16/Zechariah 11:12; Matthew 26:47-56, 27:3-10; John 6:70-71, 13:21-30, 17:12b, 18:1-4; Acts 1:18-20.

58. Matthew 26:30-35, 69-75; Mark 14:26-31, 66-72, Luke 22:31-34, 56-62.

59. Psalm 8:4; Ezekiel 2:1; Mark 14:21; Luke 21:27; Matthew 26:64; Mark 14:62; Luke 22:69.

60. Matthew 26:57-68; Mark 14:53-65; Luke 22:66-71.

61. Matthew 27:11-14; Mark 15:6-15; Luke 23:1-25; John 18:33-38, 19:1-16; Matthew 27:37; Mark 15:26; Luke 23:38; John 19:19.

62. Matthew 27:32-34; Mark 15:16-32; Luke 23:32-38; 2 Corinthians 5:21; Colossians 2:13-14; 1 Timothy 1:15; 1 Peter 1:18-20.

63. Matthew 20:28; Mark 10:45; 1 Corinthians 6:20, 7:23; 1 Timothy 2:6.

Throughout, he kept the wholeness of his bones and of his consciousness, refusing a sedative.[64]

13

All sinning originated in covetousness. In every present the Lord calls all to account for this active covetousness in his foreordained presence.[65]

V

Sinning misses the mark of righteousness and holiness.[66]
    Sinning occurs through ignorance.[67]
    Sinning is revolution, rebellion, and transgression.[68]
    Sinning is to be wrong or perverted, even do wrong or act perversely.[69]
    Sinning displays inner badness, worthlessness.[70]
    Sinning is to be wicked.[71]
    Sinning lacks integrity and rectitude.[72]
    Sinning breaks out against authority.[73]
    Sinning follows evil courses.[74]
    Sinning incurs guilt and is the door to hell.[75]
    Sin is lawlessness.[76]

---

64. Deuteronomy 21:22-23; Psalms 34:20, 69:21; Mark 15:23; Luke 23:36.

65. Genesis 3:1-7, 4:8-12; Romans 8:7-8.

66. Exodus 10:16, 32:33; Deuteronomy 1:41; Matthew 7:6; Luke 15:18; 2 Peter 2:10a-22.

67. Exodus 23:33; Numbers 14:41; Deuteronomy 4:28; Psalm 58:3; Acts 17:30.

68. Leviticus 16:21; Numbers 16:1-50; 1 Kings 12:19; Isaiah 66:3-5; Jeremiah 11:9-13; Ezekiel 3:4-11; Daniel 8:1-14; Amos 1:1—2:3; Acts 5:39, 7:51-53; 2 Peter 2:4.

69. Genesis 19:15; Isaiah 24:1-3, 32:3; Colossians 3:25; 2 Timothy 3:1-9.

70. Genesis 38:10, 48:17; Deuteronomy 15:9; Matthew 12:45, 16:4; Luke 13:6-9.

71. Psalm 1:4; Isaiah 57:20; Zechariah 5:5-11; 1 Peter 3:17.

72. Isaiah 65:11-12; Matthew 10:32-33, 12:30; Mark 7:18-23; Luke 11:23; James 2:10.

73. Number 12:1-8; Proverbs 4:24; Jeremiah 17:9; Matthew 15:19; Luke 6:45; Hebrews 3:12.

74. Genesis 3:1-7; Isaiah 48:8; Jeremiah 14:10, 18:12; 1 John 3:4.

75. Deuteronomy 24:16; 2 Chronicles 25:4; Ezekiel 18:10-13; Matthew 5:22, 18:7-9; Romans 6:23, 7:13.

76. First John 3:4-10.

Sinning is treasonous.[77]

V

None legitimately pleads ignorance.[78]

14

At the appointed hour on Crucifixion Day, cross-nailed and supported by his divinity, Jesus in his humanity absorbed at one and the same time tripled condemnation:

- the Father's wrath against the Church's sinning,[79]
- the Spirit's wrath against the Church's sinning,[80]
- and his own wrath against the Church's sinning.[81]

Rejected by the Church, condemned on the authority of Roman Empire, and forsaken by the Father, Jesus in agonies beyond pain created the Atonement to overcome sinners' self-righteousness. Thus he suffered the condemnation his people had earned for profaning the covenant promises.[82] For the cleansing of the Church, he shed his blood.[83]

This satisfied all divine justice for the redemption of Jesus' own.

V

---

77. Second Samuel 15:7-12, 20:1-2; 1 Kings 1:9-10, 2:13-18, 11:13.

78. Deuteronomy 21:22-23; Psalm 19:1-6; 2 Samuel 16:7; 1 Kings 2:39-46; Isaiah 55:1-5, 63:15-19, 64:8; Romans 1:18-23.

79. Romans 1:18, 5:9; Ephesians 2:3; 1 Thessalonians 5:9; Revelation 16:1.

80. Isaiah 63:10-14; Luke 12:10; Acts 5:1-11; Ephesians 4:30; 1 Thessalonians 5:19.

81. Exodus 22:21-24; Isaiah 51:17, 63:5; Jeremiah 6:11, 10:10; Lamentations 4:11; Ezekiel 13:15; Hosea 13:9; Nahum 1:6; Habakkuk 3:2; Matthew 12:31-32; Luke 12:10; Galatians 3:10, 3:13.

82. Deuteronomy 21:22-23; Psalm 22:1-2; Matthew 27:26, 27:45-50; Mark 15:15, 15:33-39; Luke 23:24-25, 23:44-49; John 19:1-16; Acts 2:22-23; Romans 8:3; 1 Thessalonians 2:14-16; Hebrews 5:7, 13:11-13 ; 1 Peter 4:1.

83. Leviticus 17:11; Matthew 26:28; Mark 14:24; John 6:53; Romans 5:9, 6:10; 1 Corinthians 11:25; Hebrews 9:13-14; First Peter 1:1-2; 1 John 1:6-7, 1:18-19; Revelation 1:5b, 7:14.

In the humility of and with the suffering on the Cross,[84] God the Son* and the Son of God** endured all hellish agonies in place of the elect.

He is the Savior.[85]

He is the Deliverer.[86]

He is the Redeemer.[87]

He is the Reconciler.[88]

He is the Christ, the Messiah.[89]

He is the Judge.[90]

He issued the First Judgment and recreates the dividing-line.[91]

---

*God the Son signifies his divinity.[92]
**Son of God signifies his saviorhood.[93]

15

Jesus' followers entombed his body, the evidence of his death.[94]

It is finished.[95]

In his death and burial Jesus sanctified respective graves, remembering the places of all bodies. While his body rested in the sepulcher, a stone

---

84. Deuteronomy 21:22–23; Joshua 8:29, 10:26–27; Psalms 16:10, 116:3; Isaiah 53:9; Hosea 13:14; Acts 2:29–36, 13:29; I Corinthians 15:3–4, 15:42–50, 15:51–57.

85. Isaiah 43:3, 11, 45:15, 60:16; Luke 2:11; John 1:9–13, 3:16–17, 4:42, 19:17–22; Acts 13:23; Romans 5:6–11; Philippians 3:20; Titus 2:11, 2:13, 3:3–7; Hebrews 9:23–28; 1 John 4:1–4.

86. Psalms 14:7, 18:2; Isaiah 59:20; Romans 11:26–27; Ephesians 1:3–14.

87. Job 19:25; Psalm 19:14; Isaiah 41:14, 44:6–8, 47:4, 60:16.

88. Romans 5:10; 2 Corinthians 5:16–21; Ephesians 2:16; Colossians 1:20.

89. Matthew 16:16, 22:42; Luke 9:20; John 1:41, 4:25; Acts 2:36; 1 Corinthians 1:24; 2 Corinthians 5:19; Ephesians 5:2.

90. John 5:27, 8:28, 9:37–39.

91. Psalms 75:6–8, 94:1–3; Isaiah 61:8–9; Malachi 4:1–3; Matthew 25:1–46; John 3:18–21, 12:31–32; Colossians 1:21–23; Revelation 14:13.

92. Matthew 11:27, 27:54; John 1:14, 3:16–17, 19:7; Romans 1:3, 8:3; 1 Corinthians 1:9; Colossians 1:13.

93. John 1:34, 49; Acts 9:20; Romans 1:4.

94. Matthew 27:50; Mark 15:37; Luke 23:46; John 19:30.

95. Matthew 27:55–61; Mark 15:42–47; Luke 23:50–56; John 19:31–42.

sealed off the enclosed space.⁹⁶ Jesus proclaimed to all in Sheol/Hades salvation and condemnation long remembered; he held the rebellious spirits accountable, offering no reprieve.⁹⁷ In the Eschaton they face, with all unbelievers living, the inescapable eternities of condemnation.⁹⁸

16

On Resurrection Day, after three days and nights of death, the Trinity revealed the Resurrection:

> Jesus created the Resurrection.*⁹⁹
> The Father created the Resurrection.¹⁰⁰
> The Spirit created the Resurrection.¹⁰¹

The Three as One executed absolute sovereignty over life and death. Thus, the Divinity created the Resurrection, glorifying the Son's humanity.¹⁰²

But someone will ask, "How are the dead raised?"¹⁰³

The Resurrection is: the recreation of Jesus' human nature, thereby breaking the bondage of sin and death, an inaccessibly complex trinitarian work, revealed only to the eschatologically bound Church. He in life and in death is her *Yes* and *Amen*.¹⁰⁴

The Resurrection reveals Jesus' conquest over sin and death, generating in his own the hope of the resurrection.¹⁰⁵

---

96. Matthew 27:62-66; Mark 15:42-47; Luke 23:50-56; John 19:38-42.
97. Isaiah 5:13-17; 1 Peter 3:19, 4:6.
98. Isaiah 26:19; Ezekiel 37:12; Daniel 12:2; Matthew 25:46; John 5:28-29; Revelation 20:11-14.
99. Psalm 116:3; Jonah 1:17; Matthew 16:21, 26:61, 28:11-10; Mark 16:1-8; Luke 24:1-12; John 2:18-22, 10:17, 18, 11:25, 20:1-10.
100. John 5:21, 25-30, 6:40; Acts 2:24/Psalm 16:9-10; Acts 2:32, 3:15, 5:30, 10:40, 13:30-35; Romans 8:9-11, 10:9; Ephesians 1:20; Colossians 2:12; 1 Peter 1:3-5.
101. Romans 1:4, 8:11.
102. First Corinthians 15:3-11.
103. First Corinthians 15:35-50.
104. First Corinthians 15:42-50; 2 Corinthians 1:19-20.
105. Psalm 118:22-23/Mark 12:10-11; Isaiah 25:8, 26:19; Daniel 12:2; Hosea 13:14; John 5:21, 5:25, 5:29; 1 Corinthians 15:26-28, 15:54-55; 2 Corinthians 4:16—5:15; 2 Timothy 1:8-10; 1 Peter 1:3-5; Revelation 1:17-20, 20:4-6 20:13.

*Jesus' authority over the dead.[106]

17

Over forty days Jesus ate and drank with the Twelve,* revealing to them the factuality of the Resurrection, which the Apostles taught the New Church.[107] Moreover, he laid the foundation of the New Church, on which he taught the essence of justification by faith and the glories of holiness.[108]

On Ascension Day Jesus ascended to his Father's right hand, his throne since the Creation.[109]

The reputable Twelve witnessed the factuality of his inexplicable ascension. Thus Jesus in his Person's divinity/humanity revealed the reunion of heaven and earth.

Within the new dispensation Jesus initiated eschatological haste:

Come, Lord Jesus![110]

His mercy is new every morning.[111]

---

*Minus Judas Iscariot[112]
and before Matthias' apostolic assignment.[113]

---

106. First Kings 17:17–24; 2 Kings 4:32–37, 13:20–21; Matthew 9:18–26, 27:51–53; Mark 5:35–43; Luke 7:11–17; John 11:38–44; Acts 9:40, 20:7–12; Hebrews 2:14–15.

107. John 7:32–36, 14:1–7, 14:18–20, 14:27–31, 16:5–11, 17:1–5, 20:11–28; Acts 1:1–5, 1:6–11, 10:41; 1 Corinthians 15:1–11, 15:20–23, 15:50.

108. First Corinthians 3:10–11; Ephesians 2:20; 2 Timothy 2:19; Revelation 21:14.

109. Psalms 24:7–10, 47:5–7; Isaiah 6:1–7; Luke 24:50–53; Acts 1:6–11; Ephesians 1:20; Hebrews 1:1–4; Revelation 5:6–10/Daniel 7:9–14.

110. Acts 2:19–21; 1 Corinthians 7:31b, 16:21; Revelation 20:1–3, 22:20.

111. Lamentations 3:22–23; Isaiah 54:9–10; Zechariah 1:12–17; Matthew 24:38–39; Luke 17:26–30.

112. Matthew 27:3–10; Acts 1:15–20.

113. Acts 1:26.

18

On Pentecost Day, the Holy Spirit descended upon the original New Testament congregation, a promise accomplished.[114]

The Spirit brings to bear on the New Church—to a people set apart and still prone to moral vice—the glory of the divine holiness.[115] He is the other Counsellor.[116]

The glory of holiness believers reflect in the humility that justification by faith inspires: trusting in Jesus Christ and believing the Trinity.

Now to a whole and integral people undiminished in righteousness:

> And in the last days it shall be,
> God declares,
> that I will pour out my Spirit on all flesh,
> and your sons and your daughters shall prophesy,
> and your young men shall see visions,
> and your old men shall dream dreams;
> even on my male servants and female servants I will pour out my Spirit,
> and they shall prophesy.[117]

In the Spirit the New Church moves on.[118]

19

In the full revelation of his holiness, Jesus, with the Father and in the Spirit, revealed himself. He is the King of kings and the Lord of lords.[119]

He is the Creator.*[120]

---

114. Matthew 3:11; Mark 1:8; Luke 3:16; Acts 1:15-16, 2:1-4.

115. Deuteronomy 16:9-12; 1 Chronicles 16:35-36; Psalms 46:4-7, 48:1-3; Isaiah 12:3-4, 45:14-17; Zechariah 4:1-10; John 15:18-25, 20:19-23; Acts 1:4-5, 2:33, 10:44-48, 19:6; Ephesians 1:15-23.

116. John 14:15-17, 14:25-26, 15:26-27, 16:7-11, 16:12-15.

117. Joel 2:28-29; John 7:37-39; Acts 2:17-18; 1 John 4:13-21.

118. Isaiah 44:1-5, 63:3-9; Acts 2:5-13, 43-47, 5:32; Romans 8:9-11, 12-17; Ephesians 1:13-14; Colossians 3:1-4.

119. Deuteronomy 17:14-20; Psalms 24:7, 29:1-11, 47:7-9, 61:6-7, 72:1-19, 99:4-5, 105:1-3, 136:1-3, 138:4-6, 145:4-7, 13; Isaiah 6:1-5, 11:3-5, 40:12-17, 41:14-16, 43:15; Matthew 21:5; Philippians 2:9-11/Isaiah 45:23; Hebrews 13:8; Revelation 17:14, 19:16.

120. Job 38:4-7; Psalms 104:24, 135:6-7; Jeremiah 10:12-14; John 1:2-3; I Corinthians 8:6; Colossians 1:15-16; Hebrews 1:10-14, 2:10.

He is the Judge.[121]
He is the Shepherd.[122]
He is the Commander.[123]
He is the Mediator.[124]
He is the Intercessor.[125]
He is the Husband.[126]

Jesus is the omniscient Prophet. Following Moses' calling, he ineffably taught and structured all to come.[127]

Jesus is the Priest. After Aaron's calling Jesus revealed himself the Sacrifice to gain the salvation of his own.[128]

His own put on holiness to honor the one Lord and Savior.

---

*God the Father also created.[129]

THE RECREATED SPACE

20

In the space granted the Church, the Lord Jesus creates faith, that inherent human capacity to believe him at his command.[130] Faith is the major constituent of the image of God in all people. By faith believers hear and trust

---

121. Deuteronomy 1:17, 24:16, 25:1–3, 32:39–42; Judges 2:16; Psalms 7:6–8, 7:11, 72:2, 98:9; Micah 4:3; Malachi 3:2–3; John 2:28–29, 5:25–29; Acts 10:42; Romans 2:16; 2 Timothy 4:1; James 4:12, 5:9; 1 Peter 4:5; Revelation 20:4–6.

122. Psalms 23:1–6, 80:1; Isaiah 40:11; Jeremiah 3:15, 23:1–4; Ezekiel 34:1–31, 37:24–28; Micah 7:14; John 10:7–18; Hebrews 13:20–21; 1 Peter 5:4.

123. Deuteronomy 25:17–19; Joshua 5:13–15; 2 Samuel 22:1–51; Isaiah 42:10–13; Revelation 19:11–16.

124. First Timothy 2:5; Hebrews 12:24.

125. Romans 8:34; Hebrews 4:14–16, 7:25, 9:24; 1 John 2:1–2.

126. Isaiah 54:4–13, 61:10–11; Jeremiah 2:1–3; Revelation 19:6–8, 21:1–4.

127. Deuteronomy 18:15–22, 34:10–12; Matthew 10:41, 11:9; Acts 3:22–26, 7:37.

128. Exodus 28:1; Psalm 110:4; Hebrews 7:11–22, 7:23–25.

129. Hosea 2:14–23; Revelation 4:11, 21:1–4.

130. Matthew 4:12–17; Mark 1:14–15; Luke 4:14–15; John 14:1–3; Acts 16:31; Romans 1:5, 16:26; 1 John 3:23.

the Lord Jesus' imputed justification, which he with the Father and through the Spirit inserts into the elect.[131]

> And you,
> who were dead in trespasses and the uncircumcision of your flesh,
> God made alive together with [the Christ],
> having forgiven us all our trespasses,
> having cancelled the bond which stood against us with its legal demands;
> this he set aside, nailing it to the cross.[132]

Faith thus begins in the Church, finds motivation at home, and gains intellectual maturity in worship and through schooling. Faith generates earnestness in living, joy too.[133] Faith endows thinking, learning, speaking, working, and emoting with the vigor of holiness.

Believing Jesus' history motivates serving the Lord and Savior in consecration. Believers then abandon all powers of covetousness and press onwards for total sanctification.[134] Believing fights hesitation and doubt.[135]

In the second dispensation the Lord Jesus, with the Father and in the Spirit, leads the believing Church into the Eschaton. All others he leaves behind, gathering the evidence of reprobation.[136]

21

Christ Jesus from earliest times revealed his office: King, Prophet, and Priest. These three he distributed throughout the Church for her structure and organization.

> He is the King.[137]
> He is the Prophet.[138]
> He is the Priest.[139]

---

131. Romans 3:21–26, 4:11–12, 4:16–25.

132. Acts 10:43; Galatians 2:19–21; Colossians 2:13–14.

133. Acts 10:34–43, 15:8–9; Romans 4:9, 6:1, 10:8–9, 10:17/Isaiah 52:7; 1 Corinthians 5:7; 1 Thessalonians 5:12–22; Hebrews 11:1, 12:12–17; James 1:21, 2:14–16, 4:8; 2 Peter 1:9–11; 1 John 1:9.

134. Philippians 2:12–13, 3:12–16; Colossians 3:12–17; 1 John 3:3; Jude 3.

135. Matthew 6:30, 8:26, 14:31, 21:21; Romans 14:23; James 1:5–7, 2:14–26; Jude 22.

136. Isaiah 29:10; 2 Thessalonians 2:11–12; 1 Timothy 4:1; Revelation 17:17.

137. Zechariah 9:9/Matthew 21:5; Luke 1:33; Revelation 17:13–14, 19:16.

138. Matthew 13:57; John 1:18, 15:15; Acts 3:22/Deuteronomy 18:15, 7:37.

139. Psalm 110:4/Hebrews 7:17; John 1:29; Romans 8:34; Hebrews 9:11–14,

In the Church, Jesus rules each congregation by office bearers:

Elders he mandates with oversight of the preaching, discipline, and missions.[140]

Ministers he mandates with prophesying, in his name to proclaim all great doctrines and all holy living.[141]

Deacons he mandates to alleviate hunger, poverty, homelessness, and dispossession, first among a congregation's own widows, orphans, and sojourners to unify the Body.[142] Deacons care for hurting neighbors too, even calling governments to commit to social justice for the poor and marginalized.[143]

By elders, ministers, and deacons—men Spirit-equipped for office bearing—the Christ leads the Church out of moral depravities into the Eschaton, in the process transforming his people into communities of wholeness.[144]

For strengthening the faith founded on and build up by the preaching Jesus added sacraments:

22

The Church administers baptism once in the name of the Triune God; Jesus commands the sprinkling by or immersion into water for all members of the Church, thus to impress on each, as soon as feasible, the covenant sign and seal.[145] Parents thereto engage in self-examination preparatory to the

---

10:11–14; 1 John 2:1; Revelation 5:6.

140. John 4:35–38, 17:20–26; 1 Corinthians 5:9–13; Galatians 1:6–9; 1 Thessalonians 5:12–13; 1 Timothy 1:8–11, 3:1–7, 5:17–22; Titus 1:5–9, 10–16; Hebrews 12:3–11/ Proverbs 3:11–12, 13:17; 1 Peter 2:11–12, 5:1–5.

141. Isaiah 45:22–23, 48:3–5, 6–8, 49:5–7, 52:7, 55:10–11, 56:6–8, 60:1–3, 66:2; Jeremiah 1:10; Ezekiel 3:16–21, 18:1–32, 33:1–9; Matthew 7:15–20, 13:1–8, 28:16–20; Mark 4:1–9; Luke 8:4–8; John 8:47, 8:51; Acts 5:29, 20:26–29; Romans 10:14–21; 1 Corinthians 4:1, 15:12–19; 2 Corinthians 2:14–17; 1 Timothy 3:14–16, 5:17b; Hebrews 3:7–11, 4:11–13, 13:7; James 1:16–18.

142. Numbers 18:1–32; Psalms 68:5–6, 82:3–4, 146:5–9; Proverbs 30:7–9; Isaiah 10:1–4, 58:6–9; Jeremiah 7:5–7; Amos 4:1–3, 8:4–6; Zechariah 7:8–14; Malachi 3:5; Acts 4:32–37, 20:35; 1 Timothy 5:3–8, 9–16; James 1:26–27.

143. Ecclesiastes 4:1–3; 1 Timothy 3:8–13.

144. Psalm 68:32–35; Exodus 19:22; Numbers 17:1–11; Acts 2:43–47, 4:32–37; Galatians 6:10.

145. Genesis 17:9–14; Luke 1:59, 2:21; Acts 2:39; 1 Corinthians 10:1–5; Titus 3:3–7; 1 Peter 3:21–22.

sacrament and believing adults submit to this sacrament in a responsible manner. Baptism is circumcision reformed.[146]

This sacrament declares the way ahead:

> We were buried therefore with him by baptism into death,
> in order that, just as Christ was raised from the dead by the glory of the Father,
> we too might walk in the newness of life.[147]

Every baptism in the congregation reminds and strengthens justified-by-faith believers—to walk through the stresses of sanctification.

23

The Lord's Supper Jesus instituted to reform the Passover.[148]

Upon justification by faith this sacrament fortifies believers to persevere in sanctification, perpetually focusing attention on the source of the Church's origin, life, and vigor; that is, Christ Jesus' incarnation, death, resurrection, and his continuing rule accentuate the new and eternal life given to believers. For this the Lamb gave his life.[149]

Self-examination precedes partaking of the bread and the cup, in the light of the Scripture finding increased evidence of imputed holiness: in personal commitment, in family solidarity, in educational obligations, and in ecclesiastical responsibility, together to push onwards in sanctification.[150]

24

In each congregation and throughout the Church, vigor in sanctification appears in mutual discipline.[151]

---

146. Deuteronomy 10:16, 30:6; Jeremiah 4:4; Romans 2:29, 4:1; Colossians 2:11–12.

147. Genesis 17:10; Acts 8:26–40, 16:25–34; Romans 6:4; Colossians 2:11–15; Titus 3:4–6.

148. Exodus 12:1–13; 2 Kings 23:21–23; 2 Chronicles 30:1–27, 35:1–19; Ezra 6:19–22; Matthew 26:20–29; Mark 14:17–25; Luke 22:14–23; I Corinthians 10:14–22, 11:23–26.

149. Leviticus 1:10–13; Isaiah 53:7; John 1:29, 1:36, 6:35–65, 13:1–35; Revelation 5:6–14, 14:1–5.

150. First Corinthians 5:6–8, 11:27–32; 1 Peter 1:18–19.

151. Leviticus 24:10–23; Numbers 15:32–36; Proverbs 17:17, 27:17; Matthew 18:15–20; 1 Corinthians 5:1–5; Ephesians 4:1–16; 2 Timothy 3:1–9; Hebrews 10:19–25, 12:1–2; James 5:7–11; 1 Peter 4:1–6.

Communal love validates eschatological hope. All members of each congregation, beginning with the communicants, assist the office bearers in sanctifying the congregation, the men in the capacity of headship with the women helping.[152]

Sinning within each communion and by the entire Church is intolerable.[153] All hypocrisy and nominal membership must be rooted out of heart and hope.[154] Duplicities of self-righteousness must give way to the fear of the Lord, its accountability a joy.[155]

All of Christ recognize that sins against the Holy Spirit lead into damnation, its hellish fires fearsome.[156]

Also, persecution always threatens the Church, if not from the inside then from the outside.[157] Paul's persecutions and sufferings are evidence.[158]

25

In the Church's eschatological journeying, the Lord Jesus draws many to himself; always he imbues a remnant with wholeness.[159] Remnants he reg-

---

152. Genesis 2:18; 1 Corinthians 11:2-16.

153. Isaiah 48:9-11; Lamentations 3:31-33; 1 Timothy 6:3-10.

154. Deuteronomy 9:4-12, 13:6-18, 17:2-7; 1 Kings 13:18; Psalms 78:32-37, 119:120; Proverbs 30:12; Isaiah 43:22-24, 46:8-11, 50:10-11; Jeremiah 7:16-26, 12:2, 34:8-22; Ezekiel 33:30-33; Amos 5:21-24, 6:4-7; Micah 3:9-12; Haggai 1:7-11; Malachi 1:6-14, 2:13-16, 3:6-12; Matthew 6:1-4, 6:5-6, 7:1-5, 15:1-9, 16:24-28, 21:23-27, 23:1-39; Mark 7:1-13, 8:14-21, 11:27-33; Luke 6:46-49, 11:42-52, 12:41-48, 19:20-26, 22:1-8; Acts 15:1-5; Romans 2:1-11, 17-24; Colossians 2:16-19, 20-23; 1 Timothy 1:3-7; Titus 3:8-11; Hebrews 3:12-19, 13:9-10; James 1:5-8, 3:13-18; Revelation 2:13-17, 2:19-29.

155. Deuteronomy 4:9-14, 6:1-3, 10:12; 1 Samuel 12:14, 24; Psalms 25:11-15, 33:18-19, 34:7-9, 11-14, 89:5-8, 111:9-10; Proverbs 1:7, 9:10, 14:27; Ecclesiastes 12:13-14; Isaiah 8:13, 29:13-14, 33:5-6; Jeremiah 2:19; 2 Corinthians 5:11.

156. Matthew 12:31-32, 13:49-50; Luke 12:10; Acts 5:1-11, 7:51-53, 11:1-18; Hebrews 6:1-8, 10:26-31; 1 John 5:16-17; Revelation 14:17-20, 20:14-15.

157. Mark 13:9-13; John 15:18; Acts 8:1-3, 9:1-9, 13:48-52, 14:19-23, 17:5-9, 21:7-14, 23:12-15; Romans 12:14-21; Galatians 4:28-31; 2 Thessalonians 1:5-12; 2 Timothy 2:11-13, 3:12-13; Hebrews 2:10-18, 11:32-38; 1 Peter 3:13-22; Revelation 2:9-11.

158. Acts 8:1, 9:1-9, 22:20, 26:9-11; Galatians 1:13-14; 1 Timothy 1:12-14.

159. Deuteronomy 33:26-29; 1 Chronicles 16:13; Ezra 9:6-9; Isaiah 10:20-23, 46:3-4; Jeremiah 6:9; Lamentations 3:22-23; Ezekiel 11:13; Micah 2:12-13, 4:6-7, 5:7-9; Haggai 1:12-15; Zechariah 2:6-12; Malachi 1:2-4; Matthew 7:21-23, 11:25-30; Luke 10:21-22, 13:22-30, 14:15-24; John 6:37; Acts 1:15, 2:41; Romans 11:5; Ephesians 1:3-10; Revelation 7:4-8.

istered in the Book of Life, reforming them as the light of the world.[160] All whom he gathers he purifies in the light of holiness, constantly cleansing and reforming.[161] As the Lord Jesus separates each remnant to himself he repositions the dividing-line between the Church and the world.

All others he bypasses; these prove, by life-long sinning, the justice of reprobation.[162]

For this holiness he preserves, in every generation of the Church, a remnant, a people holy to him and qualified by grace to will and to live the typically Christian love.[163] Each remnant by way of the dividing-line the LORD separates to himself, giving each a new name.[164]

26

Christ Jesus heart-holds the Church in holiness; from out of the trinitarian union the Son affirms her consecration. As she travels to the Eschaton he cleanses and reforms her. By removing every trace of covetousness he recreates his own.[165] As in the Old Testament dispensation, equally in the New, he identifies the covenant community.

The Church is his Temple.[166]
The Church is his Bride.[167]

160. Numbers 26:1-62; Matthew 5:14-16; Luke 10:20; Romans 8:28-30, 9:1—11:36; Revelation 20:12.

161. Deuteronomy 26:16-19, 32:10-14; 2 Chronicles 7:1-3; Psalm 5:11-12; Ecclesiastes 12:11-12; Matthew 19:16-22; Mark 13:24-27; John 6:37, 6:44, 15:16, 15:19; Romans 12:9-13; Ephesians 1:11-14; Colossians 3:1-4; 2 Thessalonians 2:13-15; 2 Timothy 2:19; Hebrews 3:7-11/Psalm 95:8-11; Hebrews 12:5-6/Proverbs 3:11-12; 2 Peter 2:4-10.

162. Psalms 5:9-10, 73:15-20; Isaiah 6:9-10; Luke 20:18; Acts 28:25-28; Romans 9:32-33; 2 Thessalonians 2:11-12; 1 Timothy 1:19-20, 4:1-5, 5:24-25; 2 Timothy 2:16-18; Hebrews 4:1-7; 1 John 2:18-25; Revelation 9:1-8.

163. Deuteronomy 33:29; Psalms 33:20-22, 100:1-5; Isaiah 10:20-23, 11:11, 28:5-6, 41:8-10; Haggai 1:14-15; John 15:18-25.

164. Genesis 17:5, 17:15, 32:28; Isaiah 62:2, 65:15; 2 Peter 1:3-22; Revelation 2:17, 3:12.

165. Psalm 93:5; Proverbs 9:1-6; Hosea 14:4-9; Joel 3:18; Amos 9:11-15/Acts 15:16-17; Habakkuk 3:17-19; Zephaniah 3:11-20; Matthew 16:13-20; Mark 11:15-19; Acts 2:43-47; Romans 12:3-7; Ephesians 1:15-23, 3:20-21; 1 Timothy 3:14-16; Revelation 1:17-20.

166. Exodus 25:40; 1 Chronicles 28:11, 19; Ezekiel 40:1—48:35; 1 Corinthians 3:16-17; Hebrews 3:6.

167. Isaiah 61:10-11; Ephesians 5:32-33; Revelation 19:6-8, 21:1-4.

The Church is his Body.[168]
The Church is his Flock.[169]
The Church is his Army.[170]
The Church is our Mother.*[171]

In church renewal, his people look to him for more evidence of salvation:

relative to life,[172]
relative to food,[173]
and relative to the space of the covenant.[174]

The Lord Jesus gathers the evidence of eternal life for his people.[175]

---

*The Church as Jesus' mother.[176]

27

With the Father and by the Spirit the Son in holiness created the heavens and the earth, the whole his universal rule, the Earth his global Kingdom.[177] At the heart of the Kingdom the Lord Jesus placed the Church.[178]

168. Romans 12:3-8; 1 Corinthians 12:12-31.

169. Psalm 80:1a; Isaiah 40:11; Jeremiah 31:10-14; Matthew 9:36, 10:6, 26:31; John 10:11, 21:15-19; Hebrews 13:20; 1 Peter 5:2.

170. Genesis 32:1-2; Joshua 5:13-15; 1 Samuel 7:10, 17:26, 36, 45, 47; Psalm 2:1-11; Revelation 19:11-16.

171. Galatian 4:26.

172. Genesis 15:12-15; Jeremiah 31:27-28; Ezekiel 37:1-14; Matthew 19:16-22; Luke 10:25-28, 23:43.

173. Exodus 15:24-25, 16:13-25; Psalms 78:15-16, 21-31, 104:27-30, 136:23-25, 144:12-15; Matthew 14:13-21, 15:32-39; Mark 6:30-44, 8:1-10; Luke 9:10-17; John 6:1-14; John 21:4-14; Revelation 22:1-5.

174. Exodus 3:7-8; Deuteronomy 34:4; Isaiah 54:1-3; Romans 4:13-15/Genesis 17:8.

175. Psalm 12:6; Isaiah 59:21; Jeremiah 31:31-34; Ezekiel 11:17-21, 36:22-32; John 3:16-17, 31-36, 5:24, 6:25-34, 68-69, 10:27-28, 12:25, 17:1-5.

176. Revelation 12:1-6.

177. Psalms 19:1-6, 24:1-2, 145:10-13; Matthew 13:24-33, 44-50, 19:13-15, 23-30, 20:20-28; Mark 1:14-15, 4:26-32, 10:23-31; Luke 11:20, 13:18-21, 17:20-21, 18:15-17; Romans 14:17-18.

178. Numbers 2:1-34; Matthew 16:13-20; Mark 8:27-30; Luke 9:18-22; John

As the omnipotent Lord, Jesus—by fiat—revealed the first creation; over six days by speaking he created all, from the farthest circling galaxy to the minutest spinning photon.[179] After the Fall, beginning in the Church, Jesus recreated the eschatological Kingdom rooted in the Old Testament.*[180] Now comes the Recreation, the wholeness of the new heavens and earth: such is the power of the proclaimed Word.[181]

As the resurrected and ascended Lord seated at the right hand of the Father, Jesus sanctifies the Church, the heart of the Recreation. From out of the Church he opens the heavens to his own.[182]

---

*The LORD summoned David to reinitiate the Kingdom.[183]

THE RECREATED TIME

28

In the beginning the LORD, by dividing the light and the dark, created time, day and night, each cycle measurable in twenty-four equal units.[184] In the moving of the days, today, believers redeem the time, persevering.[185]

They who take history's off-ramps slowly fade into circularities, carrying within them creative destruction.[186]

6:67-69; Ephesians 1:15-23; Colossians 1:15-20; 1 Timothy 3:14-16.

179. Genesis 1:1-31; Job 38:4-7; Psalms 33:6-7, 104:5-9; Proverbs 8:22-31; Isaiah 40:25-26; John 1:1-4; 1 Corinthians 8:4-6; Colossians 1:15-16; Hebrews 1:10, 2:10.

180. Second Samuel 8:15-18; Deuteronomy 2:34-35; Isaiah 65:17-25; Ezekiel 37:1-14; Zephaniah 3:14-20; Matthew 12:22-30, 18:1-6.

181. Matthew 19:28; Romans 8:18-25, 10:14-17; 2 Corinthians 5:17; Ephesians 2:11-22, 4:22-24; Colossians 3:10; 1 Peter 1:10-11, 22-24; Revelation 1:6, 11:15.

182. Psalms 21:1-13, 99:1-5, 111:2-4; Ezekiel 40:1—48:35; John 14:1-7; 1 Thessalonians 4:13-18; Hebrews 3:1-6; 1 Peter 1:3-5; Revelation 1:12-16, 4:1—5:14, 21:1—22:21.

183. Second Samuel 7:10-11; Psalms 20:6, 89:1-4, 132:11-12; Matthew 1:1; Acts 15:16-17; Romans 1:3.

184. Genesis 1:3-5.

185. Psalms 31:15a, 39:4-6; Ephesians 5:16; Colossians 4:5; Hebrews 11:1-40; 1 Peter 4:7; Revelation 14:12, 20:2.

186. Isaiah 40:21-24; Romans 13:11-14; Revelation 12:12.

To know one's place in time and history relative to the Christ's Return excites consecration.[187]

29

Over days, weeks, years, centuries, and millennia the Lord Jesus, sovereign and omnipotent, creates history every day. Daily he lays down the route for the Church's gratitude.[188]

In and with the Scriptures the Lord Jesus gave knowledge of the past, therewith in the present to interpret the future.[189]

Covetous peoples and empires, reactionary in being and ignorant of the common good, walk away from the main route and seek histories at variance to Jesus' lordship.[190] Off the main road these engage unforgiveable sinning, the refusal to believe and live the Gospel.[191]

Jesus, the LORD God, from out of the first dispensation alerted the Church to the consequences of sinning.[192] In cleansing the world he warned the nations to beware.[193]

In the BC and AD millennia, Jesus locates the Church on her way to the Eschaton. The Church is basic to the times; in her—shepherd-wise*—Jesus enfolds his own and for her structures history.[194]

---

187. Job 7:7; Psalms 39:11, 144:4; Ecclesiastes 3:1-9; Isaiah 64:1-3; Daniel 10:10-14, 11:2-45; Matthew 24:14; Mark 13:13; Luke 21:29-33; Romans 8:31-39; 1 Corinthians 7:31b; 2 Corinthians 6:2; 1 Thessalonians 5:1-11; Hebrews 6:1-8; 1 Peter 1:13; 2 Peter 3:8-10.

188. Genesis 50:20; Leviticus 26:1-13; Deuteronomy 5:6-21, 28:1-14; Joshua 24:1-13; Ruth 4:18-22; Esther 9:1-15; Luke 1:14-17, 1:32-33; Romans 15:21; Ephesians 2:10; 2 Peter 3:11-13.

189. Romans 13:11-14; 2 Corinthians 4:16-18; Hebrews 12:25-29; 1 Peter 4:7-11, 5:10; 1 John 2:7-11, 2:18-25; Revelation 1:7, 6:9-11.

190. Exodus 10:1-2; Esther 3:7-15; Jeremiah 18:15, 23:12; Matthew 6:32-33; Luke 12:27-31; 1 Thessalonians 5:1-3.

191. Matthew 12:31-32; Mark 3:28-30, 9:42-50; Luke 12:8-12; Hebrews 6:4-8; James 1:13-15; 2 Peter 3:15-16; 1 John 5:16b.

192. Leviticus 26:14-39; Deuteronomy 28:15-68.

193. Psalms 2:1-11, 22:27-28, 33:10-12, 37:20; Isaiah 13:1-8, 9-16; Jeremiah 18:1-11, 19:1-15, 25:15-16; Joel 3:9-21; Amos 1:1—2:16, 4:6-13; Micah 7:11-13, 16-17; Zephaniah 2:1-15, 3:8-1; Zechariah 9:1-8; Romans 1:18-23, 1:24-25; Revelation 10:11, 12:7-12, 14:6-8, 9-11, 16:16, 20:11-15.

194. Psalms 93:1-2, 100:3; Isaiah 40:9-11; Micah 5:2-4, 7:14; John 10:10b-11; Acts 20:28-31; Hebrews 12:18-24; 1 Peter 5:2-3; Revelation 7:1-8, 14:1-5.

To demonstrate universally and historically the fairness of divine justice,[195] he begins the Judgment in the Church.

---

*Bad shepherds are warned.[196]

30

Over millennia sinfulness penetrated the created order. The Lord Jesus, however, preserved the whole, the Earth specifically, for the sake of the Church and for the coming of the Kingdom.[197]

To beat down evils attacking the Church he reveals his wrath. In the first dispensation he sent sword, pestilence, and famine.[198] In the second dispensation he sends calamities.[199] Thus he initiates the punishment of unbelievers.[200]

Thus also he tests believers' faithfulness.[201] As the Son of Man he wills accountability first from office bearers.[202] By manifesting his people in holiness, sanctifying all, he reveals the centrality of the Church, the Kingdom, and the salvation of his people. Hence he provides for his people.[203]

---

195. Psalms 34:16, 98:7-9; Isaiah 63:3-9; Amos 7:7-9; John 9:39; Acts 17:30-31; James 5:9; 1 Peter 4:17.

196. Jeremiah 23:1-4; Ezekiel 34:1-31; Zechariah 10:3-5, 11:4-6, 13:7-9; John 10:13.

197. Genesis 9:12-17.

198. Deuteronomy 7:17-26; 2 Samuel 21:1; 1 Kings 8:37-40; 2 Kings 8:1-3; Psalm 11:6; Isaiah 24:1-23, 26:21, 66:6, 15-16; Jeremiah 14:11-12, 15:2, 24:10; Ezekiel 7:1-9; Joel 1:4-12; Amos 3:13-15, 4:4-12, 9:5-8, 9-10; Obadiah 1-21; Micah 1:2-7; Nahum 1:1—3:9, 3:19; Habakkuk 2:15-17, 3:1-16; Haggai 2:15-19; Zechariah 5:1-4.

199. Matthew 24:1-44; Mark 13:1-36; Luke 21:5-28; Acts 2:19-21; Revelation 6:1-17, 7:1-17, 8:1-13, 9:1-21, 16:1-21, 19:17-21.

200. Deuteronomy 6:16-19, 9:4-5; 1 Samuel 2:10a; Psalms 22:29-31, 55:9-11, 92:5-9; Matthew 11:20-24, 12:38-42; Luke 10:13-15; 2 Timothy 3:1-9.

201. Psalms 11:4, 66:8-12, 78:41, 56-57, 139:19-20; Isaiah 3:13-15; 1 Corinthians 10:6-13; 2 Corinthians 9:13-14, 13:5-10; Galatians 6:1-5; Hebrews 10:32-36, 12:5-6; James 1:2-4, 1:12-15.

202. Psalm 8:3-4; Ezekiel 2:1-7; Daniel 7:13-14; Matthew 9:1-8, 11:19, 12:8, 16:13-20, 26:64; Mark 8:31-33, 9:9-13, 30-32, 10:32-34, 13:26, 14:21, 62; Luke 5:24, 9:22, 26, 12:8-12, 17:22-27, 18:8, 31-34, 19:10; John 1:51, 5:22-23, 26-27, 6:62, 8:28, 9:35, 12:23, 34, 13:31-32; Acts 7:56; Revelation 14:14-16.

203. Exodus 16:13-21; Numbers 13:25-27, 21:16-18; Deuteronomy 7:12-16,

COVENANT ESSAYS: TWO

THE RECREATED PENITENCE

31

For purifying the Church, Christ Jesus commanded all to trinitarian prayer. True to his pardoning work God the Son hears penitential prayer.[204] Due to Jesus' atoning work the God the Father hears penitential prayer.[205] Through Jesus' atoning work the Holy Spirit leads in penitential prayer.[206] In the humility of penitence believers submit to the unsettling pain of repentance, confessing upwelling Adamic sin.

> For godly grief produces a repentance that leads to salvation
> and brings no regret,
> but worldly grief produces death.[207]

In the freedom and cleanliness of holiness believers lay out before the Judge all cruxes of covetousness and hearts of sinfulness; they do so communally and personally.[208] In the Father and with the Spirit Jesus upholds the trinitarian bond for praying.

32

At the command of the Lord and Savior believers humbly bow also before the Father, confessing covetousness with respect to the Kingdom. Every image bearer who seeks to own (parts of) the Kingdom—an empire, a country, a business, a property—finds perverse glories.[209] Such image bearers sooner or later stand before the Lord, fully accountable. All in Christ

---

8:1–10, 12:20–28; Joshua 5:10–12, 23:14–16; 1 Kings 4:20, 25; Psalms 67:1–6, 84:5–6; Isaiah 30:23–26; Joel 2:23–29; Zechariah 10:1; Matthew 14:13–21, 15:32–39; Mark 6:37–44; Luke 12:22–31.

204. Exodus 2:23–25; 1 Kings 8:33–34; Psalms 32:3–5, 44:23–26, 65:1–4, 79:8–10, 130:7–8, 145:8–9; Isaiah 58:1–5; Jeremiah 4:1–4, 14, 14:7, 25:1–7; Joel 2:12–14; Micah 7:18–20 ; Matthew 7:7, 9:13; Luke 5:32 ; 1 Timothy 1:15; 1 John 1:5–10, 5:14.

205 Matthew 6:7–13; Luke 11:1–4. Matthew 6:6, 14–15; John 14:6, 13, 15:16, 16:23–24.

206. Romans 8:12–17, 26–27; Ephesians 6:18–20; Jude 20.

207. Exodus 9:27; Jeremiah 2:26–28; Matthew 26:41; 2 Corinthians 7:10; Revelation 3:18–19.

208. John 8:36; Galatians 5:1–12, 17.

209. Genesis 13:10–11, 25:29–34; 2 Kings 18:28–35; Daniel 4:29–30, 5:2–4; Matthew 19:16–22, 20:20–21, 21:12–13; Luke 12:16–21, 15:11–13, 16:14–15, 19–31, 22:3–6.

Jesus renounce this perversion of the image of God. He wills to break such hardness of heart.[210]

> I am the way, and the truth, and the life.[211]

With his redemptive work, Mark 1:14–15, Jesus reclaimed the Kingdom; he sanctifies his for the Father and his people. In the Lord's reign—evidence of holiness—every form of ownership serves one goal, by the image of God to manage (parts of) the Kingdom, every proprietary interest stripped even of covetous taints.[212] Through ownership covenantally recreated believers in prayer confess improper interests in (parts of) the Kingdom, thus to sacrifice every property to the Father and the Son in the Spirit.[213]

33

The Church at prayer easily submits to the divine will, always only to walk by the Spirit.

In Christ believers confess every travesty of willing, never again to gratify its demands.[214]

Nevertheless, believers en route wage tiresome skirmishes, the human will against the divine. The human will is powerful in its familiarity.[215] Mercifully the divine will breaks down the covetousness of the human. This dying and death hurts. In each generation new creations appear in the light of holiness.[216]

The persevering Church as one petitions:

> Teach me to do your will,

---

210. Psalms 9:5–6, 66:18–19; Isaiah 59:1–2; Haggai 1:1–6; Malachi 1:14; John 9:31; James 4:3; 1 Peter 3:7.

211. Genesis 17:1; John 14:6; Acts 8:26–40, 16:25–34; Romans 6:1–3; Colossians 3:11.

212. Genesis 12:1; Leviticus 25:8–22; Deuteronomy 15:11; Psalms 8:1–9, 41:1; Isaiah 25:4; Jeremiah 22:16; 2 Corinthians 8:1–7, 96–14.

213. Exodus 23:10–11, 25:1–9; Judges 6:25–27; Matthew 17:24–27, 18:23–35, 22:15–22; Luke 3:10–14.

214. Proverbs 19:21; Matthew 6:10b, 7:21–23, 12:46–50; Mark 3:31–35; Luke 8:19–21; Romans 7:13–20; Galatians 5:16; Ephesians 4:15–16, 5:17; 1 Peter 4:1–2; 1 John 2:17.

215. Exodus 5:20–21, 14:10–12; Numbers 14:1–3; Psalm 7:12–16; Matthew 6:2–4, 7:3–5, 21, 11:16–19, 15:8–9/Isaiah 29:13, 26:41; Philippians 3:17–21.

216. John 3:8; Romans 6:4, 8:10; 2 Corinthians 5:16–18.

for you are my God!²¹⁷

With the human will covenantally recreated, believers in prayer sacrifice respective wills to the Father and the Son, in the Spirit.²¹⁸

34

From the beginning the LORD God provided his own with food.²¹⁹ Throughout the first dispensation since he provided the essentials, leaving all unencumbered and free to serve him.²²⁰

In the second dispensation Jesus commands believers to petition also the Father for sustenance. This ordering of reality the Spirit presses home. In the trinitarian manner God grants the recreated Church the necessities—food, drink, clothing, shelter—as he promised.²²¹ Such dependence upon the Father and the Son runs against the grain. Trust in seasonal rains suits better.

Nevertheless by faith the Church attends to the sowing and harvesting, rejoicing at every ingathering:

> The earth has yielded its increase;
> God, our God, has blessed us.²²²

With the essentials covenantally promised, believers cleanse each congregation and heart of covetous spirits.²²³

35

At the command of the Christ: believers burdened by injustice(s) seek justice from him and the Father, trusting that the Father and the Son are eminently qualified to invoke righteousness.

Beloved,

---

217. Psalms 40:8, 143:10a; Romans 14:19; 2 Corinthians 3:2–3.

218. 1 Kings 8:22–53; Matthew 16:24–26; Romans 12:1–2; 1 Corinthians 7:17–24; Ephesians 6:5–9; Philippians 4:8– 9; Titus 2:11–14.

219. Genesis 1:29, 3:19, 9:3.

220. Exodus 16:13–21, 17:1–7; Leviticus 26:3–5; Numbers 11:31–35; Deuteronomy 8:3, 26:1–4, 12–15, 28:1–6; Joshua 5:10–12.

221. Matthew 6:11, 32, 10:10; Acts 2:43–47; Philippians 4:11–13; 1 Timothy 6:7–8.

222. Psalms 65:9–13, 67:1–6.

223. Romans 14:1–9.

> never avenge yourselves,
> but leave it to the wrath of God,
> for it is written,
> "Vengeance is mine,
> I will repay,
> says the Lord."[224]

Still, in the Church, yearnings for retribution endure.[225]

Believers now put to death this perversion of the image of God. With justice covenantally recreated, all in Christ prayerfully leave retaliatory satisfactions to the Father and to the Son. In fact, believers set the norm for pardoning,

> ... forgive us our debts,
> as we have forgiven our debtors.[226]

For this, Jesus revealed the standard.[227]

36

The Lord Jesus' command stands firm: he and the Father forbid coveting all seductions of the darkness.[228] In prayer the Church asks that in the Spirit she remain strong, to prevent defeat in sin and shaming the Father and the Son. Hence, all journeying to the Eschaton seek fortification against enemies, Satan's fiery arrows specifically.[229]

> No temptation has overtaken you that is not common to man.
> God is faithful, and he will not let you be tempted beyond your ability,
> but with the temptation he will also provide the way of escape,
> that you may be able to endure it.[230]

---

224. Leviticus 19:18; 1 Kings 8:31–32; 2 Kings 13:4, 19:35–37; Psalms 12:7–8, 37:1–4, 5–6, 55:22; Matthew 5:38–42, 43–48; Romans 12:19; 1 Corinthians 4:11–13; Hebrews 10:30; 1 Peter 2:23.

225. Genesis 27:41; 2 Samuel 3:26 30, 13:23–29; Luke 9:51–56, 13.6–9, 22:49.

226. Matthew 6:14–15, 7:12, 18:21–35; Luke 6:31.

227. Mark 11:25; Luke 7:36–50; Romans 15:1–6; 2 Corinthians 2:5–11.

228. Genesis 13:10–11, 19:26, 38:15–18; Deuteronomy 5:21, 7:25; 1 Samuel 30:22; 2 Samuel 12:1–6, 15:1–6, 24:1–4; 2 Kings 5:19–27; Micah 2:2; Haggai 1:1–6; James 4:2.

229. Psalms 25:2, 53:5; Acts 7:52; Ephesians 6:16; 1 Peter 5:6–11.

230. First Corinthians 10:13; James 1:13–14.

With conquering power covenantally recreated, all in Christ prayerfully overcome and destroy temptation.[231]

37

It is the will of the Lord Jesus that his people cease coveting (parts of) the Kingdom, craving its power and its glory. Only, Satan and his pretend they own the Lord's radiant dominion.[232] Bartering lives for a dust mote of the Kingdom appeals.[233] Nevertheless,

> Better is a handful of quietness than two hands full of toil and a striving after wind.[234]

Aggressive and passive human capacities to own the Father and the Son's world, whatever the damages socially and ecologically, find the shame of destitution.[235] With ownership of the Kingdom in holy hands, believers in prayer denounce boundless cravings.[236]

38

All in real amendment know the pain of repentance; each repudiates satisfactions of hypocrisy.[237] Believers therefore in the Spirit validate the holiness welling up from within hearts of flesh.[238]

> Your decrees are very trustworthy;
> holiness befits your house,
> O LORD,

---

231. Ezra 9:6-15; Nehemiah 1:4-11, 9:6-38; Matthew 6:13, 26:41; 1 Corinthians 7:5; 1 Timothy 6:9.

232. Numbers 14:4-10; Deuteronomy 8:11-20; Isaiah 14:12-21; Ezekiel 28:1-10; Daniel 4:10-12; Matthew 4:8-10, 10:39, 19:23-24; Luke 4:5-7; 12:13-21.

233. Matthew 16:24-26; Luke 14:27.

234. Psalm 90:13-17; Ecclesiastes 4:6; Philippians 3:8; 1 Timothy 6:6-8, 17-19.

235. Psalms 73:16-17, 74:9-11; Joel 2:20; Amos 4:10; Luke 16:19-31; 1 Timothy 6:10; Hebrews 13:5; Revelation 11:18p, 20:1-3.

236. Philippians 3:12-16.

237. Numbers 12:9-16, 14:17-19, 21:7-9; Nehemiah 8:11, 9:1-3; Psalms 34:15-18, 19-22, 51:3-9; Ezekiel 20:1-8; Micah 6:6-8; Luke 18:9-14.

238. Psalm 77:13; Ezekiel 36:22-32; John 6:63; Acts 20:24; Romans 8:12-13; 1 Corinthians 3:1-4; Galatians 5:19; Philippians 3:8-9; Colossians 3:5.

forevermore.²³⁹

Jesus taught that no matter how often one (an individual, a congregation, the Church) sins he, the Savior, hears genuine repentance and, in oneness with the Father, forgives.²⁴⁰ Forgiveness then creates freedom to make real amends. At issue is not the divine readiness to remit sins, but believers' willingness and ability to repent.²⁴¹

Now, out of love for the Lord Jesus and the Father, in the Spirt all of the Church, in consecration, engage the Ten Commandments with renewed vigor.²⁴² Members of Christ orient inner and outer selves, as does each congregation, to that which glories in the eschatological future,

THE RECREATED GRATITUDE

39

Gratitude runs forever, glorifying the Trinity into all eternity.²⁴³ Beginning here and now in the sanctifying way the powers of grace bear fruit. All in every congregation walk in the light of holiness, thoughts, words, and deeds expressive of the love of the Lord, in the fear of the Lord for accountability.²⁴⁴ Hence,

> To the teaching and to the testimony!²⁴⁵

Christ Jesus, by the imposition of the Law, forms and reforms consciences, until all his abide by the same ethical standard.*²⁴⁶ Hence, again, gratitude in good works opens up holiness in righteousness.²⁴⁷

---

239. Leviticus 4:1–35; Psalms 19:11–13, 20:6, 93:5; 1 Thessalonians 3:11–13.

240. Psalm 78:38–39; Isaiah 43:25–28, 48:17–19, 59:16–20; Jeremiah 3:11–18, 24–25; Matthew 18:21–35; James 5:16.

241. Matthew 6:14–15.

242. Romans 12:1–2; Colossians 2:8–15.

243. Exodus 19:18–20, 20:1–17, 32:15–16; Leviticus 18:1–5, 26:13, 46; Deuteronomy 5:6–21, 6:1–3, 7:1–5, 10:1–5; Hosea 6:6; Malachi 4:4.

244. Deuteronomy 32:44–47; Psalms 19:7–10, 36:1–12, 97:11–12, 119:1–176 ; 2 Corinthians 10:5–6; Galatians 3:23–29; Hebrews 8:8–12.

245. Isaiah 1:18–20, 8:20a; James 1:22.

246. Psalm 103:15–18; Proverbs 28:9; Matthew 5:17–20; Luke 16:16–17; James 2:8–13.

247. Matthew 5:14–16; John 14:21; Romans 13:8–10; 1 Corinthians 6:9–11, 7:17; Colossians 2:6, 3:12–17.

The way of gratitude starts in the Church, always.[248]

---

*The Law also exposes sin, apparent ten times in the exposition of the Commandments.

40

The Lord Jesus tolerates gods neither next to him nor to the Father and the Spirit; displacement of the Persons of the Trinity garners his wrath.[249] The I AM wills all honor for the Three-in-One of whom he is one.[250]

Yet religiosities, sects,* and cults** push the Persons of the Trinity aside, covetously to claim prohibited glories in self-justification.[251] All idolatries face a grievous future, condemnation sure; moreover idolaters become what they worship.[252] Beginning in the Church, hatred for idolatry gathers strength.[253]

---

*Sect: a schismatic break to pioneer a more than holy church formation.

**Cult: an enforcement of a religious idea, its leader(s) recruiting followers from the Church.

---

248. Isaiah 35:8, 40:3–5, 43:14–21, 49:8–23, 62:10–12; Acts 9:2, 19:23, 22:4, 24:22.

249. Exodus 32:7–8; Deuteronomy 4:15–24, 32–40, 16:21–22; Joshua 23:6–11; 1 Corinthians 8:4–6, 10:14–22.

250. Exodus 22:20, 23:23–25; Numbers 25:1–5; Deuteronomy 10:1–5; Psalms 81:6–10, 96:1–6, 97:6–9; Isaiah 65:1–7; Matthew 4:10; Luke 4:8; 1 Corinthians 10:6–13; 1 John 5:21.

251. Exodus 34:11–17; Deuteronomy 9:13–21, 12:1–4, 29–31, 32:15–18, 19–22; 1 Kings 11:1–8, 12:28, 14:23–24; Isaiah 2:12–19.

252. Leviticus 18:21, 19:4, 31, 20:1–5, 6–9, 27, 26:1–2; Deuteronomy 4:25–31, 27:15; Judges 2:1–5; 1 Samuel 15:23a; 2 Kings 10:18–27, 17:7–18, 23:26–27; 1 Chronicles 9:1b, 16:26; Psalms 115:3–8, 135:15–18; Romans 1:18–23, 1:24–25; 1 Corinthians 6:9–11; Revelation 19:1–6.

253. Psalm 16:4; Isaiah 41:5–7, 44:9–20, 46:5–7, 66:17, 22; Jeremiah 2:9–13, 3:6–10, 7:30–34, 8:1–3, 23:12–15, 16–17; Ezekiel 8:7–13; Daniel 3:1–30, 4:1–37; Hosea 2:1–13, 5:5–7; Habakkuk 2:18–19; Zephaniah 1:2–6; Zechariah 1:1–6, 3:1–5; 1 Corinthians 12:1–3.

41

Even as denominations schismatically multiply the Lord Jesus wills concord in worship; as the Head of the Church he is the Liturgist and the Exegete who unifies the worshiping Church.[254] Jesus, according to his will, instituted the acceptable way of worship; none dare substitutions and devices of human imaginations to pervert liturgies—much by less Satan's suggestions—to remove attention from the proclamation of the Word.[255] Communal worship centers on reading the Scriptures and the proclamation of the Word.*[256]

They who break up the Body, the Bride, the Flock, and the Army of the Christ, to idolize inventions and projections of the imagination, find that beginning in the Church Jesus wills worship without compromise and hypocrisy.[257]

Fathers, son(s), grandson(s), and great-grandson(s) who disbelieve the Christ's headship, covetously moved, discover the fierceness of his wrath to the third and fourth generation; they also simultaneously experience the social costs. [258]

---

*Acceptable congregational worship includes teaching, admonishment, psalm/hymn singing, prayer, and sacramental observances with thanksgiving and in humbleness.

42

As the Church breaks down, blasphemy rages, accompanied by foul language.[259] Blasphemers consistently despise the Persons of the Trinity, cov-

---

254. Psalm 95:1-5; John 17:6-19; 1 Corinthians 1:10, 14:33; Revelation 1:12-16.

255. Deuteronomy 12:5-7, 10-14; 1 Kings 12:25-33; Isaiah 1:12-17; Habakkuk 2:20; Matthew 4:10; Luke 4:8; John 4:23-24; 1 Corinthians 11:2-16, 14:33-36.

256. Exodus 25:1—31:18, 35:1—40:38; 1 Kings 6:1-38; 2 Kings 12:9-16; 2 Chronicles 29:3-36; Ezra 6:13-18; Nehemiah 10:32-39; Ezekiel 40:1—48:35.

257. Exodus 32:1-6; Deuteronomy 12:8-9; 2 Timothy 2:8-14; Hebrews 12:18-24.

258. Exodus 34:6-7, 14; Deuteronomy 7:9-10; Isaiah 45:22-23, 48:1-2, 55:1-2, 66:22-23; Luke 1:11-12; John 4:23-24; Ephesians 6:4; Colossians 3:21; Hebrews 12:29/ Deuteronomy 4:24.

259. Matthew 12:24-28; Mark 3:22-27; Luke 11:15-20; 1 Corinthians 12:1-3; Ephesians 5:4; Colossians 3:8; James 3:9-10.

eting the downfall of the Son, of the Father, and of the Spirit.[260] Hence, in the Church, the more members push the Name asunder the worse the profanities.[261]

All who are in Christ Jesus reverently and humbly uphold the trinitarian names.[262] In all times and in all situations the people of the Lord, beginning in the holiness of worship, utter the divine names with reverence.

> Shout, and sing for joy, O inhabitants of Zion,
> for great in your midst is the Holy One of Israel.[263]

Now, by calling upon the name of the Lord, oaths carry weights of integrity.[264]

43

With covetously pursued labors, pleasures, and "good" causes, idolizing spirits erode the worth of sabbath rest; blending rest by enculturation into evil is to worship other gods, the social costs of which immense.[265]

In the first dispensation the covenant people rested each Seventh Day, to know themselves in the glory of divine holiness and in the fear of the Lord. In the second dispensation, on First Days, Christ's members called together—to know themselves in the divine holiness of the eternal sabbath—rest in the fear of the Lord preparatory to the week ahead, thus generating sanctity.[266] These are the primary days for the Word.[267]

In these days of rest, all in Christ gather for inspiration by the love of God.[268] On the Seventh Day in the Old Testament the Lord's people listened

---

260. Exodus 22:28; Leviticus 24:10-23; Matthew 27:39-44; Mark 15:17-20, 29-32; Luke 23:35-37; John 19:3.

261. Leviticus 5:4; Numbers 14:15-16; Job 2:9; Ezekiel 36:20-21; 39:7-8; Amos 8:11-12; Romans 3:14.

262. Job 1:5; Romans 16:25-27; 2 Corinthians 13:11-14; Galatians 3:1-5; 2 Timothy 1:8-10.

263. Isaiah 12:6.

264. Genesis 24:3; Joshua 2:12-14, 9:18; Matthew 5:33-37; Hebrews 6:13; James 5:12.

265. Numbers 15:32-36; Nehemiah 13:15-18; Isaiah 58:13-14.

266. Leviticus 19:30; Nehemiah 13:19-22.

267. Isaiah 55:6-9, 56:6-8, 66:22-23; Jeremiah 17:19-27; Matthew 12:1-8; Mark 2:23-28, 3:1-6; Luke 13:10-17, 14:1-4; John 5:10-18, 7:21-22, 9:13-14; Revelation 1:10.

268. Exodus 23:12-17, 34:21, 35:1-3.

to him. On First Days in the second dispensation they hear him. They integrate the Fourth Commandment into the holiness of the Church, celibacy, marriage, families, education, work, and even recreation.

44

By disparagement of the Scriptures and with jealously guarded individualism, each person covetously becomes a decisive authority. This is the perceived norm. Consequentially, for the consecration of each congregation, the Lord Jesus commands:

> children to honor parents,[269]
> parents to honor the Lord,[270]
> and office bearers to honor the Office Bearer.[271]

Beginning in the Church the norms for authority stand out clearly:

> for parents and teachers,[272]
> for office bearers,[273]
> and for governments, courts, and police.[274]

All in all,

" ... [submit] to one another out of reverence for Christ.[275]

45

The Lord Jesus created life and upholds the first covenant promise.[276] Where Christianity fades, neighbors' lives cheapen; then covetous forces, huge with collateral damages, assume control.

---

269. Exodus 12:26-27, 21:15, 17; Leviticus 19:3; Deuteronomy 21:18-21, 27:16; Joshua 4:21; Psalm 144:12; Proverbs 1:8, 4:1, 10:1, 19:13, 20:20, 23:22; Matthew 21:28-31; Ephesians 6:1-3; Colossians 3:20.

270. Psalms 22:4, 78:1-8, 127:3-5, 128:1-8.

271. Matthew 18:1–5; Mark 9:36 37; 1 Timothy 5:17; Hebrews 13.7.

272. Psalm 78:1-4; Ephesians 6:4; Colossians 3:21; James 3:1-5.

273. Matthew 21:23-27; 1 Timothy 3:1-13; 1 Peter 5:1-5.

274. Numbers 12:1-16, 16:1-50; Matthew 22:15-2; Romans 13:1-7; 1 Peter 2:13-17.

275. Ephesians 5:21.

276. Genesis 18:9-15; Psalm 139:13-18; Matthew 10:39, 16:24-25; Luke 1:14-17, 17:33; John 1:4, 5:21, 25, 6:35, 11:25, 12:25, 17:3; 2 Corinthian 5:4; Colossians 3:4;

COVENANT ESSAYS: TWO

      War[277]
     Homicide[278]
  Abortion ... Eugenics ... Euthanasia
     Suicide[279]
    Carelessness[280]
    Cannibalism[281]
   Substance Abuse[282]
     Hatred[283]
     Pollution[284]

 Beginning in the Church, through sanctification believers hold neighbors high.[285]

 They who disparage neighbors' lives show thereby the condemnation they face.[286]

46

From the beginning, the Lord God and Almighty Creator ordered the man-woman bond and aligned sexuality; with clarity he defined the genders.[287]

Revelation 2:7, 22:1–2.

 277. Genesis 14:1–12; Joshua 9:1–2, 10:1–21, 11:1–15; Judges 4:12–16, 9:42–49; 1 Samuel 17:1–11, 29:1–5; 2 Samuel 8:1–14, 18:1–15; 1 Kings 8:33–34, 20:26–30; 2 Kings 19:35–37; Psalm 46:6.

 278. Genesis 4:8, 9:6; Exodus 2:11–15; Deuteronomy 19:11–13, 27:24–25; 1 Samuel 22:11–19; 2 Samuel 1:15, 2:23, 3:27, 4:7, 11:14–17, 13:23–29, 18:14–15, 20:10a; Matthew 5:21–26.

 279. First Samuel 31:4–5; 2 Samuel 17:23; 1 Kings 16:18–19; Matthew 27:5/Acts 1:18–19.

 280. Exodus 21:12–14; Numbers 35:9–14; Deuteronomy 19:1–10.

 281. First Kings 3:16–22; 2 Kings 6:28–31; Ezekiel 5:10.

 282. Genesis 9:20–21; 1 Samuel 25:36–38; Isaiah 28:7–8; Jeremiah 13:12–14; Daniel 5:2–4; Amos 4:1–3.

 283. Proverbs 14:30; Matthew 5:21–26; Romans 1:29, 12:19; Gal 5:19–21; 2 Timothy 3:1–5; James 1:20; 1 John 2:9–11, 3:15.

 284. Isaiah 10:15–19; Revelation 6:1–17, 8:1—9:21, 14:17–20, 16:1–24.

 285. Exodus 23:4; Matthew 5:5, 43–48, 7:12, 22:39; Luke 6:36; Romans 12:9–13, 18, 20, 13:8–10; Galatians 6:1–2; Ephesians 4:1–3; Philippians 2:1–4; 1 Peter 3:8.

 286. First John 2:9, 2:11.

 287. Genesis 1:27, 2:21–25; Romans 7:1–3; 1 Corinthians 7:1–9, 39–40, 11:2–16; Ephesians 5:21–33; Colossians 3:18–25; 1 Timothy 2:8–15; Hebrews 13:4; 1 Peter 3:1–7.

He condemned extra-marital sexuality. They who seek fornicative gratifications cause guilt and cost for themselves and others.

Homosexualism/Lesbianism[288]
Bestiality[289]
Adultery[290]
Divorce/Remarriage[291]
Bisexualism[292]
Pornography   Surrogacy   Cohabitation   Transgenderism
Polygamy[293]
Polyamory[294]
Premarital Sex[295]
Prostitution[296]
Incest[297]
(Statutory) Rape[298]
Bigamy[299]
Exogamy/Intermarriage[300]

Fornicative human beings find themselves in the fires of condemnation.

---

288. Genesis 19:4–5; Leviticus 18:22, 20:13; Deuteronomy 23:18; Judges 19:22; 1 Kings 14:24, 15:12, 22:46; Romans 1:26–27; 1 Corinthians 6:9–11.

289. Exodus 22:19; Leviticus 18:23, 20:15–16; Deuteronomy 27:21.

290. Genesis 16:1–6; Leviticus 18:20, 20:10; Deuteronomy 22:22; 2 Samuel 3:7, 11:2–5, 16:20–22; Proverbs 6:32; Matthew 5:27–30.

291. Deuteronomy 24:1–4; Matthew 5:31–32, 19:3–9; Mark 6:17–19, 10:2–12; Luke 3:19–20, 16:18; Romans 7:1–3; 1 Corinthians 7:10–11, 15.

292. Deuteronomy 22:5.

293. Genesis 20:17, 28:6–9, 35:23–26; 2 Samuel 5:13, 12:7–9, 16:20–23; Esther 2:12–14.

294. Genesis 20:17–18; 2 Samuel 3:2–5; 1 Kings 11:1–8.

295. Exodus 22:16–17; Deuteronomy 22:13–21, 28–29.

296. Leviticus 19:29, 21:9; Deuteronomy 22:20–21, 23:17–18; Hosea 4:13b–14; 1 Corinthians 6:12–20.

297. Genesis 19:30–38, 20:2, 12, 35:22, 49:4; Leviticus 18:6–18, 20:17–22; Deuteronomy 27:22–23; 2 Samuel 3:6–11, 13:14, 16:20–23; Ezekiel 22:10–11; 1 Corinthians 5:1–5.

298. Genesis 34:1–7; Leviticus 19:20–22; Deuteronomy 22:23–29; 2 Samuel 13:14.

299. Genesis 4:23–24, 16:1–6, 44:23–24; Exodus 29:21–30; Leviticus 18:17, 20:14; Deuteronomy 21:15–17; 1 Samuel 1:1–2, 25:43–44; Matthew 14:1–12; Mark 6:14–29.

300. Genesis 38:1–5; Deuteronomy 7:3–4; Joshua 23:12–13; Ezra 9:10–15, 10:1–5; Nehemiah 10:28–31, 13:23–27; 2 Corinthians 6:14–7:1.

In the Church, believers through sanctification create respect for and trust in respective spouses, to lead next generations to glorify the Lord in human sexuality for the marriage of the future.[301]

47

The Lord Jesus from the beginning established clear boundaries by dividing neighbors' goods. All thievery he therefore hates.

> Of money[302]
> Of goods[303]
> Of fraud/identity theft[304]
> Of usury[305]
> Of robbery[306]
> Of kidnapping/trafficking[307]
> Of insider trading[308]
> Of bribery[309]

Beginning in the Church and in the sanctification of all justified by faith, they who break the boundaries of ownership, coveting what belongs to others, experience in the end its terrible social shame.[310] Hence, everyone in Christ Jesus serves the welfare of others, with trust and respect building community.[311]

---

301. Genesis 2:24-25; 1 Corinthians 7:1-7; 1 Thessalonians 4:1-8; Revelation 19:6-10.

302. Jeremiah 6:13-15, 8:8-13; John 12:6.

303. Leviticus 6:1-7, 19:11 ; Luke 12:41-48.

304. Leviticus 19:13, 35-36; Deuteronomy 19:14, 24:14-15, 25:13-16, 27:17; Joshua 9:1-27; Proverbs 11:1; Luke 19:1-10; Acts 5:1-11; 1 Corinthians 6:7-8.

305. Exodus 22:25-27; Leviticus 25:35-38; Nehemiah 5:7; Psalm 15:5.

306. Exodus 22:1-2 ; Proverbs 1:7-19.

307. Exodus 21:16; Deuteronomy 21:10-14, 24:7; Amos 2:6.

308. Matthew 26:14-16; Mark 14:10-11; Luke 22:3-6; John 18:2-3.

309. Exodus 23:6-8; Deuteronomy 10:17, 27:25; Isaiah 5:23; Amos 5:12; Acts 24:26.

310. Luke 16:19-31.

311. Second Corinthians 4:16-18; Galatians 6:10; Ephesians 4:28.

48

The Lord Jesus, beginning among his own, ordered his people to love, basic to which building up the reputations of others.

In court[312]
In church[313]
In family situations[314]
In the neighborhood also by way of social media[315]

He therefore condemns also the guilts and social costs of:

slander/gossip,[316]
bullying,[317]
and scapegoating.[318]

Every abuse of others disparages neighbors' good names.

All who are in Christ seek the wellbeing of neighbors as evidence of sanctification, however strong temptations may be for verbal abuse.[319]

49

Through the Adamic sin the Devil moves people to oppose the Christ with ingratitude but the Lord Jesus condemned every covetous action, whether of heart, soul, mind, or hand.[320] Beginning in the Church, believers, moved by the Word and the Spirit, through sanctification cease giving in to

---

312. Leviticus 5:1, 19:12, 19:15-16; Deuteronomy 19:15-21, 27:19; Proverbs 6:19, 14:5; 1 Corinthians 6:1-8.

313. John 8:44, 55.

314. Exodus 21:17; Leviticus 19:3; Deuteronomy 27:16; Proverbs 4:24, 5:3, 6:12-15, 10:32, 19:1.

315. Jeremiah 9:4-6; Ephesians 4:29.

316. Exodus 23:1-3, 6-8; Psalms 12:1-4, 3-4, 31:18, 37:12-13, 41:6-7, 64:1-6; Proverbs 7:1-20; Matthew 26:61, 27:40; Mark 14:57-58; James 4:6-12.

317. First Kings 21:8-14.

318. Matthew 27:39-44; Mark 15:29-32; Luke 23:35-37; John 11:49-52, 18:14.

319. Philippians 2:14-18; Colossians 4:5-6; 1 Thessalonians 3:11-13; James 1:19-21, 3:1-12, 4:11-12; 1 Peter 3:8-12, 14-18.

320. Genesis 13:11; Exodus 22:29; Numbers 14:20-25, 16:31-35; Ezra 4:1-3; Proverbs 6:16-19; Hosea 4:4-6; Micah 2:1-5, 6:9-14, 7:1-7; Haggai 1:1-6; Malachi 1:8; Matthew 20:20-28; Mark 10:35-45; Luke 9:46-48.

covetousness. Sins of opposing the Lord Jesus and harming neighbors bear condemnation.[321]

Sins against the commandments are identifiable, except for the Tenth. Coveting is a matter of the heart where the Lord Jesus judges, condemning even least traces of refusal and failure to respect the divine will.[322] Resistance to sanctification in holiness turns bad.[323]

50

The great law of love for the Christ breaks forces of hatred. Beginning in the Church the Lord Jesus wills the holiness of his people, therefore, to love the Father and the Spirit also.[324] The primary obligation of love is: the commitment of heart to place the Persons of the Trinity first, whatever the exigencies of life.

The great law of the love of neighbors breaks forces of hate. The Lord Jesus wills in the Church the holiness of his people, wherein the love of neighbors also with respect to pollutions.

The primary obligation of love is: the commitment of heart to place neighbors first, whatever the exigencies of life.[325]

51

The Lord Jesus builds the redeemed community through gratitude, gratitude by way of the Law; this way of life only meets his holiness. In holiness

---

321. Deuteronomy 11:18-25; Psalms 31:19-20, 37:10-11, 18-19; John 15:10; Ephesians 6:10-17; Philippians 1:6; Hebrews 12:12-17.

322. Psalms 10:10-11, 12-13, 94:7; Isaiah 29:15-16; Galatians 3:10-14; 2 Timothy 2:19.

323. Second Kings 17:1-18, 19-20; Micah 2:6-11; Mark 12:38-40; Luke 12:1-3, 13-21, 14:25-33, 22:24-27.

324. Deuteronomy 6:4-5; Psalm 31:23-24; Matthew 22:37; Mark 12:29-30; Luke 10:27a; John 14:21; 1 Timothy 6:15-16; 1 Peter 1:8-9.

325. 1) Exodus 22:21-24, 23:9-11; Leviticus 19:9-11, 14, 17-18, 32, 19:33-34, 23:22; Deuteronomy 15:7-8, 15:11, 24:19-22, 27:18; Matthew 22:39; Mark 12:31a; Luke 10:27b; John 13:34; Romans 13:8-10; Galatians 5:13-15, 6:1-5; Philippians 2:1-11; Hebrews 13:1-6.

2) Second Corinthians 5:17; James 2:8-13; 1 Peter 3:8-12, 5:6-11; 1 John 2:7-11, 3:11-18, 4:7-12, 5:1.

he creates renewal in every generation.[326] The Scriptures reveal the way for numerous generations.[327]

The holy way of life glorifies him, the Father, and the Spirit. Hence, he presses the Church into sanctity, and for the interconnectivities of the Kingdom wills that his followers incorporate—to his glory!—agricultural, mechanical, and technological inventions.[328]

Hence, believers work together against assimilation and accommodation; standing together they refuse any equilibrium: so much for God, so much for covetous selves. World conformity has no part in sanctification. Thus, beginning in the Church, Jesus creates the way into the Eschaton gratitude.

THE RECREATED ESCHATON

52

At the end of time and history, with the work that the Trinity set out to do completed, the Eschaton breaks open:

> The Armageddon battle[329]
> The resurrection of the dead[330]
> The final Judgment based on the Golgotha Judgment[331]
> The unbelievers' eternal damnation[332]
> The marriage feast and the consummation of the Christ and his Bride[333]

At the revelation of the wholeness of the Body, its numerical 144,000 complete, she enters into the totality of sanctification: [334] immortality in holiness.

---

326. Leviticus 18:24-30; Deuteronomy 4:32-40.

327. Second Samuel 22:23; Psalms 22:22, 37:5, 77:13; Isaiah 26:7, 30:21, 35:8, 55:6-7; 1 Corinthians 12:31; Revelation 21:1-4.

328. Joshua 3:5; Proverbs 3:11-12/Hebrews 12:5-6; Proverbs 6:6-11; 1 Corinthians 15:58; Ephesians 4:25-32, 5:1-20; 1 Thessalonians 4:9-12; 1 Timothy 5:25, 6:3-10.

329. Jeremiah 1:15 16; Revelation 16:16.

330. Daniel 12:2; Isaiah 26:19; 1 Corinthians 15:50, 15:51-57; 2 Corinthians 4:16—5:10.

331. Revelation 20:1-3, 11-15.

332. Psalm 102:25-28; Matthew 25:31-46; Revelation 19:1-6.

333. First Corinthians 15:51-57; 1 Revelation 19:6-10.

334. Matthew 25:14-30; Revelation 7:1-12, 14:1-5.

See, now, the Bride, the Body, and the Flock entering the eternity of holiness.[335]

In the Eschaton, all in Spirit's surround, see the Christ and the Father in the glory of holiness.[336]

---

335. Matthew 5:8; 2 Corinthians 12:1–5; Revelation 21:1—22:19.
336. Matthew 5:8; 2 Corinthians 12:1–5.

JONAH EXPOSITION

1

JONAH INTERPRETATION

2

JONAH IN BRIEF

3

JONAH—A BOOK OF CONTRASTS

4

THE JONAH PROPHECY

COVENANT ESSAYS: TWO

JONAH INTERPRETATION

Abuse of the Christ's Jonah-book comes through eisegesis, eisegetes forcing their own interpretations into the account. Such biblical *thinkers* have pushed and shoved every sort of folly and fiction onto the text to find matters of relevancy. One found in this brief history a motivational missionary message. Another put the listening congregation with Jonah into the boat, everyone fleeing to Tarshish. One found the fish a type of the Christ rescuing a sinner, barely. Another forced the account into parable-mode, moralizing (not to have a heart as Jonah's) and exemplarizing (to obey as spontaneously as the Ninevites). One saw here an inclusion of Gentiles into the believing community. Another discovered here the Gospel's global range. One ascertained in the Jonah-book God's universal love and mercy. Another perceived in the third chapter the largest (Evangelical) revival of all time. Each eisegete thus struggled to unearth consequential matters, any and all, in the Jonah-history, except the one that the book itself exudes.

One obvious fact of the Jonah-book is this: nothing of the Gospel shines forth from this historical document. What does stand out, every exegete finds, is judgment, utter condemnation, upon reprobate Northern Israel.

V

I have read works about Jonah and heard four-part sermon series on the son of Amittai, each with eyebrow-raising surprises at the moralizing and exemplarizing, fictionalizing variations predicated upon the imaginations of authors and preachers. Worse frustration emerged when these *interpreters* forced the Gospel into the text or from it extracted some gospel-good. But squeezing any sort of good news out of the Jonah-document not only sounds artificial; each attempt is false. There is simply nothing of the Gospel in the Jonah-book.

Now, after lengthy reflection, I broke with centuries of tradition in specific ways:

In the first, I identify the LORD as the Messiah of the Old Testament, the Christ of the New Testament. Rather than work with the Old Testament's Messiah-name, I took the Christ-name to carry the relevance of this book into the contemporary Church. This exegesis makes the interpretation of the account more credible.

In the second place, the Christ with sovereign authority issues judgment and gathers the people on his right hand and left, Matthew 25:31–46,

13:36–43, 47–59; Revelation 20:11–15; etc. This exegetical factoring, relevant since Adam's Fall, acknowledges the LORD as the Christ, the only legitimate way to explicate Jonah's prophetic work Christologically.

Moreover, in the third place, I am convinced that this narrative must be considered in its entirety, not piecemeal according to superficial chaptering.

Fourthly, upon completion of his office in Nineveh the Christ had Jonah narrate major aspects of the mission, reciting even parts of his assumed praying, to listeners, at least one of whom then recorded the narrative. From that account Northern Israel had to know its ineradicable doom and the Church through her generations to recognize the mighty work of the predestination documented here.

In the fifth place, I identify Jonah's "God of heaven" as an idol represented in Northern Israel by two golden calves. Consistently I pinpoint this deity as Jonah's god(s). Had he believed the Messiah, the Christ, he would never have fled into the direction of the Western Mediterranean.

Moreover, in Jonah 2:1 the prophet addressed his own god(s), the golden calves Jeroboam I set up in Dan and Bethel, 1 Kings 12:28, the two whom the Northern Israelites continually worshiped, the sin which Jeroboam caused Israel to sin. The Christ's conflict was with these metallic statues. Hence when the prophet in 2:2, 6, 7, and 9 called upon the lord he had those two things of gold in mind and at heart, not the Christ from whom he had fled and with whom he argued throughout the fourth chapter.

The name, lord, was typical in the ancient Middle East for addressing also idolic objects of worship.

To the point now, translators (also of the ESV) erroneously identified the Christ with Jonah's god(s).

Lastly, the Christ considered Northern Israel until its end in extreme violence a covenant community.

V

At various times I worked on the Jonah-book with different interpretive models to remove follies of moralizing and exemplarizing, typologizing, each of which left heavy deposits of dissatisfaction.

JONAH IN BRIEF

In the Jonah-narrative the Author juxtaposed the Lord's spokesman first with a ship's crew. At the height of the tempest those pagans believed the

God of heaven who made the sea and the dry land, and feared him. Jonah, on the other hand, attempted to run even farther from the LORD, Israel's Christ, and demanded that the sailors toss him overboard. Death by drowning seemed preferable to life in obedience. Momentarily the contrast between the son of Amittai and the seamen stood in stark relief. Then the reprobates, ship and all, disappeared over Mediterranean horizons, uncircumcised. Jonah's unfaithfulness, however, set the pace in the first part of this history; even the rescue by and sojourn in a fish failed to convert him.

Jonah remained an awkward fit among the Old Testament prophets; in his case the LORD God selected during Jeroboam II's reign an unbeliever to speak for him, 2 Kings 14:23-29.

Jeroboam II, 782-753 BC.

Upon a simple foretelling the Ninevite citizens up to and including the king believed Jonah and repented of unspecified evil. The feared Assyrian heart, Nineveh, bowed before the LORD, while Northern Israel stayed true to its idolatry, its unfaithfulness in comparison to the Assyrian *repentance* painfully condemnatory. However, as the sailors, the Ninevite males remained uncircumcised, reprobates. The *conversion* of the Ninevites occurred during the reign of Ashur-dan, 773-755 BC.

Subsequent to the Jonah-history mighty Assyrians ruled, 2 Kings 16:7, 9, 10-16, 17:7-18, 24-28, 18:9-12, 19:8, 36 as

Tiglath-pileser III, Pul, 745-272 BC.
Shalmaneser V, 727-722 BC.
Sargon II, 722-705 BC.
Sennacherib, 705-681 BC.

Those rulers, cruel to extremes, overran and depopulated the Ten Tribes, 722 BC, not the work of an empire that had wholeheartedly turned away from evil to worship the LORD.

V

In the Jonah-book terrible tensions between the LORD God, the Messiah, and reprobate Northern Israel became apparent. Despite his longsuffering and continual summons to faithfulness, this people refused conversion, comforts of idolatry more appealing.

The *conversions* of the sailors and the Ninevites contrasted sharply to the Ten Tribes' perseverance in idolatry.

JONAH-A BOOK OF CONTRASTS

The Lesser Contrast
Jeroboam II's reign
782–753 BC
2 Kings 14:23–29
Jonah's escape from office
origin of storm
Jonah and the sailors
sailors—an idolatrous lot
the sailors asked a question and Jonah answered specifically to that question
sailors believed Jonah, along with the cargo they threw him overboard
calming of the sea and the sailors' sacrificing in thankfulness
no circumcision and adoption for entry into covenant community
the reprobate sailors disappeared forever

V

with the fish the LORD bound the two parts together

V

The Greater Contrast
Jonah and Ninevites
Ninevites—an idolatrous and rapacious lot
Jonah's prophecy and Assyrians' response
by repenting Ninevites believed Jonah
Jonah sulking on hilltop
no circumcision and adoption into covenant community
the reprobate Assyrians disappeared in the crush of empires, Egypt and Babylon
fall of Samaria
722 BC

V

> since the LORD governed the sailors, the fish, and the Ninevites
> why no repentance in Jonah and Northern Israel?
> though the LORD God capably worked temporary repentance in sailors and Ninevites
> he bypassed Northern Israel, from whom he refused to lift reprobation
> 2 Kings 17:6–18

THE JONAH PROPHECY

Throughout the first dispensation the Christ sovereignly cleared the way to his Incarnation and prepared the ground for his Crucifixion. For that purpose, at the conclusion to the Old Testament era and at the beginning of the New he positioned the Cross from which to issue the first and great Judgment. Preparatory to the Golgotha-judgment he directed peoples and nations to his right hand or his left, pronouncing clearly the grace of election and the eternity of reprobation. On his left hand he also gathered Northern Israel, Jonah's people, 1 Kings 12:19. From the founding of Northern Israel to its violent destruction by Assyrian forces the Christ accumulated sufficient evidence to support his reprobation of this people, its national cup of iniquity brimming. In thematic summary of the Jonah-narrative now, the Christ revealed its one and only significance, the final confirmation of the Ten Tribes' eternal condemnation. *He had doomed this people forever.* The Christ announced prophetically that judgment throughout the Jonah-account, the whole characterized by the fleeing, praying, and raging prophet. The Christ with the Jonah-history attested in the ongoing Church and before the world the timeliness of Northern Israel's fatal destiny.

THE FLEEING PROPHET

Dynamics involving the Jonah-history started at King Solomon's death, 932 BC. The Christ because of King Solomon's idolatry split the kingdom and assigned the northern part to Jeroboam, 1 Kings 11:26–40. Lamentably, Northern Israel's first monarch, Jeroboam I, immediately and purposefully devoted the new nation to idolatry that he symbolized with two golden calves. The god(s) represented by these images, 1 Kings 12:28, had to withhold the Northern Israelites for attending the great covenant feasts, which the Christ had commanded, Deuternomy 16:1–17. As Jeroboam and his people settled comfortably between the images positioned in Dan and Bethel they willfully broke the Christ's First Commandment, "You shall have no other gods before me." This bowing in worship to those images made his condemnation upon the Ten Tribes darkly ominous.

To prepare Northern Israel for its looming peril the Christ had sent Elijah, Elisha, Hosea, and Amos who summoned the Ten Tribes to repent of sinning, recommit to faithfulness, and believe the covenant promises. Each of the four prophets had, whatever the social and political exigencies, completed respective mandates. And had Northern Israel listened?

Later, nearer the Ten Tribes' doom in death, the second Jeroboam ruled, 782–753 BC; that was a time of political stability and economic prosperity, which drove those people into more intense dependency on the golden calves. Did not the flourishing economy and the bountiful peace up and down the Eastern Mediterranean prove the inexhaustible generosity of the god(s) over which the Northern Israelites obsessed?

To grant this prosperity and regional harmony the Christ had, for a brief season, weakened Northern Israel's main enemy, the fierce Assyrians, which gave the Ten Tribes opportunity to reflect on the nation's pressing doom that Elijah, Elisha, Hosea, and Amos had prophesied. Those people, under the spell of arrogance, misidentified the source of its blessings, comparative affluence, and relative peace. In consequence to that hardness of heart the Christ—persevering to a new extreme—at that time summoned one of Northern Israel's own, Jonah, to the prophetic office and by way of the *last* Old Testament foreteller to Northern Israel pronounce its overwhelming darkness. In that decisive setting the son of Amittai had one primary mandate, to speak audibly a prophetic message in and to Nineveh, the heart of the mighty Assyrian empire of the day. Even though the Christ held Assyria in its weakened state, because of its reputation for cruelty Jonah had reason to hesitate and flee away from Nineveh as far as possible.

V

Jonah's flight to the western end of the Mediterranean, the Great Sea, had a cause other than fear of death at Assyrian hands. On account of his own idolatry he attempted the escape from the responsibility of office bearing. As all of Northern Israel the son of Amittai too was a common unbeliever, no more than an every-day sort of covenant breaker. Out of a contentious loyalty to his own god(s) he refused to oblige in the sovereign Christ's messaging service. For the Christ to interfere in the idolatry of his own heart Jonah found abhorrent. For the Christ to interfere in Northern Israel's idolatry Jonah found repugnant. Deep down the man sensed that his work in the Assyrian capital had a worse impact on himself and for his people.

Idolaters in that age too were extremely sensitive to the Christ's intervention in their religiosity, which they found intrusive meddling. Rather than hurrying as a duty-bound servant and do as commanded, Jonah purchased an escape ticket, hopefully far beyond the Christ's range of influence.

The Christ, persevering, with the divine strength of will intended that his wayward man walk into the Assyrian capital and accomplish his mission. To make him turn to the task at hand, the Christ hurled a tempest over the Great Sea, therewith to bring the recalcitrant to his senses and to his assignment; he stopped the ship amidst increasingly turbulent winds and waves. The sailors in frights of terror failed to gain a helping hand from respective gods and in desperation cast lots, to find the suddenly shaken awake prophet the center of this life-and-death predicament. Conscious of the cause of the punishing weather and still rebellious to the core the man identified himself as an idolater. "I am a Hebrew, and I fear the god of heaven who made the sea and the dry land." On the surface these credentials gave off a reputable sound. But then, note, had he feared the Christ, the actual God of heaven who made the sea and the dry land, what was he about in a merchant ship bound for the Western Mediterranean? Jonah had identified his own god(s), which intimidated the sailors frightfully. The gods they worshiped failed to offer help. Jonah's god(s) had caused the wild turbulence. Then those sea-roughened men trembled in the presence of an idolatrous deity apparently mightier than the ones to which they had appealed. They asked, What to do? Jonah still in flight-mode tested the Christ's resolve with idolatrous impertinence and ordered the seamen to cast him overboard. Better assisted suicide in obedience to his own god(s) than serving the Christ. Besides, once dead, he was beyond the Christ's reach. Even as the seamen sought a way out from committing murder, wilder winds and waves persuaded them to homicide, thereby to save themselves from terrors of the deep. After the cargo they also tossed the unfaithful office bearer into the raging seas.

As Jonah had promised the ship's crew, immediately the Christ stilled the waves and the winds. In that tranquil weather event the sailors out of fear for Jonah's god(s) offered him sacrifices of thankfulness.

Was that calling upon Jonah's god(s) evidence of conversion, idolaters calling upon the name of another idol?

The men had not heard the Gospel, not from Jonah. Also Jonah's god(s) had not commanded captain and crew to undergo circumcision, forthwith with the empty ship return to Joppa, and enter Northern Israel's covenant community, such as it was. Those seafaring idolaters briefly experienced in the stilling of the tempest a measure of the Christ's mercy, which they mistook as a work of Jonah's god(s), and then faded away into walls fogs on Mediterranean horizons.

THE PRAYING PROPHET

The Christ with incredible patience and almighty perseverance still intended that his prophet speak the assigned words among and to the Nineveh citizens. To rescue the man descending beneath suddenly subdued seawaters he directed a large enough fish to swallow and hold him. How Jonah survived physically and mentally for the seventy-two hours in that creature affirms a minor miracle. Perhaps by his praying he maintained sanity. More important, in the belly of the fish the unbeliever served the Christ by foretelling the Resurrection, Matthew 12:40. As Jonah endured deep darkness in the fish, the Christ physically suffered throughout three days and three nights hellish agonies of damnation. Without minimizing Jonah's *resurrection* when the fish spewed him out onto dry land, the Christ by this event projected into the consciousness of the Church a foretelling of the new heavens and earth; in the recreation people and animals cooperate, animals as the fish freely and fearlessly serving the new humanity. Other prophets, too, gave pointers in that direction, Isaiah 11:6–9, 65:25 thereof the more memorable.

V

More open to inspection than Jonah's residency in the fish is his recorded praying, which gives the impression that, whatever his faults and shortcomings, something covenantally good still resided in the man. With that in mind, he spent the seventy-two hours speaking to his god(s), the god(s) represented by Northern Israel's golden calves. Even superficial examination of this nine-part semblance of calling upon a god leads to the acknowledgment of its brokenness and shambling shallowness, if not hypocrisy. If the man drew the pieces from the Psalm-book he severed each one from its context. The Psalmist(s) called upon the Christ from out of persecutory suffering. Jonah's pain in isolation resulted from his hatred of the Christ. Moreover, most of the nine, if from the Psalm-book, were ill-remembered and, hence, ill-quoted. Take the first:

> I called out to the lord, out of my distress, and he answered me;
> out of the belly of Sheol I cried, and you heard my voice.
> Psalms 18:3a; 31:22b; 2 Samuel 22:6a

This sounds like Psalm 18:3a poorly recited, and totally out of context. The other eight segments also, upon inspection, show similar weaknesses and laxities, if not blasphemies.

> For you cast me into the deep, into the heart of the seas,
> and the flood surrounded me;
> all your waves and your billows passed over me.
> Psalms 88:6a, 42:7b

At Jonah's request the sailors threw him into the wilding seas; thus he planned to escape the Christ after all, and forever.

> Then I said, "I am driven away from your sight;
> Yet I shall again look upon your holy temple."
> Psalm 32:22a

He was not driven away from the Christ. Obsessed by idolatry he fled of his own volition, also into the depths of the Mediterranean. Besides, what did he want at the Temple in Jerusalem? The Christ willed this flight from reality to demonstrate thereby his perseverance in patience first with Jonah, next also with Northern Israel.

> The waters closed in over me to take my life;
> the deep surrounded me; weeds were wrapped about my head at the roots
> of the mountains.
> Psalms 18:4–5, 69:1

> I went down to the land whose bars closed upon me forever;
> Yet you brought up my life from the pit, O lord my god.

True, the Christ preserved the man from Sheol, temporarily, only to fulfill his and the Ten Tribes' condemnation after the completion of this mission.

> When my life was fainting away, I remembered the lord,
> and my prayer came to you, into your holy temple.
> Psalm 18:6b

If Jonah petitioned as here presented, he remembered only his own god(s), never the Christ dwelling with omnipotent authority in the Jerusalem Temple.

> Those who pay regard to vain idols forsake their hope of steadfast love.
> Psalm 31:6–7

All the while Jonah called only upon the god(s) of heaven represented by the golden calves. He hated the Christ too much.

> But I with the voice of thanksgiving will sacrifice to you;
> what I have vowed I will pay.
> Ps 50:14

Nothing is recorded of a vow, nor of any thanksgiving after the fish spat him out upon dry land. Jonah was incontrovertibly hardened in idolatry.

> Salvation belongs to the lord!
> Psalm 3:8

Coming from Jonah this exclamation sounds strange. What then of his burning anger before and after prophesying in Nineveh?

V

On the surface this façade of praying sounds sincere, as sincere as any unbeliever can exploit the Psalms for his/her own exigency in pain. Frankly, the prayer, if from the Psalms, resembles at best a caricature, a patchwork of ambivalent quotations.

While praying, if that accurately describes these collections of words, Jonah experienced a foretaste of death; with that sampling of Sheol in his mouth he wanted to live after all. For a moment, cowed by the darkness of death, he desired to move on, even by way of a detour through Assyrian Nineveh, as the Christ required of him. Was Jonah's new will to live a conversion experience? There was nothing of the Gospel in nor from the fish. The man remained no more than a common unbeliever surrounded by the protection of his god(s), the golden calves, from a country populated by covenant breakers. Despite the promises to Abraham's seed they refused to honor the obligations. In that anti-covenant, pro-idolatry world the Christ had no right to interfere, not with Jonah's god(s), not with Jonah's heart, and not with the Ten Tribes' fate. In fact, on the way to Nineveh the man seethed with hatred for his mission and for the Christ.

Because of a renewed will to live Jonah bowed temporarily to the divine command. He had no free will to resist. Afterwards he counted on the liberty to worship his own god(s) in the *freedom* of idolatry.

COVENANT ESSAYS: TWO

THE RAGING PROPHET

Jonah's impatience with and hatred for the Christ grew arguably stronger. Blinded to the proficiency of divine interference in realms of idolatry the man raged intensely; in his fury he cared little for the Assyrians and, if possible, less for his own people. With the typical temperament of a reprobate confronted by the actuality of the Christ, he waited impatiently and hoped for Nineveh's overthrow.

V

Jonah had entered the expansive city by way of a gate and (repeatedly as well as audibly) proclaimed in a hostile place and to an idolatrous people, "Yet forty days, and Nineveh shall be overthrown." Simply that, without an evident trace of the Gospel. Even with no enemy in sight, no storm on the horizon, no pestilence ready to pounce, and no drought in the forecast, this foretelling caught attention, as the Christ intended; the judgment raced fleet of foot through the city's wards, for the residents sensed deep down they deserved this divine antipathy. Precipitously, then, the entire population up to and including the king clothed itself in the fashion of grief and bowed repentantly, not before the Christ, but before Jonah's god(s), an idolic force apparently more forceful than any in the Assyrian pantheon, notably its Ashur. To demonstrate the sincerity of this pagan remorse the lord of the Assyrians dictated a declaration. "By the decree of the king and his nobles: let neither man nor beast, herd nor flock, taste anything. Let them not feed or drink water, but let man and beast be covered with sackcloth, and let them call out mightily to god. Let everyone turn from his evil way and from the violence that is in his hands. Who knows? God may turn and relent and turn from his fierce anger, so that we may not perish." Out of an overruling fright for an idol seemingly more powerful than even Ashur the Assyrians neglected the old gods; they halted the worship of the traditional divinities. Life in repenting Nineveh ground to a standstill. All believed Jonah's god(s). This bound the population with a fiery catalyst of fright, as the sailors had experienced earlier.

At Nineveh's *repentance* the Christ too repented. Jonah 3:10 stressed the full extent of the divine remorse, for he immediately called off the destruction of the enormous metropolis with its numerous men, women, children, and animals.

Had the Christ, then, sovereign in holiness, sinned when he laid a conditional condemnation on Nineveh to strike the immensely large city with implacable disruption and death? He had issued a conditional verdict, which the Assyrians believed, although they attributed the warning to Jonah's god(s). Because of the metropolitan-wide sorrow the Christ cancelled for the present his purposed annihilation. He had brought about this Assyrian repentance for a purpose that involved Northern Israel directly.

V

From eternity but more specifically over the centuries of its existence the Christ had directed the Assyrian nation to his left hand, its reprobation certain. In the moment of its sorrow he did not draw this people into Northern Israel's covenant community, such as it was. Much less commanded he the Ninevite males to undergo circumcision, the necessary sign of covenant membership. Therefore, this movement in repentance has another than missional significance or evidence of universal love. That became apparent to all with eyes to see. Any missionary intent remains starkly absent in the Jonah-history. The forty days became the final testing period for the Ten Tribes.

Remember the sailors. By way of a violent tempest the Christ persuaded the ship's crew to realize his purpose, cast the fleeing man overboard. Similarly Nineveh's repentance also accomplished his will. During the forty days of testing the Ten Tribes remained unimpressed on all counts by this remarkable event in the midst of the fiercest enemy. Nineveh's repentance revealed that he, the Christ, had the power to lift the darkness of idolatry as well as seal the Ten Tribes eternally in the hell of reprobation.

What then was the sense of Assyria's repentance? With that passing sorrow the Christ revealed to Jonah, to Northern Israel, and above all to the Church in every generation that he, and he alone, with undisputable sovereignty over heaven and earth, as well as with unimpeachable omniscience, distributed eternal life and eternal death. Not the Assyrian pantheon and not Northern Israel's golden calves owned that authority; such deities only led the way into darker depths of reprobation. For all the world to see, to Northern Israel he displayed also after the forty days of testing that the nation had earned its doom.

V

All the while Jonah's rage increased to towering proportions, his heart an autocratic pit of malice towards the Christ. For forty days he had witnessed a hitherto unimaginable measure of mercy for a pagan nation and he reacted negatively as his people had with respect to the Gospel. Over the decades of the ministries of Elijah, Elisha, Hosea, and Amos the Christ had revealed mercies uncountable, to which the Ten Tribes answered with deep-seated unbelief. As the Christ worked the Assyrians' powers of tempering regret, Jonah exposed his implacable hatred of heart for the Gospel; he sternly clung to his own god(s). As he experienced the Christ's right to interfere with his heart and Northern Israel's idolatry he, argumentive, wanted death now more than ever. "O LORD, is not this what I said when I was yet in my country? That is why I made haste to flee to Tarshish; for I knew that you are a gracious God and merciful, slow to anger and abounding in steadfast love, and relenting from disaster. Therefore now, O LORD, please take my life from me, for it is better for me to die than to live." Worse than before, the man wanted to flee as far as possible, even into eternal death, forever away from the sovereign Christ. Jonah, technically a man of the covenant, and Northern Israel, formally a covenant nation, wanted nothing of the Gospel. The man in his soaring rage at and impatience with the Christ dramatically represented his people and opened up the convicting evidence of sinning unforgivably. In this manner through the Jonah-account the Christ prophesied for the last time the radical destruction of a once covenant nation for its idolatry, its reprobation proven by relentless idolatry.

V

When Jonah saw and Northern Israel later heard of Nineveh's astounding moment of pity and therein perceived the Christ's authority to elect and to reprobate, they still presumed themselves safe in the neighborhood of the golden calves. Over the decades they had refused Elijah, Elisha, Hosea, and Amos. At the last they also shut out the Jonah-impact.

In the end Jonah was a harder man, more resentful of the Christ's assault on his personal reality; the death of a shadowing plant to blunt the heat of the sirocco troubled him more than the destruction of a city with at least 120,000 infants. See: Deuteronomy 1:39.

Together, Jonah and Northern Israel wanted nothing of the Gospel. Such was the man's soaring rage and the Ten Tribes' negligence.

In fact, the man's impatience with the Christ aroused in every generation of the Church the difficulty of the Jonah-book: the Christ's sovereignty to destroy radically a once covenant nation with its idolatry and settle the Ten Tribes forever in the hell of damnation.

V

After the forty days the Assyrian men discarded the sackcloth and returned to serving the imperial pantheon by warring up and down the Eastern Mediterranean. In 722 BC an Assyrian army overran Northern Israel, one pagan nation destroying another, killing numerous many and forcing thousands into captivity, beginning thereby the Exile. Thus the Christ imposed eternal condemnation upon the Ten Tribes.

Soon thereafter, in 612 BC, the more cruel Babylonian, Nebuchadnezzar II, crushed Assyria and its chief god. In this manner Assyria entered its damnation, never to rise again.

Conclusion

For the Church through her generations to believe that the Christ for the reprobation of Northern Israel governed this prophet, the tempest, the sailors, the fish, and Assyria opens the Jonah-book, which exegesis encircles the Church in every generation with the awe of stillness.

In the Old Testament he prepared the way to the Incarnation and cleared the ground of impediments forestalling the Crucifixion, in the process of which he directed Northern Israel to his left hand; at the time of Jonah the national cup of iniquity overflowed. Northern Israel then had nothing to complain about when Assyrian hordes overran the country and the golden calves proved to be no more than empty hopes.

Now the Jonah-history stands in the Scriptures and lives in the Church as a warning to all reprobates, also those still hiding in her congregations: the Christ will have the justice of reprobation and he will have the grace of election, with due respect for each aspect of his eternal predestination. Only in believing his Gospel shines the eternity of grace.

In summation yet, perhaps no more than a belated thought:

The Jonah-book when exegeted and interpreted must be taken as one straightforward statement on predestination, which eisegetes under cover of learnedness seek to avoid by typologizing.

V

I thank Rev. Mr. D. Shin for his perspicuous critique of this Jonah-essay; rather than submit the essay to *time-honored* typologies, he quietly and patiently with sharp insights forced me to reevaluate this work.

V

Responses to thoughtful protests:

One. The connection the Christ drew from Matt 12:38–42, Jonah, to himself began in the Old Testament dispensation. He appointed the man prophet and commissioned him specifically to declare judgment upon Nineveh, calling for repentance. Upon one such proclamation the city as a whole repented (temporally), whereas Northern Israel after the long ministries of Elijah and Elisha, compounded by the unyielding prophecies of Hosea, Micah, and Nahum, hardened itself in defiance. Out of the Jonah-history the Christ pulled as *productive* the prophet's three days and three nights to illustrate his three days and three nights in the grave.

Jonah's unbelief and status as unbeliever stemmed from several features. Rather than enter upon his unique as well as dangerous commission, when faithful prophets spoke as commanded, he ran away. Rather than ask the sailors to return him to Joppa, he asked for assistance in death by suicide, which indicated how far he wanted to escape from his commission and the Christ. Rather than sympathize with the Ninevites he waited for the divine damnation to consume the entire city. Rather than at the end to repent, he wished to die, that is, put eternal distance between himself and the Christ. Not a trace of faithfulness distinguished the man. In that faithlessness he personified Northern Israel.

The Gospel is the Good News of salvation. The Christ sent hardship upon Jonah, not to call him to repentance and faithfulness, but to demonstrate thereby the hardness of his heart, even as Northern Israel's, 2 Kgs 17:7–18.

The Christ, in effect, verified the hardness of Jonah's heart and the recalcitrance of Northern Israel.

Jonah is a difficult book. Students want to find the Gospel in it, when the only good for the ongoing Church is the Christ's perseverance in condemning unrepentance in covenant people.

THREE ARRESTING THEMES

ISAIAH 65:17-25 (17)

THE WORD AND THE NEW CREATION

IN THE MIDST OF Old Testament times the Christ declared in and to the Church, " . . . behold, I create new heavens and a new earth." Herewith he announced the Recreation. Speaking prophetically in the first dispensation he promised by the power of the word to recreate the entire universe, the earth included. Again, at the beginning of the New Testament times he proclaimed, Revelation 21:5, "Behold, I make all things new." In the Church struggling with sin and in the world dark with sin *the Creator God revealed the recreative power of the word.*

THE CREATION OF THE UNIVERSE

In the beginning the Creator God, the Christ, spoke. Out of nothing he created the heavens and the earth.

On the first day he spoke, "Let there be light." And light broke forth, shining over the heavens and the earth.

On the second day he spoke again, "Let there be an expanse/canopy in the midst of the water and let it separate the waters from the waters." This expanse or canopy he called Heaven, space.

On the third day, by speaking, he separated the dry land and the seas.

On the fourth day he called forth all stellar lights. "And God made the two great lights—the greater light to rule the day and the lesser light to rule the night—and the stars."

Five, six, seven, eight times the Creator God spoke and out of nothing brought forth the whole of the first creation. By the word, speaking, the LORD God created the entire universe.

V

Look now with the naked eye into the night sky and see the stars. Through a telescope look farther and see galaxies. Look at red shifts in time exposures from the Hubble Space Telescope and see circling constellations.

Of the galaxies the Milky Way holds together as many as 250,000,000,000 stars. The nearby Sagittarius Galaxy, 10,000 times less massive than the Milky Way, has about 100,000,000,000 million stars. In the observable universe as many as 100,000,000,000 galaxies orbit in the stillness of outer space, some of which follow respective trajectories fifty, one hundred, two-hundred light years distant from the earth. Of these galaxies many contain more stars than the Milky Way. According to Job 9:9–10, the Christ " . . . made the Bear and the Orion, the Pleiades and the chambers of the south; who does great things beyond searching out, and marvelous things beyond number." Job 38:31; Amos 5:8. The Creator God made the entire universe, the earth included, by speaking. From the beginning he revealed the power of the spoken word.

Look now to the earth, the planet on which the LORD God distinctly concentrated; out of all stars, planets, and moons he selected this planet and its people as the center of his attention. Plainly, the Christ affirmed the earth central to the universe, the center of his providential rule, uniquely prepared for conditions of life.

Look now to Adam and Eve, both wonderfully made. The Creator God spoke, Genesis 1:26–27, "Let us make man . . . male and female he created them." The LORD created Adam and Eve righteous, capably doing only his commands. He created both holy, competently willing only his commands. Both he created image bearers, fully qualified to govern Eden in his Name. Therefore he exhorted, Genesis 1:28, "Be fruitful and multiply and fill the earth and subdue it and have dominion over the fish of the sea and over the birds of the air and over every living thing that moves on the earth." Both he placed in Eden, a garden of beauty. Both Adam and Eve he placed on the earth, a planet of beauty. Both he placed in the universe, an immense sphere of beauty. The whole creation throbbed with vitality, everything very good and fully functioning.

In the vastness of the universe, in the largeness of the earth, and within the limitations of Eden the Christ concentrated specifically on Adam and Eve.

V

In the masterfully created universe, on the earth, and within Eden sin mysteriously ruined the very goodness of the Creator's workmanship. Eve and Adam out of an inscrutable hunger wanted of the forbidden fruit more than all of life with and for which he had made them. They had twisted intrinsic righteousness into unrighteousness, no longer capably doing only the divine commands. They had perverted integral holiness into unholiness, no longer capably willing the divine commands. They were no longer gifted to hear the commands of the Lord. Now strangely covetous, the two preferred the fruit of the knowledge of the tree of good and evil. The two became sinners, a people condemned to death who as the first image bearers took the earth and the universe down with them. With the anomaly of the Fall Adam, following Eve, first ruined Eden, its attention to beauty and harmony in unity violated.

At following the Serpent, Adam soaked the earth with sinfulness and the Christ cursed the ground into its depths, Genesis 3:17p. The natural beauties of this planet through the (four) seasons henceforth failed to hide the fact that death overpowered life, the wages of sin evident everywhere. The violence of war, the suffering of pestilences/pandemics, the hunger of starvation, the thirst of drought, the brokenness of family life, the deformity of marriage, the horror of addiction, the madness of racial hatred, and the process of aging weighed heavily throughout the world. The LORD made death its identifying mark.

The heavens—sun, moon, and stars—to the farthest galaxies also suffered the impacts of the Adamic sin. Despite raw splendors of stellar phenomena, immensely huge dust clouds soaring up, and supernovas streaming light waves, the celestial sphere too lost its edenic grandeur. Space became a domain of death. With approving Adam on his side the Satan placed the stamp of his rule even over the most remote galaxies. When Adam, the first image bearer, sinned all of creation collapsed into the Devil's death grip.

From the people, through the earth, and unto the farthest boundaries of the universe life as created ceased.

V

In the death-ridden universe, on the sin-bound earth, and into evil-oriented Judah, the Church at that time, the voice of the Lord through the mouth of Isaiah broke forth, " . . . behold I create new heavens and a new earth." Christ himself called this "the regeneration," Matthew 19:28. Speaking in the midst of death the Christ proclaimed the Recreation, indeed, the reconstitution of the heavens as well as of the earth. The Old Testament Church had come to its lowest in sin. Throughout the monarchies of Uzziah, Jotham, Ahaz, and Hezekiah, kings of Judah, the people of the covenant had over generations forsaken the LORD God in favor of idols, seeking a life in and a future from idolatries, wherewith they defied the living God and wherein they succumbed to Sheol.

Among his condemned-to-death people the Christ through Isaiah proclaimed the hope of the Recreation. To the unbelievers he revealed the glory of the new heavens and earth from which they were shut out. To the remnant of believers he gave hope. For a people who walked in darkness he promised a great light. Upon that remnant dwelling in a land of deep gloom he shone light. To his own he imputed the strength to hope and persevere in the Faith.

Believers responding in hope had to cleanse themselves from the cloying powers of idolatry.

By means of proclaiming the new heavens and a new earth he contrasted the hopelessness of life in sin and the hopefulness of the Gospel, the Gospel only defined by the focal point of the Old Testament, the Incarnation.

V

In the dying and death of Judah, the Old Testament Church the LORD God, speaking, created the future for his people to hang on to and move further in faith.

THE RECREATION OF THE UNIVERSE

To reveal the Recreation through the power of the word starting in the Old Testament Church the Christ prophesied the Incarnation and by hearing him speak through the prophets a remnant believed his enfleshment, his *Immanuel* glory.

> For to us a child is born, to us a son is given;

> and the government shall be upon his shoulder,
> and his name shall be called
> Wonderful Counsellor, Mighty God,
> Everlasting Father, Prince of Peace.
> Isaiah 9:6

Because of the power of the spoken word those whom the Christ selected believed his advent in the flesh.

Again, to reveal the Recreation by the power of the word in the Old Testament he spoke of the Crucifixion; by hearing from Isaiah the remnant that believed the Incarnation also believed his agonizing death.

> He was despised and rejected by men;
> a man of sorrows, and acquainted with grief;
> and as one from whom men hide their faces he was despised,
> and we esteemed him not.
> Isaiah 53:3

Throughout the long Old Testament millennia all who heard the prophets and believed the word lived for the Incarnation and the Crucifixion.

V

In the course of the New Testament dispensation the power of word became more direct, centered about the Crucifixion. At the appointed time the Lord and Savior had Roman soldiers sink the Cross into rocky Golgotha. From that place, lifted up between heaven and earth, he earned the Atonement for his people, issuing the truth of justification, justification by faith, the whole majestically affirmed by the Resurrection.

In Christian congregations the proclamation of the Gospel in its simplicity and grace sounds forth in the spoken word, *You are justified in Christ Jesus*. You were dead in your sins and trespasses in which you once walked. Because you hear the spoken word and believe your justification, you are now alive in Christ Jesus, regenerated, a people still striving against sin, but capable in righteousness to do only the good of the Commandments and in holiness to will only the good of the Commandments. In the Romans 10:17 manner you believe the spoken word, "So faith comes from hearing, and hearing through the word of Christ." Out of believing the word of the Christ, the proclamation of the Church, the Holy Spirit recreates you and binds you actually together as congregation. A believing people is the first evidence of the Recreation.

V

This work of gathering his people together into a holy congregation he began at the Sinai. In extreme thunder and lightning, to the sound of the divine trumpet, the Christ spoke the almighty and irresistible affirmation.

> I am the LORD your God,
> who brought you out of the land of Egypt,
> out of the house of slavery.
> Exodus 20:2

By that word he bonded Israel into his congregation. Through Moses and later David the Christ brought forth the Recreation. Prophets as Isaiah, Jeremiah, and Ezekiel kept the Church alive in faith through the spoken word.

Now in the New Testament dispensation the Christ calls congregations into life for the proclamation of the word. Remove the preaching and each congregation slowly collapses into a social club, its worth practically negligible, salt that has lost its saltiness, to be thrown out and trodden underfoot. It is through the word that the Christ calls more people out of death into the life of the Recreation and instructs members in the great doctrines of the Scriptures; then with these teachings in heart and mind through the Holy Spirit he motivates the righteousness and holiness wherewith to glorify him, the Christ.

The power of the word structures the Church, each congregation of which now displays the beginning of the recreation of this planet. Because of the significance of the Church, the second evidence of the new creation, to the people whom he gathers at his right hand he declares again and again the worth of Isaiah 51:16p, "You are my people." Through his people he makes the new earth here and now in the shape of congregations. In effect, all the congregations, which as the one Congregation, are the vanguard that shapes history, moving evidence of the authority of the word.

As the Christ completes his work on this planet and finishes gathering the Church, he will speak again. Then by the power of the word he will totally renew the earth, and with the earth the entirety of the universe, all of space. In that hour he makes the Milky Way and Sagittarius, and the millions of other galaxies orbiting about even a hundred or more light years away with a beauty and a goodness greater than Eden's in the beginning. In that hour with open-mouthed awe we will behold the Christ recreating the earth and the heavens into a splendor more glorious than Adam and Eve beheld at the Genesis start, for the Recreator in that glory provides the third evidence of the power of the word in the most radiant fashion.

In the fullness of the Eschaton, in the joy of all believers and faithful angels, in the rejoicing of this earth, in the praise of all stars, the Christ speaking once more joins the original creation, recreated, to the heavens of heaven, where stands the divine throne from where he with the Father and in the Spirit rules, with the newly recreated earth along with the galaxies. Then he accomplishes that which Isaiah declared long ago, 65:17b, " . . . the former things shall not be remembered or come to mind." Eternally the darkness of death with its violence shall pass away.

V

Though limited by sin the new radiance broke through. Isaiah 60:19, "The sun shall be no more your light by day, nor for brightness shall the moon give you light; but the LORD will be your everlasting light, and your God will be your glory." According to Revelation 21:22–25 then,

> And I saw no temple in the city, for its temple is the Lord God Almighty and the Lamb. And the city has no need of sun or moon to shine on it, for the glory of God gives it light, and its lamp is the Lamb. By its lights will the nations walk, and the kings of the earth will bring their glory into it, and its gates will never be shut by day—and there will be no night there.

The whole may be summed up as the Spirit does in Revelation 21:1–4 to provide hope and endurance for the generations of the Church.

> And I saw a new heaven and a new earth, for the first heaven and the first earth had passed away, and the sea was no more. And I saw the holy city, new Jerusalem, coming down out of heaven from God, prepared as a bride adorned for her husband. And I heard a loud voice from the throne saying, "Behold, the dwelling place of God is with man. He will dwell with them, and they will be his people, and God himself will be with them as their God. He will wipe away every tear from their eyes, and death shall be no more, neither shall there be mourning nor crying nor pain any more, for the former things have passed away.

V

Now to live in and for the Recreation as it takes shape in the Church the Christ through Apostle Peter started a perennial exhortation. Second Peter 3:11–13,

> Since all these things are thus to be dissolved, what sort of people ought you to be in lives of holiness and godliness, waiting for and hastening the coming day of the God, because of which the heavens will be set on fire and dissolved, and the heavenly bodies will melt as they burn! But according to his promise we are waiting for new heavens and a new earth in which righteousness dwells.

To a congregation struggling with sin and overcoming a stridently disobedient and alienating world the Christ declared the Recreation the focal point of living; all in Christ through the Spirit take hold of the hope and cleanse themselves from every impurity of sinfulness. The hope of the Recreation is more significant than oxygen, more than water, more than food, more than even life itself.

Rev. Mr. T. Bailey critiqued the immediately above *essay* in a heartening and positive way. For this I gave him a hearty thanks.

Revelation 20:11–15
John 12:20–36 (31–32)

TWO JUDGMENTS: THE FIRST AND THE LAST

In the Eschaton the Son of Man presides over the last and glorious judgment. For that day of grandeur it is written, Revelation 20:11–12,

> Then I saw a great white throne and him who was seated on it. From his presence earth and sky fled away, and no place was found for them. And I saw the dead, great and small, standing before the throne, and books were opened. Then another book was opened, which is the book of life. And the dead were judged by what was written in the books, according to what they had done.

The two books, one of which the book of life, contain the names of all people whom Jesus while on the Golgotha Cross summoned in the first and great judgment to his right hand and his left. In and with the Crucifixion the Son of Man judged all who had lived, lived in that day, and will live. In effect, then, *the Son of Man forever judged all human beings.*

THREE ARRESTING THEMES

THE FIRST AND GREAT JUDGMENT

One. Jesus announced in the hearing of the nearby Twelve and some Greeks to a crowd of Passover worshipers that he within the week planned the first and great Judgment. For that momentous event he revealed himself the Son of Man—the Son of Man is Jesus and Jesus is the Son of Man—who is the Judge of all the earth. God the Father commissioned Jesus in his divinity and his humanity to reveal the double verdict involving the entire human race, John 5:27. Believers and unbelievers had to hear, do have to hear now, and will have to hear the inclusive word of judgment.

The Son of Man revealed the main fact of the day of judgment. He was to be lifted up, a synonym then current for crucifixion, and deeply experience the fearful Roman death. This lifting up recalled Moses' bronze serpent, John 3:14–15; Numbers 21:4–9; 1 Corinthians 10:9, by which the LORD at that time distinguished between the living and the dead. For the hour of judgment the Son of Man planned to draw all human beings before him, the people of Israel first and also the entire number of the Gentiles at that moment represented by some Greeks. By pulling the entire human race before him for sentencing the Son of Man revealed that he, not the ruler of this world, the Devil, owned and controlled the world's population—those of the past, those of that present, and those of all futures who yet had to see the light of day. In the first and great judgment Jesus promised to reveal his omnipotent rulership.

On the Cross, lifted up between heaven and earth—rejected by the Church and forsaken by God the Father—the Son of Man with finality judged every man, woman, and child for eternity, a decision never open to repeal. For the hour of judgment he pulled all whose names he had by grace written in the book of life to his right hand and drove all others in condemnation to his left. Thereto he declared, John 12:23, "The hour has come for the Son of Man to be glorified." Matthew, Mark, and Luke stressed the Son of Man on the Cross in the agonies of his suffering to make the Atonement. John, on the other hand, revealed him in his glorying, the exaltation of the first and great judgment beginning with Israel, the Church at that time, and including all Gentiles to God the Father's praise.

The Son of Man petitioned the Father that he in the critical hour also glorify his name. God the Father responded as with a thunderous sound, John 12:28p, "I have glorified it, and I will glorify it again." The Father had glorified his name at the Incarnation, sending his only-begotten Son into the world and he willed to exalt it again in and with the Crucifixion that specifically the men, women, and children at the Son of Man's right hand—who had venerated him, were venerating him, and will venerate him—receive the grace of the Atonement. The Atonement constituted the magnified and magnificent moment in the history of the Church and consequently pertinent for the world at large, the whole of which that crucial day concentrated in Jerusalem and on Golgotha. In and with the execution of the sentencing the Son of Man handed down 1) he blessed with grace those on his right hand, declaring each and all righteous, 2) he held those on his left accountable for every sin committed, and 3) he clarified for all eternity that the Satan never had, did not, and never will own the world, no matter how at times he engulfs many with evil.

By the first and great judgment the Son of Man separated whom the Father had given him from those who faced eternal condemnation. To all on his right hand and on his other he left no one in doubt with respect to the future in the Eschaton.

V

Two. Moreover, in and with the hour of the Crucifixion the Son of Man announced as well as designed the casting out of heaven the ruler of this world. Throughout the Old Testament dispensation this fearsome archangel, terrible in his fallenness, presumed that he owned the earth and ruled over its people. To round off this presumption he had to rid the world of certain people, Job for one and Israel for another. 1) To seek Job's destruction he pointed out to the Judge of all the earth that Job only served him out of covetousness, what he got out of it in material goods. The Judge permitted the Accuser to take Job's possessions away and test the depth and sincerity of the man's righteousness, Job 1:12. At another occasion, Zechariah 3:1–5, the Accuser pointed out to the Son of Man that Israel represented by the high priest was filthy, unworthy of atoning grace. To actually own the earth Satan had to remove such persons as Job and Israel. And by removing the Old Testament believers God the Son no longer had a reason for the Incarnation and create the Atonement. By preventing the Atonement he then confirmed his presumptive ownership of the earth.

By evicting Satan the Son of Man then no longer allowed him access into heaven. Throughout the Old Testament dispensation mighty archangels served the Son of Man, at his command to minister in and to the Church, Isaiah 6:1–5; Luke 1:26-27. The Satan on the other hand had moved at will from heaven onto the earth and from the earth into heaven to bring accusation against the believers and function as a prosecutor by which to remove them from the right hand of the Son of Man and erase their names from the book of life. Now this two-way access was shut, never to be opened again. The first meaning of the eviction was that the Satan no longer had access to the divine throne and accuse the people of the Lord of sinfulness. The second meaning of the expulsion was this: he had never owned the earth or its people in the first place. The Son of Man in his majesty ruled all people either for grace or for condemnation. In both ways the glory of the Son of Man stands out, also of the Father who not only sent him but also strengthened his humanity to withstand the pain of the Atonement.

You may ask, legitimately, wherefore the Son of Man and the Father set the Crucifixion date to that day on Golgotha before expelling Satan from ever approaching the throne of grace again and creating the grace for all eternity. What of the time of Noah and the Flood, of Moses and the Exodus, or of Solomon and the Temple, key events in the history of the Church and for the world? Totally independent of human preferences, the Son of Man with the Father and in the Spirit, one God, chose that day for the glorification of the Trinity and the defeat of the ruler of this world, as prophesied in Genesis 3:14–15. The Crucifixion followed by the Resurrection proved also to Satan's followers the Son of Man the Victor in glory.

V

Upon the Devil's primary defeat the Christ prepared the Church to withstand the desperation in which he seeks to regain governing control. Revelation 12:12, "... rejoice, O heavens and you who dwell in them! But woe to you, O earth and sea, for the devil has come down to you in great wrath, because he knows that his time is short." Now in this world the signature of his presence is evident in three ways—insecurity, doubt, and coldness.

One way the Satan writes his signature is through insecurity. He demonstrates the mark of his presence through wars, droughts, famines, plagues/pandemics, aging, illness, and bereavements to upset believing the victory that the Judge of all the earth wrought on Golgotha. Every uncertainty speaks of Satan's winning way to spread insecurity in the Church, all on the Christ's right hand, and thus prove that the Resurrection did and does not reveal the victory over sin and death. On the other hand, for those on the left this is the very fear for which they have no answer.

Another way he still seeks to put his mark upon the community of the covenant is through sowing seeds of doubt with questions that suddenly come out of nowhere. Do you think that you a really a good enough person to be on the Son of Man's right hand? Are you convinced deep down that you have earned enough good works to be one in the community of the righteous? Are sins of the past really covered? Those on the left do not care much; the Devil makes sure they have idols in which to trust until the last hour. But the people on the right hand of the Son of Man he will have by spreading doubt.

In a third way he chokes off interest in the Gospel and the Church. Did not the Christ reveal that the faith of many will grow cold, Matthew 24:12b? For those on the left hand of the Son of Man this indifference is normal; the Devil makes sure they have enough interesting idols for whom to live until it is too late. But if he can convince members of the Church that the grass on the other side of the fence is greener, he wins little victories in this manner too.

Through the means of insecurity, doubt, and indifference he still seeks the defeat of the Son of Man and he uses people to achieve his goal. For now he is certainly at home in this world.

THE LAST AND GLORIOUS JUDGMENT

Three. At the last and glorious judgment the Son of Man will publicize all names in the two books or registries before him, first of those on his left hand. In the silence of the courtroom setting these men, women, and children will hear their names read off as determined before the foundation of the world; they are eternally hell-bound. The Judge will also read off the names of all registered in the book of life. He began compiling that registry in the Old Testament dispensation, witness Moses' reference, Exodus 32:31–34, and Jesus' exhortation to the Twelve to rejoice in the fact that their names were written in heaven, Luke 10:20. On the Cross the Judge inscribed in the court records the names of all on his right hand—those who had lived, those living, and those who still had to face the reality of birth. he declares each righteous on account of atoning grace. To have the entire human race listen to the reading of the names the Son of Man in the Eschaton will call forth the general resurrection of the dead.

In the Eschaton the Son of Man gathers the human race, missing none. In this courtroom setting he will explain the grounds for the double verdict, the fair and equitable grounds. He will measure each person with the same measurement, "according to what they had done." What can be more just than that standard? By what each has done? Unbelievers face condemnation for unbelief and hypocrites undergo exposure for the insincerity they treasured. In distinction, believers see the fruit of living the Faith. Now in the approach to the Eschaton with its last and glorious judgment all know on what hand of the Judge they will stand, on the right or the left. Long before the names are read off, unbelievers and hypocrites know they are headed for the left hand and believers will know they are placed on the right hand.

The Son of Man calls the believers to appear before him Sundays in every worship service to hear the judgments of grace, lest they slip off into doubt and insecurity with respect to the Faith or take pleasure in self-righteousness. In every worship service congregations of Christ come before the throne of grace to hear to the royal assertion with respect in the last and glorious Judgment. Over the 1,000 years between the Ascension and the Eschaton the Judge declares grace for all he placed on his right hand.

Over these 1,000 years the Devil tempts to catch believers off guard. For one thing, he sows more doubt, pressing hesitations into believers. Am I really saved? Is my faith strong enough? For another thing, he scatters insecurities. Is Jesus both God and man? Was his death on the Cross sufficient to atone for my sins? How can I believe the Trinity, the One-in-Three? Is the Bible the Word of God trustworthy, inerrant? Are there not contradictions in the Bible? And for a third thing, Satan wants that we work our own justification, make up a list of good works to persuade ourselves that we are good people and that the Judge will see us a people who meant well and even tried to live in a Christian way. If the Devil over the time left to him can persuade us of doubt, of insecurity, and of works-righteousness he has his hooks in to do real damage not just to any of Christ, but to Christ himself. His anger and frustration at being cast out of heaven is real and he wants revenge the only way possible, through attacking the members of the Church by unbiblical preaching and teaching, untrustworthy friendship, illicit entertainment, etc.; actually the ways of deceit are manifold.

In response to every and all demonic attacks the Judge in every worship service repeats the sentencing from the first and great judgment that all on his right hand know without doubt, insecurity, or pride in self-righteousness what he thinks of them.

Living now between the judgments the Church as a whole and her members live towards the Eschaton to hear the Son of Man read our names from the book of life. The joy of walking day by day toward the last and glorious judgment shows in our loving the Son of Man with all of heart, soul, and mind. In the life journey—direction the Eschaton— we show this joy of loving our neighbors as ourselves. That joy stands out in the eagerness of feeding the hungry, giving water to the thirsty, welcoming strangers, clothing the poor, caring for the sick, and attending to the imprisoned, first those oppressed by persecution. The joy of the life before the Judge we demonstrate in the care for the earth. It further shows in respect for governing authorities. Moreover, as we look forward to stand before the Judge at the glorious conclusion to history all on the Judge's right hand seek him and the Father as well while he shapes the history of the world for the sake of the Church and the coming of the Kingdom. That is the work of the Holy Spirit in each Christian congregation.

The Spirit convinces all in Christ to do as he commands, to do all good works, which God prepared beforehand, that we should walk in them, not according to day-planners or at our conveniences.

In the Christian walk to the last and glorious judgment this is the time to interrogate the Scriptures and ask, What sort of people ought you to be in lives of holiness and godliness? For now in this dispensation yet Satan through the power of death is strong. But someday, for the final time two rhetorical questions will sound forth.

> O death, where is your victory?
> O death, where is your sting?
> 1 Corinthians 15:55; Isaiah 25:8; Hosea 13:14b

This victory over death begins every Sunday again at hearing the grace recorded indelibly in the first and great judgment.

Isaiah 1:1–20 (18)

THE TRIAL OF A LIFE TIME

The Christ through the Prophet Isaiah called Israel out, planning to prosecute his case against the Old Testament Church. The covenant people in the approach to the long-promised Incarnation had buried themselves under layers of self-righteousness, even trained new generations to copy this form of hypocrisy. They persuaded each other that the omniscient Christ was pleased with their outward displays of Sabbath observances and feast day celebrations. To alert the people, Isaiah quoted the Christ.

> Ah, sinful nations, a people laden with iniquity,
> offspring of evildoers, children who deal corruptly!

By calling Israel out, the Christ closed off every escape route; the people had to appear before him. In his courtroom *he intended Israel to hear the eternal judgment.*

THREE ARRESTING THEMES

THE RIGHTEOUS SUMMONS

Towards the end of the eight-century BC ferocious and rapacious Assyrian armies gathered on the northern horizon to invade Canaan. These hordes of aggressive and unmerciful armed men served as the Christ's scourge upon Israel, or what was left, Judah. In the calamity of the age Isaiah, prosecuting, summoned the whole of Judah to acknowledge the divine indictment, "Hear the word of the LORD, you rulers of Sodom! Give ear to teaching of our God, you people of Gomorrah!" Judah, the Church, had fallen low, to the level of Sodom-and-Gomorrah's morality. At heart the people had turned thoroughly idolatrous and Isaiah, as the prosecutor, intended to get a conviction.

V

To cover over this Sodom-and-Gomorrah sinfulness Judah generated enthusiastic displays of religiosity. But Isaiah pressed the case by quoting the Judge.

> What to me is the multitude of your sacrifices? says the LORD;
> I have had enough of burnt offerings of rams and the fat of well-fed beasts;
> I do not delight in the blood of bulls, or of lambs, or of goats.
> Isaiah 1:11

The Christ perceived the sinning that Judah attempted to cover up under enthusiastic ceremonies of sacrificing and excitements of corporate worship. But his patience had come to an end.

The Church driven by fear of death at the hands of the Assyrians crowded the Temple courts on the Sabbaths and the feast days, the Passover, First Fruits, and the conclusion to the harvest. With animated worship they proved to themselves and to the Judge that they were good people, not worthy the destruction and death at the hands of the Assyrians. Every Sabbath without fail they gathered for the reading of the Law, Exodus 31:12–17. Three times per year, as the Christ commanded, the men appeared before him in Jerusalem and filled the Temple courts with fervors of worship, Exodus 23:14–17; Deuteronomy 16:1–17. The Passover in the New Testament became Crucifixion and Resurrection Days. First Fruits in the New Testament became Pentecost Day. The end of the harvest they celebrated with the Feast of Tabernacles. Moreover they held convocation on the appearances of New Moons. Outwardly, the Church's enthusiastic fulfillments of the divine commandments showed that the Judge had no complaints with his people.

As the zeal of worshiping came to its climax, Isaiah quoted the indictment.

> Bring no more vain offerings; incense is an abomination to me.
> New Moon and Sabbath and the calling of convocations—
> I cannot endure iniquity and solemn assembly.
> Your new moons and your appointed feast my soul hates;
> they have become a burden to me;
> I am weary of bearing them.
> Isaiah 1:13–14

Step by step the prosecutor laid out the evidence of the Church's evil-doings, her Sodom-and-Gomorrah style sinning, then covering this with undue excitements on the Sabbaths and during the great convocations. The Judge had had enough, the conviction of great guilt prepared. This the Prophet stated,

> When you spread out your hands, I will hide my eyes from you;
> even though you make many prayers, I will not listen; your hands
> are of blood.
> Isaiah 1:15

That is, blood from numerous murders of innocents. With this the evidence the prosecutor had made the guilty conviction extremely convincing.

V

Because the people feared the Assyrians massing on northern horizons they nervously congested the Temple courts for Sabbath services. By attending to the commands of worship they found that that made them righteous. The people of the Church set standards by which they found themselves righteous, self-righteous. This is always the same for achieving self-righteousness. Church people, Old Testament as well as New, select a few parts of the Commandments, keep these "perfectly," and, presto, they are self-righteous in their own eyes. The Christ saw through this fakery and refused to accept further offerings and prayers.

For years, if not decades the people of the covenant commemorated main convocations and all Sabbaths with an eye to detail and celebratory demeanor, to fool the Christ into thinking that self-righteousness was the same if not better than the biblical standard for righteousness. And by outer appearances the Christ could not have wished for a better, more upright people. Isaiah's trial was a waste of time.

In fact, callously, as a nation and each individually, the heart of all overflowed with sinfulness. At home they did was evil in the sight of the Christ, according to the despicable practices of the nations that he had driven out before Israel at the time of Moses and Joshua. On the outside they looked good. Inside, away from the three great convocations and on the Sabbaths they were pagan as pagans serving Baal, bowing to the Asherah, worshiping the host of heaven, sacrificing children, listening to fortune-tellers, and believing the predictions of the mediums. In the eyes of the Christ, the Judge, they had become a hateful people.

Under these circumstances and with such collective guilt to come before the Christ on the Sabbaths and the greater as well as lesser convocations was foolhardy in the extreme, a daring only the self-righteous risked. What could the Judge find wrong? Such hypocrisy! What arrogance! Pretending to be good, sincere, and honest on the outside, while sinful to the core on the inside, praying to and confessing the name of the Christ and then go home to serve other gods that were not gods?

Judah as a whole and the men individually covered this sinfulness with the enthusiasm of religiosity. Superficially they worshiped the Christ in all of life. Internally they worshiped idols, typically pagan with envy, pride, and covetousness, by which hypocritical acts they hoped for the Christ to turn back the Assyrian armies.

V

Even though the prosecutor had presented enough guilt to secure the conviction and the Judge was ready to convict he—merciful and gracious, slow to anger and with abounding love for thousands, forgiving iniquity, transgression, and sin—once more, unbelievably, called the people to complex and complete repentance.

> Wash yourselves; make yourselves clean;
> remove the evil of your deeds from before my eyes;
> cease to do evil,
> learn to do good, seek justice, correct oppression;
> bring justice to the fatherless, and plead the widow's cause.
> Isaiah 1:17

Deep and painful silence followed upon this sovereign call to repentance.

COVENANT ESSAYS: TWO

THE GRACIOUS VERDICT

In the agonizing stillness the Prophet in the name of his Lord inserted the kicker.

> Come now, let us reason together, says, the LORD.
> Isaiah 1:18a

Upon this exhortation all of Judah, the whole Church, had to make a choice. In self-defense they could excuse themselves. We did not mean anything bad by this idolatry. Idolatry is not such a terrible sin. Others worship idols. Here they had a golden opportunity to lay out in public the benefits of idolatry. They had in that moment the possibility to prove that the Christ had failed them and they, to survive, needed to support of other gods to get through a difficult time in the life of the nation. In the Judge's courtroom they had every break to explain themselves, to make excuses, or even blame the Judge himself for their inversion of the First Commandment.

Or they could commit to that which is most difficult, repentance.

In effect, the Christ exhorted, Argue your case before me, dispute with me, prove me wrong in my covenant faithfulness.

The choice was plain: either the Judge, the Christ, or the idols.

V

As tensions within tensions gripped Judah, the Old Testament Church, one thing became clear; no justification for sinning against the First Commandment had even a slight measure of success. No excuse sufficed. No legal gimmickry prospered.

The Christ placed the covenant people at the crossroads of eternity. He had penetrated their hypocrisy and exposed the shabbiness of their self-righteousness.

And the people of the Church stood before the Judge, unable to reply.

V

In the heart-breaking silence the Judge proclaimed the Gospel in one of its Old Testament formulations, perhaps even the most memorable. For this people he was coming into the world. For this people he was going to the Cross. For this people he had planned from before the creation of the world to move through the glory of the Incarnation to create the Atonement.

> Though your sins are like scarlet, they shall be white as snow;

Though they are red like crimson, they shall become like wool.

The glory of the Gospel hidden as it was in the Old Testament times shone forth. With this Gospel the Judge placed Israel at the main intersection of life, Isaiah 1:19, "If you are willing and obedient, you shall eat the good of the land," meaning you shall live; the Assyrians shall no more steal your crops, herds, and flocks. On the other hand, "if you refuse and rebel, you shall be eaten by the sword," signifying more trouble, more devastation, and death at the Assyrians' hand. Isaiah, speaking as the mouth of the LORD, placed the Church where eternal life and eternal death part ways.

The divine call to decide was not an opening to the exercise of free will. He alone and in righteousness made separation. Those he bypassed, it became obvious, left the divine courtroom to worship the old idols under cover of self-righteousness and hypocrisy. They pretended that they owned final authority, which added self-deception to their culpability. These members asserted positive self-images; inside they looked good to themselves, aiding by a few easy rules for self-justification. Nothing changed in their lives or reason for living. To others, responding with repentance—the work of the Holy Spirit in the Church—he imputed grace and forgiveness. That repentance was the act of the Judge who is the Christ. The separation of the two peoples in the Church came through the decision-making authority of the Judge, not from those who stood before him. The pronuncation of grace and guilt is the righteous and holy juridical act of all times.

This greatest of all decisions the Judge revealed on Golgotha; on the Cross he separated people—eternally—to the condemnation based on reprobation and the salvation founded on predestination.

From Isaiah's declaration of the Gospel not what church members think of themselves but what the Judge thinks of them only counts.

V

In any language the Gospel as Isaiah declared stands out with memorable clarity. What does that transition from scarlet to white and crimson to wool look like? Or how that changing of the colors presents itself.

For the Old Testament Church as well as the New believing Isaiah's declaration of the Gospel begins with brokenness of heart. The Christ seeks the sacrifice of a broken spirit, broken and contrite, Psalm 51:17. People of broken heart and contrite spirit give the first evidence that the scarlet of sin is washed white, and that the crimson of guilt changes to the color of wool. The doubling of the transition indicated already in the Prophet's day the seriousness of obeying the Gospel.

This breaking of spirit and contriteness of heart happens on Sundays when each congregation meets before him, the Judge, in worship. To insist that attendance at worship services makes people good was already a despicable allegation long ago, a condemnable works-righteousness with which unbelievers deceive themselves. The same applies to annual feast days—Incarnation Day, Crucifixion Day, Resurrection Day, Ascension Day, Pentecost Day—each of which reveals an aspect of the New Testament Gospel. Each is designated to break hypocrisy and generate brokenness of spirit and contriteness of heart. Unbelievers want to come before the Lord in worship to hear they are worthy of the Judge's admiration and clemency, acquitted of any guilt. However, the Judge calls people to look beyond silly self-images and hear what he thinks of each and all.

V

Were the Assyrian armies the immediate threat to Judah's existence, in this day and age other fierce militants as socialists and rabid communists who through the destruction of Western civilization seek to undo the Church. As these citizens of the world seek autonomy, topple statues, change names, and nihilistically erase history to *create* a better world they go for the jugular of Christianity.

As world powers face off to find out which is the strongest the foundations tremble.

As killer viruses decimate both the weak and the strong pandemics shake even the strongest with fear.

As terrorizing annihilation gathers ferocity, the commands Isaiah issued in the name of the Judge and for the exposition of the Faith remain the same. This then is what Gospel believers do:

They cease to do evil, renounce idolatries tied in with reliance on Western civilization, mammonism for one, hedonism for another.

They learn to do good relative to love of neighbors, in humility counting others more significant than themselves, looking not only to one's own interests, but also to the interests of others.

They seek justice for the oppressed and the repressed minorities, to do justice and love kindness, thus to walk humbly with them before the Lord Jesus, undo white privilege and advocate in word and deed the equality of all before the law.

They work to create justice for the fatherless first in the Church, then also and equally for the orphans among the indigenous and the persecuted.

They plead the cause of the widows that they are cared for and fit in.

Whatever the threats from the rioters for a burnt-out West and a socialistic/communistic world, believing the Gospel and the evidence of broken hearts and contrite spirits remains the same.

Now, then, this is the day in which to give evidence of the grace of the Gospel.

ERRORS IN THE NICAENO-CONSTANTINOPOLITAN

THE PURPOSE OF THIS essay: to lay out the origin and the nature of two errors firmly lodged in the Nicene Creed, the Niceano-Constantinopolitan. With every recital of this statement of faith the catholic Church confesses doctrines at odds with the Scriptures, first respecting God the Son[1] and second respecting God the Holy Spirit. The italicized phrases locate the points of conflict.

We believe in one God, the Father Almighty,
Maker of heaven and earth,
of all things visible and invisible.
And in one Lord, Jesus Christ, *the only-begotten Son of God,*
begotten of the Father before all ages;
God of God, Light of Light, very God of very God;
begotten, not made,
of one substance with the Father;
through whom all things were made.[2]
Who, for us men and our salvation,
came down from heaven and became incarnate by the Holy Spirit of the
virgin Mary
and was made man.
He was crucified for us under Pontius Pilate;
he suffered and was buried;
and the third day he arose, according to the Scriptures,
and ascended into heaven, and sits at the right of the Father,

---

1. The God-the-Son naming stresses his divinity: Matthew 3:17, 11:27; Mark 1:11; Luke 3:22, 10:2; John 14:8–11; Galatians 4:8; 1 John 2:19–23; etc. The Son-of-God naming lays emphasis on his atoning work: Luke 1:35; John 1:34, 49, 3:18, 5:25; etc.

2. God the Son was involved in the work of creation with the God the Father, 1 Corinthians 8:6.

and he will come again with glory to judge the living and the dead;
whose kingdom shall have no end.
And we believe in the Holy Spirit, the Lord and giver of life,
who proceeds from the Father and the Son;
who with the Father and the Son is worshipped and glorified;
who spoke through the prophets.[3]
And we believe one holy catholic and apostolic church.
We acknowledge one baptism for the forgiveness of sins;
and we look forward to the resurrection of the dead,
and the life of the world to come.
Amen.

God the Son's *generation* and God the Spirit's *spiration* form this essay's foci. Both assertions defy the Scriptural accounts of the incarnational and the pentecostal revelation.

THE SON'S GENERATION

During the third-century AD Plotinus' Neoplatonism dominated the philosophical landscape, infiltrated Christ's Church, and structured theological thinking. This paradigmatic close-mindedness colonized biblical interpretation to the detriment of believing the Trinity according to the Scriptures, first now by misinterpreting the bond between God the Father and God the Son, the interest in which suspended attention on the Christ and the Atonement.

Origenist Eisegetics

Origen of Alexandria, apologist, AD 185–254, wholly absorbed by Plotinus' Neoplatonism, forced himself rationally within the trinitarian mystery, distorting the filiation between God the Father and God the Son to misshape Christology for the coming centuries. With Neoplatonism he moved the basic referent reprehensibly into forbidden territory, into the eternity and immutability of the relationship between God the Son and God the Father, before the Holy Spirit revealed in the New Testament the connectivity between the two, thus submitting its unintelligible mystery to rational inquiry.

---

3. Rusch. *The Trinitarian Controversy*, 4, "A special debt was owed to the Jewish philosopher Philo of Alexandria, who taught that the divine Logos had spoken through the prophets and had been the subject of the theophanies of the Old Testament."

Following through upon the filiation and explaining the eternally immutable bond between God the Father and God the Son, he ingeniously invented *eternal generation*, or *eternal begetting*. By this ceaseless filiating Origen, without attention to the historicity of the Incarnation, intended to clarify "the [only-begotten] Son," John 1:14, 3:16, 3:18, and "the [only-begotten] God," John 1:18. Through rationally probing into the Trinity he served the preferment of Greek philosophy at the expense of the glory of God, both the Father and the Son, and believing the Atonement. Neoplatonic inquisitiveness, typically Greek philosophy, knew neither limit nor modesty.

Eternal filiation fitted into a larger eisegetical expanse—subordination, presupposing God the Son's inferiority to God the Father—that made the Son a lesser god in comparison to the Father, suordinationism. Along with such as Philo, Justin Martyr,[4] and Clement of Alexandria, Origen subscribed to and assumed for God the Son an inferior divinity and eternity—God the Father *ágennetos*, uncreated, and God the Son eternally *gennetos*, created. This subordination of God the Son gave the identity of the Trinity a monotheistic slant, if not definition. That God the Son was the lesser in divinity and other in eternity than God the Father fitted well into Neoplatonism, deranged the filiation between God the Father and God the Son, then subsequently prepared the way for inventing *eternal generation*, which metaphor no Greek philosopher understood and which analogy resisted biblical revelation with respect to intratrinitarian bonding.

At that time and with that "subordinate" idealizing, thinkers as Origen struggled rationalistically with fundamentals belonging to the doctrine of the Christ and of the Trinity, seeking language constructs with which to confess the One as well as the Three in a manner suitable to Greek philosophy. In the Eastern Church radiating out from Constantinople leaders chose two conventional descriptives with which to reflect on the Trinity, *ousia* and *hypostaseis*.[5] In Rome, however, *hypostaseis* suggested tritheism. In the Western Church radiating out from Rome leaders evolved another

---

4. Norris. *The Christological Controversy*, 6, "Justin in effect takes up the language of John 1:14, where . . . Jesus is described as the enfleshed Logos or 'Word' of God. This Logos is God's Son, a reality distinct from the Father but begotten of him for the creation of the world."

5. Rusch. *The Trinitarian Controversy*, 22, "One of [Athanasius's] major accomplishments was a Council in Alexandria in 362, which recognized that what was critical was not the language but the meaning expressed. Because of the work of this council, the confusion over the possible meaning of *hypostasis* and *ousia* was cleared up. The formula of one *hypostasis* was endorsed as a means of stating the unity of nature between Father and Son."

trinitarian discourse, *substantia* and *personae*. In Constantinople, however, *personae* connoted Sabellianism, one god with three masks or roles. As respective Church Fathers debated linguistics, another philosophic obsession asserted attention: to know the filiation between God the Son and God the Father.

As one among others, Origen rationalized trinitarian unity and diversity, specifically the bond between God the Son and God the Father. In this respect he explicated, for instance, John 10:30 according to Neoplatonic philosophy, "I and the Father are one." One, ontologically? One, economically? Origen's metaphysical inclination settled on the ontological, the immutable nature of the being of God the Father and the being of God the Son. Quite naturally, he translated the "one" of John 10:30[6] with the neutral *hen*, "one thing." Except for the then current subordinationism the sense of the "one" approached the later powerfully significant *homoousion* descriptive of the Son's filiation. To clarify what he found in his philosophical rationalizing, Origen recommended *eternal generation*: God the Father eternally creating God the Son.[7] Apparently this profundity was acceptable to the Greek philosophy of the times.

With this eternally generative metaphor Origen, to explain the intratrinitarian bond between God the Father and God the Son, looked away from the Incarnation history, Matthew 1:22, Luke 1:35, Jesus' Jewishness, and from the factuality of the Cross-bound Savior, even the Atonement. Enthralled by speculative philosophy he with many others attempted to interpenetrate the Trinity's ontology.

Origen speculated further. He identified God the Father with the One of Neoplatonism, an idol, and recognized God the Son as an emanation of that unknown and unknowable deity, twisting therewith the way of the First Commandment, and of the Second also. This Neoplatonic, and Gnostic,[8] One endured at a far distance from the earth, a god too holy to touch matter or, worse, a god too holy to create matter. The purity of his emanative creativity trembled beyond all rationalization. The One is the

---

6. Holmes. *The Quest For the Trinity*, 44, for Athanasius this text decisively warranted *homoousios*.

7. Norris. *The Christological Controversy*, 15, "Origen believed, as against his predecessors, that God begets his Wisdom or Logos eternally—that there was never a time when the Logos did not exist (*De prin.* 1.2.9). This divine Wisdom, moreover, is the complete expression of God's being. At the same time, Wisdom is not God himself but his image, a 'second God,' subordinate to the ultimate Father of all."

8. Gnosticism developed a mental structure similar to Neoplatonism; the creator of universal matter and thus human beings occurred as the work of a lesser deity.

most absolute Absolute, an impenetrable mystery, which descriptive is already too physical a qualifier.

This begetting-metaphor described a transcendent relationship radically different from the conception-to-birth phenomenon familiar in this time-space world. No father is forever generating the same child. Origen, to gain credence for his metaphorical generation in its intratrinitarian framework—the Son *gennetos*, the Father *agennetos*—transferred finite maturation in a maternal womb into an inexplicable begetting without actually illuminating the activity of the ceaseless causation, transcending all known and knowable forms of procreation. The Son's eternal begottenness, beyond human comprehension, flickered as a far-off ideal. Only, Origen found the metaphor a working model to describe the indescribable and define the indefinable.[9]

Eternalizing God the Son's begottenness complicated Origen's working model. Following Clement of Alexandria's path[10] he equated the transcendent God the Father's unbegottenness with the Neoplatonic One, the source and cause of all that is. As the One emanates, God the Father comparably causes God the Son's ceaseless generation. This begetting-metaphor then takes filiation into metaphysical spheres, creative activity before the Genesis origins of all created reality. "For 'emanation seems to be of one substance [homoousios] with that body from which it is either an 'emanation' or a 'vapour.'"[11] The Neoplatonic One's emanating happens in a mythical realm, which gave first the authors of the Nicene Creed to say, "God of God, Light of Light, true God of true God," not to confess the Son's divinity and eternity, but to express his *gennetos*, which outdated Greek philosophy still rings false. Even though Origen with his generative ideal claimed God the Son's eternity and divinity, of the same substance as God the Father, he nevertheless projected two different divinities and eternities, the one subordinate to the other. In that perpetual begetting God the Son was at best an exemplary deity or an inspiring prophet, but not the Lord and Savior of the Gospels.

---

9. The Incarnation extends beyond comprehension; hence, the Scriptures move on to its purpose relative to the Atonement.
   Holmes. *The Quest for the Trinity*, 76, " . . . an argument from divine immutability: God does not change, and so the Father could not become the Father by begetting the Son; the Father must eternally be Father, and so the Son must eternally be."

10. Glover. *The Conflict of Religions in the Early Roman Empire*, 301, "The ideal Christian is habitually spoken of in this way, as the 'man of knowledge'—the true 'Gnostic,' as opposed to the heretics who illegitimately claim the title. A very great deal of Clement's writing is devoted to building up this Gnostic, to outlining his ideal character."

11. Holmes. *The Quest For the Trinity*, 40.

In elaborating on God the Son's begottenness Origen, ensconced in Neoplatonism, missed every appeal to the Jesus of the Scriptures.[12] Throughout his speculative maneuvering the Person of the Christ remained marginal. Without following through upon the Old Testament Christological prophecies over to the Incarnation, the Crucifixion, the Resurrection, to the Ascension, Origen even as the other Church Fathers generally sought salvation in philosophical abstraction. Seeking a syncretistic union between Neoplatonism and the Bible, the Bible lost its relevance for the Church; the Son of God depicted by the Church Fathers, Origen in particular, stood apart as an emanation to move souls into the One, not to give his life as a ransom for many.

Neoplatonic Emanating

Plotinus, AD 205–270, imagined into existence an immense reality transcending the space-time creation; its metaphysical dimensionality made sense only in the Platonic ambience of the times. According to Plato, souls belonged to a world other than this one, and by an exercise of the mind needed to return, thus leaving the prison house of the body behind. Souls freed of respective bodies became absorbed in divinity. When contemporary Epicurean[13] and Stoic[14] types of materialism failed to satisfy deepest human longings, Plotinus offered other-worldly hope, immersion into a

12. Anatolios. *Retrieving Nicaea*, 16, "Origen spoke of varying degrees of transcendence among the three *hypostaseis*, though he strictly differentiated the divine Trinity from creation." Neither the Son nor the Spirit was a creation, in opposition to Arius.

13. Epicureanism consisted at one level as an attack on superstition, hence anti-Platonic. On a more practical level, its practitioners sought modest forms of sustainable pleasure--tranquility of soul, peace of mind, freedom from fear, and an absence of physical pain. By limiting desires this mild hedonism stayed away from political involvement and military strife. To maintain this pleasure-principle, Epicureans recommended a working knowledge of this world. The narrowness of this philosophy offered no hope beyond immediate existence.

14. Stoics shunned emotions as fear and envy that destabilized equilibria of satisfaction, inclusive sexual excitements, passionate loves, each of which based on false judgments of worth. Stoic sages attained moral and intellectual strengths by seeking immunity to misfortune and finding the virtues of living sufficient. Stoics considered themselves free, all others bound as slaves to negligible passions. This mild hedonism gave no satisfaction to searching for existence beyond present confinements.
Glover. *The Conflict of Religions in the Early Roman Empire*, 72, "The Stoics in some measure felt their weakness here. When they tell us to follow God, to look to God, to live as God's sons, and leave us not altogether clear what they meant by God, their teaching is not very helpful, for it is hard to follow or look to a vaguely grasped conception."

divinity as far removed from human sensuality and earthly existence as possible. With his philosophic imagination he had the One of Plato's other world emanating and presented every soul with the ultimate journey, escape from the body into the One. Souls by gaining *gnosis* followed the way into the totally highest Being. Neoplatonic philosophizing promised release from bondage to matter, in the end freedom in that which exists beyond human terminology and comprehension.

According to this solely mental construction, the One exists in remote infinity and in utter transcendence, completely outside human comprehension. Even the identifying number, One, falls incredibly short of mentally grasping its nature. The One owned no qualifier or predicate that allowed for any subject/object explanation. This ultimate One, then, by emanating illuminated all reality and, because it exists beyond all human understanding, explains naught. Even *gnosis* to arrive at the One has a source outside the Ultimate, an emanation created for this purpose. This emanation Plotinus equated with God the Son.

V

The Neoplatonist One in its radical immateriality—without predicating materiality—continuously emanates, ceaselessly communicating qualities of eternity, *Nous* and *Psyche*. Through this existential reasoning the One thinks, spontaneously and naturally bringing forth by mentation its principle emanations.[15]

Mentating, the One by mental activity emanates *Nous*, its Mind.

Mentating, the One through Nous emanates *Psyche*, its soul; the *Psyche* too participates in radical immateriality.

Mentating, through the *Psyche* the One emanates a creation similar to Plato's *Demiurge*, which Plotinus blasphemously identified as God the Son. Following this idolatrous rationalizing: God the Father separates God the Son from himself and God the Son separates himself from God the Father, yet in eternity the two remain inseparably connected to each other; this connectivity Origen called *eternal generation*.

To account for the materiality of the earth in the One's totally spiritual creation, Plotinus transmuted Plato's *Demiurge* into a divinity that creates matter, since the One is too transcendent even to image a substance other than itself. This *Demiurge* enlivens inherently evil matter with the World

---

15. Glover. *The Conflict of Religions in the Early Roman Empire*, 288, "Neo-Platonism has its 'golden chain' of existence descending from Real Being—God—through a vast series of beings who *are* in a less and less degree as they are further down the scale."

Soul, the spirit that pervades the earth's motion and change, two qualities totally foreign to and impossible for the One. The *Demiurge*, or Plotinus's idolatrous God the Son, also fashions the Middle Soul, the stuff of which human souls. The *Demiurge* next molds innately sinful material bodies that imprison pieces of soul-substance.[16] This imprisoning function of materiality defines a timeless or pretemporal "fall," the mixing of souls into intrinsically sinful bodies to explain the effect of Adam's disobedience for himself and his posterity. Matter is outside the range of the eternally transcendent One's mentation.

V

The dichotomous soul-and-matter, matter beyond redemption, gave human beings an ill-fitting unity, the parts of the spiritual Middle Soul constantly rejecting the physical bodies. Human beings of binary perplexity experienced in Plotinus' scheme of reality constant tension, the soul discarding bodily matter to escape the fallenness of Adam's seed.

Freeing oneself from entrapment in the physicality of the prison of matter each soul sought the *gnosis*[17] the *Demiurge* provided, then motivated by this *gnosis* ascended (slowly) up the *Psyche* and the *Nous* into the One. Neoplatonist salvation, therefore, consisted in this: souls gaining release from unredeemable material bodies by garnering *gnosis* to facilitate the way through the *Psyche* and the *Nous* into the freedom and the eternity of the Absolute. Long entanglement in materiality broke down the will to ascend into the One, then forever abide in this idolatrous entity. Strengthening personal virtues of good and love indicated success in the upward climbing to the ultimate Mystery, achieving a unity that defined Plotinus's manner of deliverance from materiality.

The One eternally emanating *Nous* and *Psyche*, then through the *Demiurge* creating spiritual souls that matter trapped, communicated release to the soul substance; active souls achieved release from the physicality of respective prison houses and found the way up into the eternal One.

When Greek philosophers abandoned Epicurean and Stoic materialism, finding those belief systems unable to satisfy the longings of souls for

---

16 Rusch. *The Trinitarian Controversy*, 4, "Justin began with the idea of the *Logos spermatikos* (the seminal Word) planted in all persons incompletely and in a fragmentary manner. Before Christ, human beings had 'seeds' of the Word and could reach only fragments of the truth."

17. Norris. *The Christological Controversy*, 16, ". . . Wisdom the mediator must be mediated to the fallen spirits, and this is the point of the incarnation."

absolute and eternal unity in divinity, Plotinus's mystic immersion into an indescribable ultimacy found resonance—at least among the intellectual elite.

Arian Heresies

Arius, AD 256–336, Neoplatonist, from within that philosophical structuring found that God the Son missed out on the totality of divinity and eternity in a way more extreme than Origen's eisegesis.[18] For Origen God the Father and God the Son in some inscrutable fashion remained attached relative to divinity and eternity. Arius, on the other hand, separated God the Son and God the Father, making God the Son even more inferior to God the Father than in Origen's school of thought.[19]

Arius (with numerous followers) preferred to speak of the Word in a philosophically abstract manner to believe God the Son a creature involved in the creation of the Neoplatonic earth[20] with its human beings. Given now then the dichotomy between this god, the One, who had no interior source, and the Word, that had an external source, Arius considered that the Logos belonged to the created order,[21] a quite superior creature outranking all others. The Neoplatonic god brought him forth before all ages to function as the agent in the creation of all other creatures, matter specifically.[22] Arius

---

18. Berkhof. *Systematic Theology*, 82, "[Origen] detracted from the essential deity of these two persons of the Godhead, and furnished a stepping-stone to the Arians, who denied the deity of the Son and of the Holy Spirit by representing the Son as the first creature of the Father, and the Holy Spirit as the first creature of the Son."
Anatolios. *Retrieving Nicaea*, 17," . . . the doctrine of Arius combined Origen's emphasis on the real distinctions within the Trinity with an unflagging insistence of the utter singularity of the one unoriginated and unbegotten God."

19. Norris. *The Christological Controversy*, 17, "Logically enough, therefore, [Arius'] doctrine of the Logos was so formulated as to express two convictions: first, that the Logos cannot be God in the proper sense; second, that the Logos performs an essential mediatorial role in the relation of God to world."

20. Rusch. *The Trinitarian Controversy*, 5, "For Justin, in addition to the incarnation, the Logos functioned as the Father's agent in creation and in revealing truth."

21. Rush. *The Trinitarian Controversy*, 30, from Arius' Letter to Eusebius of Nicomedia, "And before he was begotten or created or defined or established, he was not. For he was not unbegotten."
Anatolios. *Retrieving Nicaea*, 17, "His generation from the Father is thus the first and highest instance of creaturehood."

22. Norris. *The Christological Controversy*, 18.

thus taught a radical bifurcation beyond Origen's left, totally outside the Scriptures.

To give voice to this extreme subordination Arius coined curious phraseology[23]—*en pote hote ouk en*—to assert that once there was when the Word was not or once the Father was not the Father. This "once" differs from *chronos*, regular time; it has some sense of eternity built in, a "once" in which the Father preceded the Son. Arius held fast the conviction that even though the Word was a creature, its creaturehood existing from eternity in a way different from the Neoplatonist god's eternity, a double sort of eternity free only in Neoplatonist reality.[24] He was convinced, different than Origen and other Greek-thinkers, that by *going back in* eternity far enough this godness of the One was without the Word. He held that the Word existed as a creature before the Genesis creation, in which creation attaining an eternal status—the first-born of all creation.

Eschewing any recourse to the Scriptures and speculating abstractly, Arius, typically Neoplatonic, assumed his god was a simple entity, the One, without attributes and predicates, who was unwilling and unable to defile himself with matter that obviously existed relative to the world and humanity. He needed the Word with the mandate to fashion the material world, something extremely ungodlike. Through the Word Arius explained the origin of humanity. Therefore the Word's ontological beginning is/was crucial to Arius, both theologically and confessionally.

As Arius distinguished between his god's *agennetos* and the Word's *gennetos* he complicated the bond between God the Father and God the Son by equating *gennetos* with *genetos,* came into being, thereby exaggerating the Son's creaturehood.[25] The Word as the first creation created that for which the Neoplatonic god was too transcendent. At this point, by breaking Origenist orthodoxy, Arius and Arianism became a source of controversy.

V

23. Frame. *A History of Western Philosophy and Theology*, 104.

24. Norris. *The Christological Controversy*, 18, " . . . the Logos made a human body his own in order to restore humanity to the state which God had originally intended for the human race. Human beings, constituted of soul together with body, had been created to share the qualities of God's own life by living in fellowship with their Creator—by knowing him, and through such knowledge being conformed, at their own creaturely level, to his way of being."

25. Torrance. "Being of One Substance With the Father," 52.

In the then current persuasion of subordination Arius was the first to counter Origenist orthodoxy and claim the Word's creatureliness, a "hybrid,"[26] the first creation with the authority to create, as Arius twisted John 1:3. Arius' insistence concerning the creatureliness of the Word initiated controversy; the Church Fathers, though submerged in Greek philosophy, perceived from the Scriptures that no creature arrived into existence qualified to serve as the Redeemer. Therefore third-century AD philosophers/theologians, Origenists, inveighed against Arius and Arianism, citing Origen's *eternal generation* to hold up the divinity and the eternity of the Word. Despite the difficulties engulfed in ceaseless begetting, the Church Fathers recognized that Arius' configuration of the Word was beyond any capability of saviorhood. Against all Arian opposition the Church Fathers, Athanasius notably, generated the *homoousion*, terminology in which God the Son's eternity and divinity equaled God the Father's eternity and divinity. Arius worse than Origen failed to describe the relationship between the two Persons of the Trinity in the biblical manner; only, Arius abstracted the Person of the Son more than Origen. Yet the Origenists in the approach to the AD 325 Council of Nicaea had equated the Son's divinity and eternity with the Father's.[27]

Arius even more than Origen had attempted to comprehend God the Father and God the Son in terms of the Neoplatonist One in a meaning acceptable only to Arians. More extreme than Origen and the other Church Fathers, Arius by breaking into the immutability and impenetrability of the Trinity set the Church up for severe problems.

Arianism encourages worship of a creature. Christians have long worshiped Christ as God. If Arianism were true, Christians either would have to abandon their worship of Jesus or would have to confess the sin of idolatry—giving divine worship to a mere creature.

Arianism teaches that our salvation depends on a creature, rather than wholly on God.[28]

In short, Arius with his eisegesis failed more miserably in his interpretation of God the Son's eternity and divinity than Origen. As a Greek philosopher his interest in Jesus of the Scriptures remained marginal, a name, a concept. Without the Old Testament's Christological prophecies and the Gospel's historicity, Arius developed a syncretic union between the

---

26. Gunton. "*And In One Lord, Jesus Christ, ... Begotten, Not Made*," 44, in Christopher R. Seitz, ed., *Nicene Christianity: The Future for a New Ecumenism*, Grand Rapids: Brazos, 2001, 35–48.

27. Frame. *A History of Western Philosophy and Theology*, 106.

28. Frame. *A History of Western Philosophy and Theology*, 107.

Scriptures and Greek philosophy, the Scriptures losing. Except in Arian imagination, Arianism crushes the Christian hope.

Incarnational Exegetics

The Church Fathers philosophized with rather than exegeted the *monogenous* of John 1:14, 18, 3:16, 18, terminology relative only to the Incarnation's historical context. Neither the Son, nor the Father, nor the Holy Spirit revealed prior to the Genesis creation anything of the intratrinitarian unity, except the bonding love and glory of John 17:5, 24. Instead of reading the Bible as the Word of God the second- and third-century AD Church Fathers, overwhelmingly pressured by Neoplatonism, overlooked the Incarnation's historicity; they imagined God the Son an emanation brought about by Origen's *eternal generation*, which the Church since affirmed in the Nicene, a shadow of which also lingers in the Athanasian, #22, "The Son is from the Father alone, not made nor created but begotten." Neoplatonic (and Gnostic) academics eisegeted key words philosophically, thereby forcing Greek ideals into Scripture interpretation.

In contrast to the Greek philosophical interpretation of *monogenous*, Spirit-filled John named herewith the incarnational bond between God the Father and God the Son, according to the law of primogeniture. As the *monogenous* of all creation, as Paul in Colossians 1:15, Jesus with his divinity and humanity received the primary blessing, ownership of the entire universe.

More significant than primogeniture, Apostle John in the Fourth Gospel consistently accentuated that God the Father sent God the Son into the world for the ministry of the Atonement; this sending revealed trinitarian work with regard to the Incarnation. In the Old Testament the LORD God prophesied his advent in the Incarnation, which occurred according to his will, Philippians 2:5–7. Matthew, 1:22, and Luke, 1:35, revealed that the Holy Spirit brought the Incarnation about. John, in distinction, at the conclusion to the first-century AD stressed against the rising appeal of Judaism and its Pharisaic works-righteousness that God the Father had sent God the Son without any hint that God the Son with respect to his divinity and eternity was inferior to the Father. God the Father's sending of the Son happened in sharp contrast to the Jewish god eternally locked in monotheistic isolation, John 8:44; that idolatrous being was eternally unable to filiate and forever ineffective at atoning for the sins of *his* people. Despite the humiliation God the Son experienced in and to his human nature throughout the

Fourth Gospel,[29] John gathered powers of excitement preparative to the Resurrection and the Ascension.

Rather than interpreting the Father's sending of the Son as subordination (true only with respect to Jesus' humanity) the Son according to his divinity and eternity was/is the Father's equal. By emphasizing the Son's sent-ness John affirmed his Christhood (as at the baptism, John 1:32) as well as the intratrinitarian unity of the Son, the Father, and the Holy Spirit. This unity—specific now between the Father and the Son—has nothing to do with *eternal generation*; they were one *throughout* all eternity. From the initial prophecy of the Incarnation, God the Son committed himself to a space-time life, Galatians 4:4–5; and at his baptism, Matthew 3:13–17; Luke 3:21–22, God the Father and God the Spirit alongside Jesus' divinity promised to protect his humanity in the way of suffering to and in the Atonement, which sovereign promise God the Father reaffirmed, Matthew 17:1–8; Mark 9:2–8, and John 12:27–28. Thus the Author revealed the sending of God the Son only as a giving in and with time-space, the sole arena for exegesis.

By eisegesis Origen and other Church Fathers forced a Neoplatonic thought structure onto, or into, Jesus' Person; relative to the incarnational terminology they found the *eternal generation* idea acceptable in the framework of Greek philosophy. Only in Greek philosophy did eternal emanating have a place, God the Father "birthing" God the Son in a manner similar to Zeus "extracting" lesser gods from his head and the Egyptian Atum "fathering" inferior deities from his body, which sorts of auto-generation found resonance only in pagan communities.

V

Throughout, Origenists and Arians assumed that God the Son owned this name from all eternity. However, neither God the Father, nor God the Son, nor God the Holy Spirit had these names prior to the Genesis creation; they identified themselves in this trinitarian manner specifically in the New Testament dispensation, the era of the fuller revelation of the Trinity.

---

29. Rusch. *The Trinitarian Controversy*, 22, "Eternally the Father has the Son. The Son is the eternal Son of the Father. The Father is the eternal father of the Son. Only if they are co-eternal can Jesus, in whom the Logos is present, give us eternal life."

Athanasius' Resolution

Athanasius, AD 290–373, at the AD 325 Council of Nicaea[30] (under the auspices of Alexander the Great) confronted and penetrated the seriousness of Arius' inferior god; the teaching that God the Son's divinity and eternity were of a lesser quality scandalizes the actuality of the Trinity. With the *homoousion* (of the same nature, substance)[31] as the key shibboleth throughout the controversy, Athanasius and the Council countered the Arian heresy. The divinity and the eternity of God the Son equaled the eternity and the divinity of God the Father. Not even a counter-suggestion, *homoiousion* (of like substance) sufficed to exegete the Scriptures and unify the Church with respect to the Persons of the Trinity. For God the Son to be the Son of God, Savior,[32] he had to be of same substance as God the Father. The originators of the Athanasian therefore stated, #8–9, "The Father is uncreate, the Son uncreate, the Holy Spirit uncreate. He is infinite, the Son infinite, the Holy Spirit infinite." However much the orthodoxy of the Origenist *eternal generation* functioned in Nicaea to overcome the Arian heresy, the *homoousion* served in the biblical manner to express the eternal and divine unity of the Persons.[33]

Because Arius and Arians persisted in denying the *homoousion* the Council denounced this idolatry. The AD 351 Council of Chalcedon reaffirmed the Nicaean Christology, which decision, humanly speaking, preserved the Church in her continuity. At the AD 381 Council of Constantinople the majority of the bishops confirmed the now Nicene

---

30. Rusch. *The Trinitarian Controversy*, 20, "The issue at Nicaea was the Son's co-eternity with the Father, not the unity of the Godhead."

31. Rusch. *The Trinitarian* Controversy, from Athanasius' Orations against the Arians, Book I, 70, "He is neither a creature nor a work, but an offspring peculiar to the Father's substance. Therefore he is true God, *homoousios* with the true Father."

Holmes. *The Quest for the Trinity*, 88, "Although *homoousios* was to be the decisive term later, there is reason to suppose that, for those present at Nicaea, it was understood as merely clarifying or reasserting 'from the *ousia* of the Father', which was the crucial dogmatic claim."

32. Norris. *The Christological Controversy*, 18, "This the Logos accomplishes in two ways. First, by his death on the cross he discharges the debt which had rendered human beings morally liable to physical death. Second, by his presence he enables people to share in the divine life."

33. Norris. *The Christological Controversy*, 19, "The incarnation is and must be the incarnation of one who is fully and truly God. Inevitably, then, Athanasius repudiated the teaching of Arius on christological, and not merely theological, grounds."

teaching with respect to the substance of the Persons,[34] creating the Nicaeno-Constantinopolitan.

Despite the Nicaeno-Constantinopolitan correction—the equality of the substance of the Father and of the Son—*eternal generation* still describes the unbiblical relationship between God the Father and God the Son; this unorthodoxy remains firmly wedged in the Nicaean-Constantinopolitan.

V

At issue now: the Nicaeno-Constantinopolitan and the Athanasian relative to Christology advocate a pagan teaching; nothing of *eternal generation* appears in the Scriptures. It may be that through conventional reading the Church overlooks this hypocrisy, but before the Christ his Church owes him clarity, truth-full universal creeds.

THE SPIRIT'S PROCESSION

The trinitarian Nicaean professed the facticity of the Holy Spirit following the Apostles Creed, " . . . and in the Holy Spirit." The AD 381 Council of Constantinople confirmed the AD 351 Council of Chalcedon's extension with respect to the Spirit.

> We believe in the Holy Spirit, the Lord and Giver of Life,
> *who proceeds from the Father and the Son,*
> who with the Father and the Son is worshiped and glorified,
> who spoke through the prophets.

The revelation of this procession Jesus expressed in different ways. First: God the Father sent the Spirit to the Twelve. John 14:16–17a, "And I will ask the Father and he will give you another Helper, to be with you forever, even the Spirit of truth." John 14:26, "But the Helper, the Holy Spirit, whom the Father will send in my name, he will teach you all things and bring to remembrance all that I have said to you." With all emphasis Jesus drew God the Father into the trinitarian Pentecost Day work. Second: with anticipation of Pentecost Day Jesus also *autonomously* sent the Spirit, John 16:7, " . . . if I do not go away, the Helper will not come to you. But if I go, I will send him to you." Third: the Holy Spirit also acted *independently* of the Father and the Son. John 16:13, "When the Spirit of truth comes, he will

---

34. Rusch. *The Trinitarian Controversy*, 70, "He always was and is, and never was he not. Because the Father is everlasting, his Word and Wisdom would be everlasting."

guide you into all the truth, for he will not speak on his own authority, but whatever he hears he will speak, and he will declare to you the things that are to come." Briefly then, God the Father sent the Spirit, God the Son sent the Spirit, and God the Spirit acted on his own. Acts 1:1–4 revealed a truly trinitarian work.

> When the day of Pentecost arrived, the [one hundred and twenty] were all together in one place. And suddenly there came from heaven a sound like a mighty rushing wind, and it filled the entire house where they were sitting. And divided tongues as of fire appeared to them and rested on each one of them. And they were all filled with the Holy Spirit and began to speak in other tongues as the Spirit gave them utterance.

Thus the Spirit also acted as a Person from within the unity of the Trinity, fully *homoousion* with God the Son and God the Father; in effect, he proceeds into the historical setting from both, God the Father and God the Son.[35]

Fourth, and here is the problem with respect to the procession of the Spirit, John 15:26, "But when the Helper comes, whom I will send to you from the Father, the Spirit of truth, who proceeds from the Father, he will bear witness about me." That phrase with respect to spirating from the Father, the Church Fathers eisegeted in the Neoplatonic mode, imagining that this proceeding occurred before the foundation of the world. Thus these men of old pretended they had penetrated the mystery of the Trinity and found another creative act before the Genesis account. In this manner they skewed the facts of the Scriptures as badly as earlier with respect to Christology. The attending bishops at the Council of Chalcedon read the Scriptures in a Neoplatonic manner, not in reference to the Pentecost Day outpouring.

The Spirit's *homoousios*, the same in substance as God the Son and God the Father, appeared first in the form of a dove, bringing the Three of the Trinity together, Matthew 3:13–17; Mark 1:9–11; Luke 3:21–22; John 1:32; from that moment the three—Jesus' divinity, God the Father, and God the Spirit—prepared the Son of God's humanity for the agony of the Atonement. The proceeding, however, occurred in history.

V

---

35. Smail. "The Holy Spirit in the Holy Trinity," 155, in Seitz, ed., *Nicaean Christianity*, "So the New Testament witness, expressed particularly by John but confirmed by the other evangelists, is that the Spirit is sent *by* and *from* the Father but also *through* and *by* the incarnate Son."

At issue with the Spirit's procession, first the Nicene and also the Athanasian (#23, "The Holy Spirit is from the Father and the Son, not made nor created nor begotten but proceeding.") allows pneumatologically for an erroneous reading, now wedged in the Nicaeno-Constantinopolitan. Nothing of eternal proceeding appears in the Scriptures. It may be said that conventional readers/confessors ignore the hypocrisy. However, before the Christ the Church owes him through her members truth also in her universal creeds.

Finishing Matters

One: it is possible to rephrase the Nicaean at the two italicized intersections and make this universal creed more biblical.

THE NICENE CREED

We believe in one God, the Father Almighty,
Maker of heaven and earth,
of all things visible and invisible.
And in one Lord, Jesus Christ, *the only-begotten God the Son,*
of one substance with the Father,
through whom all things were made.
Who, for us men and our salvation,
came down from heaven and became incarnate by the Holy Spirit
of the virgin Mary
and was made man.
He was crucified for us under Pontius Pilate;
he suffered and was buried;
and the third day he arose, according to the Scriptures,
and ascended into heaven, and sits at the right of the Father,
and he will come again with glory to judge the living and the dead;
whose kingdom shall have no end.
And we believe in the Holy Spirit, the Lord and give of life,
whom the Father and the Son poured out upon the Church;
who with the Father and the Son is worshipped and glorified;
who spoke through the prophets.
And we believe one holy catholic church.
We acknowledge one baptism for the forgiveness of sins;
and we look for the resurrection of the dead,
and the life of the world to come.
Amen.

V

Two: by collapsing #21–23, it is also possible to rephrase the Athanasian at the italicized intersection and bring it in line with the Scriptures.

THE ATHANASIAN CREED

Whoever desires to be saved must above all things hold to the catholic faith.
Unless a man keeps it in its entirety inviolate, he will assuredly perish eternally.
Now this is the catholic faith, that we worship one God in trinity and trinity in unity, without either confusing the persons, or dividing the substance.
For the Father's person is one, the Son's another, the Holy Spirit's another; but the Godhead of the Father, the Son, and the Holy Spirit is one,
Their glory is equal, their majesty is co-eternal.
Such as the Father is, such is the Son, such is also the Holy Spirit.
The Father is uncreate, the Son uncreate, the Holy Spirit uncreate.
The Father is infinite, the Son infinite, the Holy Spirit infinite.
The Father is eternal, the Son eternal, the Holy Spirit eternal.
Yet there are not three eternals, but one eternal; just as there not three uncreates or three infinites, but one uncreate and one infinite.
In the same way the Father is almighty, the Son almighty, the Holy Spirit almighty; yet there are not three almighties, but one almighty.
Thus the Father is God, the Son God, the Holy Spirit God; and yet there are not three Gods, but there is one God.
Thus the Father is Lord, the Son Lord, the Holy Spirit Lord; and yet there are not three Lords, but there is one Lord
Because just as we are compelled by Christian truth to acknowledge each person separately to be both God and Lord,
so we are forbidden by the catholic religion to speak of three Gods or Lords.
From all eternity the Father, the Son, and the Spirit are one,
immutably.
So there is one Father, not three Fathers; one Son, not three Sons; one Holy Spirit, not three Holy Spirits.
And in this trinity there is nothing before or after, nothing greater or less, but all three persons are co-eternal with each other and co-equal.
Thus in all things, as has been stated above, both trinity in unity and unity in trinity must be worshipped.
So he who desires to be saved should think thus of the Trinity.
It is necessary, however, to eternal salvation that he should also believe in the incarnation of our Lord Jesus Christ.

Now the right faith is that we should believe and confess that our Lord Jesus Christ, the Son of God, is equally both God and man.
He is God *equal with the Father and the Spirit* before all time; and he is man from his mother's substance, born in time.
Perfect God, perfect man composed of a human soul and human flesh, equal to the Father in respect of his divinity, less than the Father in respect to his humanity.
Who, although he is God and man, is nevertheless not two, but one Christ.
He is one, however, not by the transformation of his divinity into flesh, but by taking up of his humanity into God; one certainly not by confusion of substance, but by oneness of person.
For just as soul and flesh are one man, so God and man are one Christ.
Who suffered for our salvation, descended into hell, rose from the dead, ascended to heaven, sat down at the Father's right hand, from where he will come to judge the living and the dead; at whose coming all men will rise again with their bodies, and will render an account of their deeds; and those who have done good will go to eternal life, those who have evil to eternal fire.
This is the catholic faith. Unless a man believes it faithfully and steadfastly, he cannot be saved.
Amen.

V

Three: it is also possible to start anew by avoiding the errors of the Nicaean and the Athanasian, thus drawing all believers together in and before the Christ.

CHRIST AND CHRISTIANS

Christians believe: Christ Jesus is.
Christians believe: Christ Jesus is Lord, omnipotent and omniscient.

V

Christians believe: Christ Jesus with the Father and the Spirit created the universe.
Christians believe: Christ Jesus led the Church and the Kingdom, Israel, to the Incarnation.

Christians believe: the Christ descended from heaven.
Christians believe: he with the Father and the Spirit bonded divinity/humanity in his Person.
Christians believe: Christ Jesus suffered humiliation throughout his life.
Christians believe: Christ Jesus in the Crucifixion, by grace, created the Atonement.
Christians believe: Christ Jesus constituted the Crucifixion the first and great Judgment.
Christians believe: Christ Jesus according to his human nature died.
Christian believe: Christ Jesus in the agonies of dying and death created the Atonement.
Christians believe: Christ Jesus with the Father and the Spirit created the Resurrection.
Christians believe: in the Resurrection Christ Jesus' humanity was recreated.
Christians believe: Christ Jesus, resurrected, lived in exaltation.
Christians believe: Christ Jesus in his exaltation ascended into heaven.
Christians believe: Christ Jesus upon the Ascension initiated his thousand-year reign.
Christians believe: Christ Jesus with the Father sent the Holy Spirit.
Christians believe: through the Spirit Christ Jesus and the Father recreated the Church.
Christians believe: Christ Jesus included the Church in his sovereignty.
Christians believe: with the Church Christ Jesus started the Recreation.
Christians believe: he rules his Church by means of the Gospel and the Commandments.
Christians believe: Christ Jesus from within the Church governs his Kingdom.
Christians believe: people are chronic sinners, unable to extricate themselves from bondage.
Christians believe: Christ Jesus causes his to believe the covenant promises.
Christians believe: Christ Jesus qualifies his people to live the covenant obligations.
Christians believe: Christ Jesus heads the Church until the end of history.

V

Christians believe: Christ Jesus in the end returns.
Christians believe: Christ Jesus calls the final Judgment.
Christians believe: Christ Jesus will summon all to his right hand or left.
Christians believe: Christ Jesus will condemn all on his left to hell.
Christians believe: Christ Jesus will summons all on his right into glory.

Christians believe: Christ Jesus with the Father and the Spirit reign forever.
Christians believe: Christ Jesus lives.
Amen.

V

It is imperative that the Church confesses the Faith in wholeness and unity, thus glorifying the Lord Jesus Christ, the Father, and the Spirit, one God.

BIBLIOGRAPHY

Anatolios, Khaled. *Retrieving Nicaea: The Development and Meaning of Trinitarian Doctrine.* Grand Rapids: Baker Academic, 2011.
Berkhof, L. *Systematic Theology.* Grand Rapids: Eerdmans, 1939/68.
Frame, John M. *A History of Western Philosophy and Theology.* Phillipsburg, Presbyterian & Reformed, 2015.
Glover, T.R. *The Conflict of Religions in the Early Roman Empire.* London: Methuen & Co., 1909.
Gunton, Colin, in Seitz, Christopher R., ed. *Nicaean Christianity: The Future for a New Ecumenism.* Grand Rapids: Brazos, 2001/4, 35–48.
Holmes, Stephen R. *The Quest for the Trinity: The Doctrine of God in Scripture, History, and Modernity.* Downers Grove: IVP Academic, 2012.
Norris, Richard A. *The Christological Controversy.* Philadelphia: Fortress, 1980.
Rusch, William G. *The Trinitarian Controversy.* Philadelphia: Fortress, 1980.
Seitz, Christopher R., ed. *Nicaean Christianity: The Future for a New Ecumenism.* Grand Rapids: Brazos, 2001/4.
Smail, Thomas, in Seitz, Christopher R., ed. *Nicaean Christianity: The Future for a New Ecumenism.* Grand Rapids: Brazos, 2001/4, 149–165.
Torrance, Alan, in Seitz, Christopher R., ed. *Nicaean Christianity: The Future for a New Ecumenism.* Grand Rapids: Brazos, 2001/4, 49–61.

EXEGETICAL STUDIES

LEGAL FINDINGS

THE IMMEDIATE BACKGROUND TO the New Testament, the Pharisaic/Sadduceic offense to prevent the Christ in his ministry, occupies the exegesis of its twenty-seven books. To interpret first of all the Gospels apart from this historical framework leaves interpretation/application at best shamefully mediocre, the work of untrained students. As in *Covenant Studies: One*, I lay out the necessity to know the context of a textual unit, thus to exegete biblically.

Luke 15:1–32
Luke 15:11–32

A HEART OF FLESH AND A HEART OF STONE

The Lord Jesus, *the* Teacher, with pastoral intensity addressed also difficult members in the Church, on the one hand the young and restless, on the other the Pharisees. For this purpose he created the parable, concentrating on two equally rebellious sons and a caring father, on the father even more than the sons; indeed, he made the character of the father dominate. Over the three parables by moving from the one hundred sheep to the ten coins to the two sons, the Teacher built up tension, an intensifying concentration.

In the parable Jesus as the Creator from the beginning to the end controlled the plot and the character development; that is, both the men and the story-line are his, to do with according to his good pleasure. Word by word and scene by scene, his sovereign lordship shines through the growth of the parable. At the telling of the parable the Lord Jesus also selected the place and the audience in order to lay down the dividing-line, forever separating the two brothers. Remember, Jesus constructed the plot as well as the characters of this mini-world in which he revealed the trinitarian unity between himself, the Son of God, and God the Father.

The Younger Son

The younger son, a member of the Church and hence a man of the covenant community, duly circumcised, insisted on living according to his own desires. For that reason, with a heart of stone, he rudely and inappropriately demanded to have his portion of the inheritance due him while his father was still very much alive. Legally, since time immemorial sons and daughters received respective inheritances only upon the death of the parents, Hebrews 9:17. However, as Jesus constructed the story-line and the character of the younger son whose whole life was wrapped up in covetousness; he made the worst of this young man stand out. "Father," he commandeered, "give me the share of the property that is coming to me." According to the law of the land the share of the property came to one-third of the assets, the elder son to inherit two-thirds, per primogeniture, Deuteronomy 21:15–17. As impertinent and improper the request, yet the father consented and gave his younger son his share of the property.

> An inheritance gained hastily in the beginning
> will not be blessed in the end.
> Proverbs 20:21

V

Over several days the greedy fellow, unwilling to drag buildings, animals, land, and farm equipment with him on the planned journey, converted his share of the property into hard cash. Then by traveling into a distant country, he broke all family ties. In that other place of the parable he squandered his wealth on loose living, whatever that meant at that time and in that place, perhaps by gambling on camel races and partying. The point of the matter is: in unrighteousness he wasted his capital, which left him destitute in a strange place among, to him, foreign people.

For the sake of clarity: the young man in his poverty represented the marginalized of the Church, those whom the Pharisees and Sadducees considered the wrong sort for synagogue membership.

To make matter worse for the young man, now a penniless fellow, the Lord Jesus introduced in the parable a famine that overwhelmed the country. In these extremes of poverty and hunger the Teacher gave him a job, for the guy hired himself out to a citizen of that country, willing to work for food, a reasonable enough decision under the circumstances. However, by making that young Jew do the unthinkable, herding swine, Jesus pushed him to the limits of endurance in order to come to the one issue of the parable. The guy had to herd swine, the meat of which the LORD God, the Christ himself, had forbidden the people of the Old Testament Church to eat, Lev 11:7. While he fed the swine pods of carbo trees that served as food for animals, swine, and the destitute, the employer gave him nothing. While the pigs ate to the full, the young man starved.

For a sum so far of the hungry man's character: Jesus made him an unrighteous fellow, one who wasted his share of the family wealth, broke the family ties, and placed him starving in the midst of a swine herd, altogether as low as possible in Pharisee disparagement. The Lord Jesus presented him as one unwilling and unable to do the Commandments, the Lord's own rule for living.

V

As Jesus placed the young man at his lowest in the social order, he came to the first point of the parable. It is easy to assume that the guy chose his own troubles and then sensibly as well as rationally turned about on his own account, because of an insightful flash of intelligence. But all who make that assumption take control of the parable to rewrite the plot and this character to suit some eisegetical preferences. Jesus is the Creator of the parable and, mysteriously, turned the fellow about, in fact, gave him a new heart, a heart of flesh. Thus the Son of God, Savior, made him righteous, Isaiah 53:11; Daniel 12:3–4, altering him radically.

Remember: Jesus created the characters and gave each a life to come to the issue of this parable. By grace he made the rebellious young man righteous, willing and able to do even in the direst circumstances what is right and true in accordance with the Commandments. This life-changing work of the Lord and Savior broke through immediately. For the young man watching the swine eat more than enough recalled his father's hired men.

It is important to appreciate the turnabout as Jesus' work, this regeneration within the young man as he said to himself, "How many of my father's hired servants have more than enough bread, but I perish here with hunger!" In and by that remembering Jesus revealed the heart of flesh he had given the young man, with this understanding: the turnabout was entirely Jesus' work, his alone. The Lord and Savior declared him righteous, willing and able to do the good of the Law.

At telling the parable Jesus also created the words of repentance that welled up out the new heart of flesh, evidence of the reformed human being as he prepared to return home. Jesus put those words in the man's mouth, as if he drew them from his heart. "I will rise and go to my father, and I will say to him, 'Father, I have sinned against heaven and before you. I am no longer worthy to be called your son. Treat me as one of your hired servants.'" These humble and free-flowing words of repentance before God the Father and his own father he recited over and over on the way home.

V

On hearing and thinking through this parable the one of the lost sheep comes to mind,. As the shepherd committed himself to the task of finding the lamb, Jesus put in every effort to give the young man a new heart and a new future; the Lord and Savior extracted him from the grip of damnation and called him into the membership of the New Church.

A wise son makes a glad father.
Proverbs 10:1a

By creating the covetous character of the young man Jesus made him represent the marginalized of the Old Church, the rebellious, the angry, and the dissatisfied. Only, in making him a new creation Jesus revealed the kind of people that he began calling into the membership of the New Church.

The Caring Father

At creating the father of the parable, Jesus gave a presentation of his Father, God the Father. Since no one has seen or can see God the Father, except the Son only, the Lord and Savior carefully portrayed that earthly father as a caring man who perceived his younger son while he was still a long way off. Jesus, to stress the love of this father, exaggerated the situation by intimating that the man had stood for weeks, if not months, in his front door peering down the road, expecting. The point is: Jesus pictured that father eagerly waiting for the younger son to return, even though he had no inkling of his conversion and of his journeying home.

V

The compassionate father ran to meet the son. Running. It was not the custom of significant personages, nor of the elderly, to go at a run down the road to meet people; it was considered an undignified means of getting about in public. But this man of the Church rejected propriety and ran to embrace his son still filthy from long travelling on dusty roads.

The son immediately began his well-rehearsed confession of sin with the words Jesus created and placed in his heart and mouth, but the father cut him off; he could see into his son's heart and knew the pain of that repentance. Instead of listening and hearing his son out, he ordered a feast, at the center of which a fattened calf, an animal raised and stabled for such an occasion. Abraham had done the same with the LORD and two angels who unexpectedly stopped by, Genesis 18:7. Hear the joy in the father's commands to the servants. "Bring quickly the best robe, and put it on him, and put a ring on his hand, and shoes on his feet. And bring the fattened calf and kill it, and let us eat and celebrate. For this my son was dead, and is alive again; he was lost, and is found."

V

As Jesus structured the parable and the character of the father, he portrayed the welcome as an attribute of God the Father who accepted the work of God the Son, Jesus. In the Father of the parable, running and embracing, Jesus not only showed his own work of salvation; he also revealed the manner that the Father in heaven fully accepted his work already in the Old Church. Jesus presented God the Father running to embrace his new creation. By God the Father's recognition of Jesus' saving work, the Son of God came to the strong point of the parable, the joyfulness in heaven over one repentant sinner. The parable of the lost sheep comes to mind again. Luke 15:7, " . . . there will be more joy in heaven over the one sinner who repents than over ninety-nine righteous persons who need no repentance." The laughter over one found coin too reflects the worth of penitence.

Thus the Lord and Savior revealed the profound unity in his and God the Father's working, for those two along with God the Spirit, had the same purpose, creating the New Church out of living members drawn from out of the Old Church's dead membership. In God the Father's recognition of his work, Jesus thus revealed the second purpose of the parable, and its high point.

The Elder Son

By developing the movement of the plot-line from the younger son to the elder, Jesus made the latter the more difficult character, difficult in the sense of his decision to leave him in the deadness of the Old Church, the Church controlled by Pharisaism.

V

When this fellow arrived home after a day's fieldwork and heard sounds of feasting, he demanded from a servant the meaning of the revelry, for he had not been notified. The servant in the telling hardly contained his joy. "Your brother has come, and your father has killed the fattened calf, because he received him safe and sound." At that the elder brother's anger broke out: he refused to join in the merriment.

This elder son, also a member of the Church and duly circumcised, represented the Pharisees, those self-righteous leaders of the covenant community at that time; they found that the legalism of the Tradition of the Elders represented the Faith and hence forced its members to believe and live accordingly. The Pharisees in the centuries after the Exile had modified the Church into the Old Church. The Lord and Savior had with respect to salvation bypassed the Pharisees: no grace, no regeneration, no new hearts, no repentance for those people. In effect, Jesus left those of the Old Church symbolized by the elder son, to carry individual hearts of stone forever, into all eternity. The elder son's hardness of heart, unbelief, and self-righteousness too broke the family unity, only in a way different from the way his younger brother had done, as became apparent from the way in which he addressed his father, the father of the parable.

The father, upon hearing that his elder son had returned home, came out and entreated him to enter into the festivities of the day. "Look," that son remonstrated, "these many years I have served you, and I never disobeyed your command, yet you never gave me a young goat, that I might celebrate with my friends. But when his son of yours came, who has devoured your property with prostitutes, you killed the fattened calf for him." At this rebuke the distance between the father and his elder son broke out.

The elder son's reproach requires various explanations:

Self-righteousness works with a minimum of effort, in the case of the elder son the fieldwork his father commanded. But what of filial love, the son for his father, and of fraternal love, the brother for the brother? What of the Fifth Commandment with respect to parents. All of the Old Church intent upon self-righteousness tended not to strain themselves with matters of the heart. Jesus therefore pictured the elder son hopelessly lost.

2–5. A goat as animal was of lesser worth than a calf, particularly a fattened calf. By mentioning a goat the elder son revealed a false humility, typical of all the self-righteous.

3–5. The younger son had not devoured his father's property, for the father had freely given him his one-third share of the assets. The young man has wasted his own wealth, perhaps by betting on donkey races.

4–5. Nothing in the parable indicated that the younger brother had squandered all on prostitutes. That was slander, for the elder brother had no information about his brother's whereabouts and lifestyle while far away from home.

5–5. By referring to his brother as "this son of yours," he insulted his father and removed himself further from the family bond.

V

For a sum so far: this guy was a troublesome man who cared little for others, even the friends he mentioned. He was covetous, earning rather than inheriting his father's property. He talked down to his father and hated his brother. He was one whose presence caused strife.

The elder son calls to mind the parable of the Pharisee and the tax collector, Luke 18:11–12, the Pharisee speaking,

> God, I thank you that I am not like other men, extortioners, unjust, adulterers, or even like this tax collector. I fast twice a week; I give tithes of all that I get.

In his own eyes he was self-righteous—by comparing himself to public sinners rather than the Christ. Moreover, by tithing he hardly strained himself. In his own eyes he had established his righteousness on the cheap, claiming that his god owed him. Keep in mind that the Pharisees' god was not Jesus, much less God the Father, but another, Satan, John 8:44, or Beelzebul, Matthew 12:24–27, who had a very shallow standard for righteousness.

V

The father of the parable now pleaded with this other son. "Son, you are always with me, and all that is mine is yours." Then, once more. "It is fitting to celebrate and be glad, for this your brother was dead, and is alive; he was lost and is found." However, son senior maintained his hardness of heart. Then the caring father turned away from the elder son to rejoin the feasting for his junior son.

At this point Jesus presented dark part of the parable: he bypassed the senior son with the grace of regeneration; his heart of stone knew nothing of repentance. Thus the Lord and Savior bypassed the Pharisees entirely, except Nicodemus.

In this hard-hitting moment of the parable the father, after his appeal to the elder son, turned his back to him and reentered the house. Thus Jesus revealed that God the Father also recognized as valid his work of reprobation. Here too the Son of God and God the Father worked as one in the unity of the Trinity that the Holy Spirit impresses upon the hearts of flesh throughout the New Church.

> He who sires a fool gets himself sorrow,
> And the father of a fool has no joy.
> Proverbs 17:21

V

Now, at creating the character of the elder son and leaving him eternally with his heart of stone, Jesus made him represent the Pharisees, the self-righteous leaders of the Old Church. Bypassing the man forever, the Lord and Savior left him behind in the isolation of damnation.

Conclusion

In a way this is a joyous parable, because of the repentant younger son once dead and now alive.

In a way this is because of the elder son a rough parable.

A first conclusion: between the two men Jesus stretched out the eternal dividing-line, thus separating the New Church from the Old; this he presented with the two equally rebellious brothers.

A second conclusion: Jesus revealed the eternal unity of being and of working between him and the Father, the Holy Spirit bearing witness.

A third conclusion: the Holy Spirit works the significance of the parable in all hearts of flesh.

At issue on the parable's mini-world: through his ministry Jesus gave a heart of flesh to the one brother and left the other burdened with a heart of stone. Thus, the Lord and Savior presented salvation and damnation, both of which sovereignly just, because he is the omnipotent and omniscient Teacher as well as Savior.

P/s – Weak exegetes easily enough fail to perceive in the parable Jesus' intent relative to the immediate background of the *Gospel according to Luke*. For any relevance at all they drift off into exemplarizing and moralizing—fraternal love, family unity, sibling rivalry, monetary covetousness, sexual immorality; etc.—the sorts of buttons when pressed then draw attention away from the parable's one purpose.

FOLLIES AT FUNERALS
or ANTI-EULOGIZING

AT FUNERAL SERVICES EULOGIZERS addressing grieving family members and sympathetic friends speak to a gathering on the whole and for the moment acutely aware of human mortality. In times as these an old maxim applies: never speak ill of the dead. Aware of this social axiom eulogizers turn memorial services into celebrations of life to comfort the mourners by allaying fears of dying, if not also of death itself. A bit of humor and a good laugh at the expense of the deceased go a long way to hide the obvious and cover up the reality of life's transience, as do pompous flower arrangements.

\/

For the celebration of life eulogizers concentrate on deeds well done and traits of character well meant, on achievements reached and dispositions of character admired, each assessment seasoned with tidy qualifications, such as a sense of humor, a love for family, and an involvement in community. These eulogizing staples allegedly satisfy momentarily a captive audience and stay far away from the inevitables and unavoidables of life; that is, eulogizers skirt around the meaning of life and death through the loss of a human being, family member, friend, or neighbor. Such eulogizing demonstrates (and obituaries as well) that the dead person lived through no more than passing glories—here today, gone tomorrow, however strong the accolades. At funeral services speakers put on display the poverty of the rich and famous as well as the riches of the poor and unknown, even though the end for all is the same, which mortality the author of Ecclesiastes referenced succinctly.

> For of the wise as of the fool there is no enduring remembrance,
> Seeing that in the days to come all will have been long forgotten.

> How the wise dies just as the fool!
> Ecclesiastes 2:16

At funerals eulogizers avoid such bluntness with respect to living and dying in order that under the guise of comforting the grief-stricken family and sympathetic friends, they ease secularized consciences, whatever the actualities of the life celebrated.

V

In a secularized church setting a eulogy affirms assorted qualities and ignores mortal failures in order to assure the gathered that the lately deceased is worthy of place in heaven among the rejoicing angels. Hence, after the fact of the divine judgment at the moment of death, Heb 9:27, eulogizers over ten to twenty minutes seek to assure the gathering of their powers at *verhimmlen* or *ophemelen*, a judging that second-guesses the Judge, or, perhaps, in a church-based funeral a celebration of life focused on the deceased's good parts that comes with the intention to persuade the Judge of heaven and earth to reverse his initial decision and as yet open heaven's portals wide for the achievements accomplished, deeds done, family wholeheartedly loved, and communities enriched, or whatever eulogizers may imagine to arrive a fitting finale for the end of a life. Apparently, these celebrators of life know of the deceased what they fancy will please the consumer-oriented gathering and with shamanizing to convince the Judge through fancy pleadings and prayers to open the doors of heavens.

Of course, with respect to a place in heaven it is too late, for the lately departed at the moment of the last sigh suddenly appeared in the glory of the Judge to hear what the deceased knew along, condemnation in eternal death or resurrection to eternal life based on the first and great Judgment, the Crucifixion of the Christ. No one, except the eulogizers, is actually surprised by Christ Jesus' sentencing handed down from the Cross.

However, for the moment the loquacious words of *verhimmlen* or *ophemelen* do give caring impressions to a grieving family and considerate sympathizers, leaving an imprint also on well-wishers and curious neighbors. Yet, to present a history of the lately deceased that insults the Judge and impairs the gathered in the issues of life and death defeats the purpose of grieving. Reminiscences, the stuff of eulogizing, do nothing to ease the emptiness of wordiness, however eloquent and touching the verbosity.

V

For all in Christ Jesus, a church-based funeral service ought to have as its center piece a meditation on an appropriate biblical passage, to impress on and persuade the living to place all hope only in the love and the grace of the Son, the Lord and Savior, who with the Father and the Spirit in this life overcomes the forces of death, the last enemy, by way of the Gospel. For this purpose two mediations:

Isaiah 35:1–10 (8a)

THE WAY AHEAD

FROM THE PAST THROUGH THE PRESENT INTO THE FUTURE

In the Scriptures the LORD God, the Messiah, for the salvation of his people laid down a highway, the Way of Holiness. To this important road he pointed with emphasis in Isaiah's prophecy. As every road has a beginning and an ending, the Holy Way too; it runs from the past through every present to conclude in eternity. Day-to-day the Christ calls his people onto the road and into the life that never ends.

1–2

In deep time the LORD made the highway physically visible and accessible to Abraham and Sarah when he summoned to two out of Ur of the Chaldeans and they migrated to Canaan. By faith, Hebrews 11:8, the father of all believers and his wife took the road to arrive in the future, first Canaan, the Land of Promise.

As you read through this early part of Genesis you see the road unfolding in front of Abraham and Sarah's feet as well as sense the hope with which they looked forward.

The route the Messiah selected for Abraham and Sarah started in a land of idolatry and ended in a future alive with the grace of salvation. Once the two arrived in Canaan that section of the Holy Way had served its purpose and disappeared from sight; neither Abraham nor his descendants had the freedom to return to the land of idolatry.

V

Again, the Messiah made the great road visible and accessible when he commanded the people of Israel to leave Egypt, the house of bondage.

From Egypt he took Israel on the forty-year long journey through the terrible wilderness to Canaan, the Land of Promise. By faith the thousands upon thousands of Israel, beginning amidst Egyptian idolatries, entered upon the Holy Way.

As you read through Exodus you see the road taking shape in front of Moses and the Israelites' feet; at the same time you experience the hope with which they traveled. You will also stop with those people of the covenant and ask rebelliously, "What did we get ourselves into by walking out of Egypt?"

Daily the LORD led them by a cloud and at night by a pillar of fire, Deuteronomy 1:33. He brought his people forth from a place beginning in idolatry, Egypt, to a new life in Canaan. Once Israel arrived in that land the road long travelled faded out as winds swept away footprints in the sand. Israel had no freedom to return to Egypt.

V

Next prophetically, the LORD God through Isaiah promised once more to make this great road visible and accessible. The beginning of the Holy Way lay in Babylon, the land in which the people of Israel slowly absorbed its idolatries. There and then the LORD through Isaiah promised once more in the Old Testament dispensation the Holy Way in a physically visible and accessible manner:

> And a highway shall be there,
> and it shall be called the Way of Holiness.
> Isaiah 38:8a

In other words:
> A voice cries:
> in the wilderness prepare the way of the LORD;
> make straight in the desert a highway for our God.
> Isaiah 40:3

Again:
> I will make a way in the wilderness and rivers in the desert.
> Isaiah 43:19

And once more:
> . . . I will make all my mountains a road, and my highways shall
> be raised up.
> Isaiah 49:11

V

Then at the time of Cyrus, King of Medo-Persia—as Ezra and Nehemiah recorded—the Messiah led a remnant of the numerous exiles from Babylon to Canaan, there to rebuild the Temple. By faith this remnant took the road out of the Babylonian idolatries into the Land of Promise.

In summary of the Old Testament: at the time of Abraham and Sarah and at the time of the Exodus the Way consisted herein, and only herein that the Messiah dedicated the route to bring his own, Abraham and Sarah, the Israel of the Exodus, and then some exiles out of Babylon to magnify his glory and create the salvation of his people in the Land of Promise by laying out in each instance a physically visible road. The unclean and the foolish were unable to see the route into the future. But in his great mercy the Messiah laid out the highway from yesterday through every day to guide his people to Canaan.

2–2

In the New Testament dispensation the Messiah himself walked the Way of Holiness; according to the Gospel of Mark he with his disciples took the road from Galilee to Jerusalem, where he walked the *via dolorosa* from Pontius Pilate's court to Golgotha. There, on the Cross through the grace of the substitutionary atonement he created the total redemption of his people, all who believe in him as the Christ. For on the Cross in his human nature he absorbed the totality of divine wrath for the sins of those whom he calls his own. The Cross on Golgotha marked the importance of the Land of Promise, every destination of the Holy Way in the Old Testament.

From Golgotha the Christ created the physically visible high way for his people, the New Church, for walking to and into the second and last Judgment.

Now the great road of holiness, running from Golgotha into all eternity, is simply called the Way, Acts 9:2, 19:23, 24:24. By faith all in Christ see and walk this route, the living prescribed by the Commandments for the first reason, gratitude for the grace of salvation, and for the second, eternally magnify the Christ in his trinitarian communion.

Walking along the Holy Way according to the Commandments you see the road opening up before your feet. At times you may look back and wonder, even with a spirit of rebellion, for what purpose you strive for a still invisible future? Yet in the power of the Spirit you persevere following the way of the Christ.

Living the Commandments opens the way from the past through every present into tomorrow. It is the way of hope for the resurrection of the body. It is the way of gratitude for the great grace of salvation. It is the way the New Church journeys from her past in sin through the days of redemption into the life in the presence of the Trinity.

V

For all walking the Way, rejoice and persevere, listening to the answer that is the Psalm 143:8 petition.

> Let me hear in the morning of your steadfast love,
> for in you I trust.
> Make me know the way I should go, for to you I lift up my soul.

Are you not sure of the Way?

Out of immeasurable grace the Lord Jesus calls you to journey with his people, following the response to a plea as Psalm 25:4.

> Make me to know your ways, O LORD;
> teach me your paths.

Then together we travel over the Way of Holiness into the Eschaton and the resurrection of the dead, to live forever in the one splendor of the Lord Jesus, God the Father, and the Holy Spirit.

Revelation 14:6–16

IN THE GRACE OF THE DAY

Out of Revelation 14:13 two voices issue forth; both speakers break into the silence of the hour and raise the powers of hope. The first, of an angel-messenger, addressed the Apostle in the name of the resurrected and ascended Lord Jesus, now enthroned in the glory of majesty at the right hand of the God the Father, the place of all authority. The second voice, equally divine and equally authoritative, belonged to the Holy Spirit. In effect the Lord Jesus through the angel and the Holy Spirit, two witnesses to the one truth, demanded that the Apostle listen intently, for both revealed the abundant grace in the hour of judgment.

COVENANT ESSAYS: TWO

The Voice of the Christ

The ascended Christ through the piercing voice of a messenger revealed to the Apostle the divine care for all believers suffering persecution, definitively in the hour of death, Revelation 14:12. At the beginning of the New Testament Church, post-Pentecost, many believers suffered, even died, for they refused to recant the Faith; they believed in the Lord and Savior, King of kings and Lord of lords. However representatives of the Roman imperium little tolerated resistance against the Caesar of the day, John 18:33–34, and intended to make the believers deny the way, the truth, and the life they treasured, more than even life itself. Rome endured no rivalry to the emperor. Yet shortly after Ascension Day the Lord of lords, conqueror of death, spoke through a messenger of the grace promised the Church, specifically the hope for martyrs.

> Blessed are the dead who die in the Lord from now on.

Christian prisoners of Rome awaiting in dark dungeons the hour of execution, in a sense dead already, had to hear from the Apostle the grace of the day. In fact, through the Apostle the Christ addressed the Church in the coming ages: blessed are all persecuted and martyred by the world's powers for believing in the Christ. To the martyrs the Son of God promised life in death, light in the darkness of death, as well as hope in deepest despair, however frightening the gloom of dungeons and immediate the hour of death.

This blessing calls to mind, Psalm 31:15a, "My times are in your hand." In the same way the blessing calls forth Psalm 116:15, "Precious in the sight of the LORD is the death of his saints." In the vitality of the New Testament dispensation these Old Testament references reveal that the Christ never discards one of his own, not even if they had to die by fire, wild animals, or decapitation.

Many Christians died thus, even by crucifixion. But they even in the frightful days and hours leading up to the execution, remained faithful, uncompromising. Though rejected by the political authorities of the day and despised by the masses of unbelievers who came into the arenas to witness the spectacles of believers dying, Christ Jesus held his own, as in the palm of his hand; no persecution and no martyrdom separated believers from the Lord and Savior, Rom 8:31–39.

The angel with the authority of the ascended Jesus commanded John to write out the blessing. "Write this!" Words spoken may be twisted or forgotten. Words inscripturated as the Word of God carry the permanence of

Jesus' guarantee and therefore last forever, a clear and enduring affirmation of the divine grace imputed also in the day of martyrdom.

Voice of the Spirit

The Holy Spirit also spoke, confirming and amplifying the grace imputed on the day of death, and in the hour of execution, however terrible the discriminatory harassment.

> Blessed indeed ... that they may rest from their labors.

These labors consisted of working through the frightening fears of persecution that rolled over the seven congregations, fears increased a hundred-fold in the hour of execution. With these fears the Spirit tested all and everyone in Christ for perseverance in the Faith. Not to be afraid of persecution and anti-Christian forces? That stretches credulity. Church members then too were human, with a limit to endurance. However the works to which the Spirit referred comprised the suffering, the labors of standing up unbowed and untiring under the persecutory powers of the world for the sake of and in the name of the Christ. Therefore the Spirit informed that he, God, strengthened believers against the temptations of denying the Lord Jesus.

Each temptation comes innocently. In the early New Testament Church, to escape horrifying deaths, members had only to sprinkle a pinch of incense on an altar and whisper, "Caesar is lord." Simple. A few words and a pinch of incense stopped martyrdom and prevented further untold discrimination. However, the Spirit always persuaded believers of refuse the pull of temptation, and die in Jesus Christ. He alone is Lord, Head of the Church. In him suffering discrimination nevertheless consists of heavy labors from which believers rested only after the execution.

To be sure, standing up strong against the temptations of denying the Christ, whatever the severity of martyrdom, never earned the faithful the promised blessing of the Spirit's presence. Those labors under stresses of rejection by political authorities and masses of unbelievers—whatever the causes of death: death by fire, by crucifixion, by wild animals, or by beheading— ended in rest, the peace of living eternally in the presence of the Christ, God the Father, and God the Spirit, one God, which undeserved mercy fortifies the vitals of the Faith.

Only after martyrdom and execution the surprising thrust of grace opens up, as the last part of Revelation 14:13 indicates,

... for their deeds follow them.

It is a human expectation to come before the Christ, the Judge of heaven and earth, and in outstretched hands present the good works of overcoming the fears and the terrors of persecution. It is human to hope that he will judge by the faithful living of his people. However, what people find interesting and important means nothing; also what the early Christians accomplished under the press of persecution earned nothing of worth relative to judgment.

The *deeds* that followed believers as they appeared before the Judge consisted first of faith, believing the Savior's atoning works achieved on Golgotha, the faith imputed by grace. Out of that faith proceeded the works that actually glorified the Lord and Savior. Thus what followed believers into judgment consisted of the works of faith, the results the commitment of love for the Savior. Throughout that living not even the worst of rejection by earthly powers deleted those of endurance and perseverance. Thus, the deeds referred to started already long before persecution started and increased under the stresses of martyrdom, the significance of which may never be underestimated, for at the last Judgment all will be judged, each one according to the deeds done while alive, Revelation 20:13. These works do not enter in as the main or even as the first evidence of righteousness. Works confirm the first Judgment and appear as the result of the declaration of imputed grace. That strength of heart refused the fakery of hypocrisy, the easing into world conformity, escaping the hazards of persecutory circumstance, or even bargaining with Jesus to make the evidence of Christianity count in the Judgment. Though consigned to martyrdom the Spirit held all in Christ—proof: faithful living—strong in endurance.

In this day hearing the angel's command to John to write also the Spirit's words as Scriptures opens up in believing the steadfastness of the Faith.

V

From the throne of authority at the right hand of God the Father and in the presence of the Holy Spirit Jesus spoke—the Father and the Spirit the two witnesses—to pierce the isolation in the hour of death with the grace of eternity.

CONCLUSION

Meditations set in a simple and unpretentious liturgy focus on the Lord and Savior to proclaim to all present the way ahead in this life, for family, relatives, and friends alike. In the ahead to know the Judge of all the earth eases the passage into death.

Hence, eulogies may be acceptable in a secular or paganized setting. In the Church of Jesus Christ the Gospel ought to be taken most seriously and the Christ, not the deceased placed first.

SEXUALITY ON AND OFF THE MAIN ROAD

Powers of human sexuality run on testosterone and estrogen; these essential hormones intrigue enormously and, if abused, destroy frightfully. For living this sexuality the Creator God laid down the main road, the connubial straightaway, Genesis 1:26–27, 2:23–24, and not because he had only two genders to work with. Early in the history of the creation the LORD God thoughtfully prepared this very good male/female sexual intimacy. To be precise, he structured the stable creation of testosterone and estrogen for the marital way.

THE MAIN ROAD OF SEXUAL INTIMACY

The Lord with all authority in heaven and on earth created monogamy, the one-flesh bond constitutive of the love-generating tie that binds a man and a woman throughout the life of both. Such is the heterosexual orientation on the main road, the indelible setting in which the currents of estrogen and testosterone oblige the love between the genders.

Upon Adam's sin the Christ recreated the way of marriage for the main road as the means in the experiences of monogamy to rule over the sexual hormones, lest these hormonal powers behave unruly. Now through every present of the Kingdom and the Church the Lord Jesus orders his own, as image bearers, to govern these hormonal necessities of life.

Off Down the One Side

Falling away from the main road because of Adam's disobedience another authority, lust, moved in to rule over human sexuality; in this off-roading men and women rebelliously compel the responsibility of image bearing to bow to another norm for testosterone and estrogen, which mobilizes damnation. This off-track abuse of human sexuality by baptized and committed/communicant members manipulates itself into the covetousness of adultery and fornication.

Adulterous Relations

When married people interact sexually with others' spouses they submit to carnal corruption. Such *love* between consensual actors in the throes of passion disarms the Seventh Commandment, "You shall not commit adultery." In the *progressiveness* of this age infidelity may be decriminalized as well as socially acceptable, yet the Christ forever condemned ruinations of connubiality, Leviticus 20:10. Long ago a Pharaoh, Genesis 12:17–20, and two Abimelechs, Genesis 20:17, 26:6–11, feared with mortal trepidation to take the wife of another man. For the same reason the LORD severely berated David for seducing Uriah the Hittite's wife, 2 Samuel 12:1–14. Even off the main road the conjugal norm of the beginning remains fully active.

Adultery carries over into another manifestation of covetousness. Often enough after divorce, or as a motivation for divorce, men and women seek remarriage, a lookalike to the original construction of the marriage institution, however sinful, Matthew 5:31–32, 19:3–9; Mark 10:2–10; Luke 16:18. Subsequent divorce, remarriage stimulates continuous adultery. As much as divorcees, bound up in the enslaving follies of the age, may grasp at freedom to *love* again, and seek the fullness of John 10:10, it is better by far to absorb the pains of celibacy. Matthew 19:12; 1 Corinthians 7:7. No amount of proof texting and fractious hermeneutics *converts* adultery of second and third marriages into main-road sexuality, Christ-approved. When remarried people engage in sexual physicality with others' spouses (remember the-till-death-you-do-part vows?) they succumb to the covetousness of carnality. Nothing can make the Bible prove the legitimacy of marrying the husband or wife of another. David's Bathsheba remained life-long first Uriah the Hittite's woman, Matthew 1:6b. Remarried men and women merely acclimatize to falling social values.

The same standard for conjugality applies to cohabitation. Common-law relations, however deeply committed, also unlock individualistic ideals inattentive to the ecclesiastical code of ethics alive in Christian congregations. Shacking up is unmindful of the divine stipulations for wedlock: a man and a woman promising life-long fidelity before the Lord Jesus and the congregation of membership.

However much adultery, divorce/remarriage, and cohabitation may tug at heart strings to approve low-road standards and values, sin is sin.

Fornicative Connections

Sexual disarray descends into immorality, the severity of which accelerates life to doom in damnation, 1 Corinthians 5:9–13. Fornicative brutalities have an opportunistic character, lustfully looking at or thinking about a naked woman or man. For unbelievers this sort of speculative cruelty (using male or female bodies for private pleasuring) may seem harmlessly digressive, but the Lord Jesus displays little patience with such vice, Matthew 5:27–28. For in the wilds of fornicative passions (adult) men and women fall victim to hungers of pornography, to the point of brutalizing children. Sexual fantasizing maliciously beguiles love of neighbors.

Malice of sexual perversity capitulates to incest, consensually planned, 2 Samuel 13:14; 1 Corinthians 5:1–5, or opportunistic, Leviticus 18:1–18, 19:12, 14, 17; etc., every instance callous disregard for the original marital norm, illicit one-flesh bonds impossible to explain before the Judge.

Much carnal willfulness falls under fornicative connectives. Physical, emotional/mental and sexual mistreatment of wives, husbands, daughters, and sons sours many marriages, even the hopes of matrimony for coming generations. The selfish fiascoes of rough sex to exert domination or unleash sado-masochistic pleasures earn condemnation. Nymphomaniacs and rapists, too, impetuous in boundless hatreds seek convenient victims to satisfy dark desires. Prostitution, despite warnings as Leviticus 19:29; 1 Corinthians 6:15, depends on perversities in men and women wallowing in the brokenness of sin, bringing about highly damnable one-flesh connections, 1 Corinthians 6:17.

V

Fornication, even as adultery, in the numerous expressions possible reaps in respective bodies commensurable irruptions of divine punishment. Promiscuity carries perpetrators along, direction eternal torments.

Off Down the Other Side

Down off the other side of the main road baptized and committed communicants live a sexual orientation different from the heterosexual; they identify as homosexuals and lesbians. Under the authority of lust, Romans 1:24–25, these people of the Church come out to belong also to the loosely organized and fractious LGBTQ+ community, a community held together mostly by external opposition to homosexuality, indeed, anti-homosexualism.

Homosexual Relations

Same-sex oriented members of the Church who have married in the *traditional* way or seek such marriage are not the godless types who suppress the truth, except in one specific area of life. They present themselves as responsible members, only with activated homosexual relations, which relations have repercussions elsewhere—regarding Jesus' lordship, biblical authority, legal obedience, congregational sanctity, exemplary living; etc., similar to the adulterous and fornicative people on the other low road. Despite these discrepancies, out of doctrinal dedication and confessional commitment they *only* seek traditional marriage with the same acceptance rate and status as any heterosexual one-flesh union. Stronger, they yearn for the blessings of divine love even as the majority, though the homosexual and the lesbian stand apart, despairing in condemnable consequences, Leviticus 18:22, 19:13; Romans 1:26–27; etc. For a relationship that may feel natural to same-sexed human beings in terms of orientation and identity, they desire quality equal to living on the main road.

Does an appeal to the radical inclusion of Gentile believers in the New Testament Church help homosexuals achieve equal standing with heterosexuals on the main road? Converts out of the Gentiles believed the Gospel and in the process of learning the doctrines of the Church they discarded pagan practices, 1 Corinthians 6:9–11. Through baptism they entered the Church's membership and adapted to the Commandments—without asking for an exception either in doctrine or in life. In contrast, no amount of proof texting and restless hermeneutics can make homosexual unions, even if antinomously solemnized in a church setting, acceptable to Christ Jesus on the main road. Still, homosexuals want to live as homosexuals as a defining feature of church membership. Inclusion of Gentiles into the Church, then, offers no precedent for legitimating same-sex unions.

Further, argumentation that society evolved, socially engineered to accept lookalikes to *traditional* marriages, and that science has explained the hard-wiring of same-sex orientation presents only assimilation to worldliness. For those members of the Church who seek and support approval for conjugal unions analogous to *traditional* wedlock run into the wall of condemnation.

Again, these church members are not necessarily godless human beings who suppress the truth; they are, so to speak, born and raised in the Church who over the years of maturing had parents who taught them the way of marriage and who listened to the proclamation of the Word also with respect to conjugality. On this foundation they desire lasting marriages—to do what heterosexuals do in the homosexual way—under the assumption that God caused the gay-ness and now ought to accommodate them by changing biblical interpretation. So they yearn for the meaning of love and sex on one of the off-roads that social engineers sweep clean of sinning. This world conformity never approaches the Scriptures relative to connubiality.

V

Homosexuals may argue that declining homophobia, pederasty, and sexual slavery allow for accepting of same-sex marriages supported by human rights legislation, however clearly the Scriptures stand on this matter.

Homosexual Connections

In this allegedly *progressive* Western society of openness, tolerance, and acceptance—homophobia on the wane, homosexual prostitution in the open, and sexual slavery at an end—same-sex connections outside committed relations gain increasingly social recognition, even approval. In the background to this approval hovers a claim that Paul, speaking out against homosexualism, condemned elite Greco-Romans who carried this perversion too far. Contrary to all twists and turns in biblical interpretation, the Scriptures clearly reveal the end of all homosexual activity.

Severe condemnation of heterosexual pornographic lusting, Matthew 5:27-28, applies no less to homosexual aches for the body of another man, or in the case of lesbianism, for a woman's. In matters of lust homosexuals are as unscrupulous as heterosexuals in breaking the Seventh Commandment on every level. Therefore homosexual sins of opportunity—prostitution, rape, pederasty, nymphomania—remain under continual condemnation, even if Western society as a whole erases sexual sins from law codes and consciences. Driven by sexual needs and desires the men and the women of homosexual orientation and identity tie themselves up in knots of one-flesh bonds insupportable before the Judge, the Lord Jesus. If heterosexual fornicators cannot reasonably explain to the Judge why they did what they did, homosexuals fail as miserably.

V

Unless homosexuals commit themselves to celibacy in a way similar to what Jesus presented, Matt 19:12, and Paul recommended under endtimes expectations, 1 Corinthians 7:7, they move along with the heterosexual adulterers and fornicators into the deadly hostility Christ Jesus revealed against all sinning.

THE HIGHROAD OF SEXUAL INTIMACY

The Lord Jesus summoned his people, even those on the low roads, onto the highroad of marital fidelity created in Eden: one man and one woman committed to the marriage vows spoken before him and his people in a solemnization of matrimony (without escaping into serial monogamy). In this heterosexual identity he calls his own to obedience in love, the deepest and strongest commitment possible between a male and a female of the human race.

The Lord calls his own to holiness in marriage, therefore also in sexuality, making sexual intercourse always more expressive of the husband/wife one-flesh union, Hebrews 13:4. In Christ Jesus life is a gift, heterosexual orientation/identity too, physically dependent on flowing hormones. Hence, for the transformation mandate on the highroad the Lord's people uphold fully functioning commitment to wedlock, despite its difficulties and complexities. Gratitude for the grace of redemption displays itself also by living the one marital standard.

In marriage on the highroad as the ardor of youth moves into the maturing of reflection, a man and a woman together in Christ recognize lust, selfishness, and power of domination. They then seek to break up these motor forces of sinfulness and upon repentance renew marriage vows. This reformation then grants groundbreaking futurity in the fullness of the John 10:10 life. Believers in covenanting communion, which involves sexuality, over the years quietly evolve in day-by-day commitment, bringing about newness in wedlock. Thus Ephesians 5:21–33,

> ... submitting to one another out of reverence for Christ.

> Wives, submit to your own husbands, as to the Lord. For the husband is the head of the wife even as Christ is the head of the church, his body, and is himself its Savior. Now as the church submits to Christ, so also wives should submit in everything to their husbands.

Husbands, love your wives, as Christ loved the church and gave himself up for her, that he might sanctify her, having cleansed her by the washing of water with the word, so that he might present the church to himself in splendor, without spot or wrinkle or any such thing, that she might be holy and without blemish. In the same way husbands should love their wives as their own bodies. He who loves his wife loves himself. For no one every hated his own flesh, but nourishes and cherishes it, just as Christ does the church, because we are members of his body. Therefore a man shall leave his father and mother and hold fast to his wife, and the two shall become one flesh. This mystery is profound, and I am saying that it refers to Christ and the church. However, let each one of you love his wife as himself, and let the wife see that she respects her husband.

In the biblical climate revealed in *the Letter to the Church at Ephesus* the renewing sense of marriage takes place. Men and women in Christ do not dare appear before him with a marriage less holy in maturing love than indicated through this marital mandate.

V

Some with poor marriages, stalled in superficiality and filled with monotony, may find in heterosexual marriage proof of self-righteousness; they presume on the basis of conjugality that they are better human beings than all suffering from homosexual inclinations and caught in (committed) same-sex relations. They look down on same-sex attractions. In a prestige of marriage impossibly grounded in the Scriptures they present wedlock as a superior status-marker cold and lonely on its pedestal.

In contrast, out of strengths of Christian mercy married church members with compassion both communal and personal draw in the congregation's homosexuals and provide them with stability necessary for and compatible with celibacy—as they do with adulterers and fornicators coming off the low road.

V

Christ Jesus in the Scriptures set for all generations of the Church inviolate norms for marriage and its intimacies. With the sexual needs and energies generated by testosterone and estrogen marriage in Christ sublimates into life-long commitment. Full of grace, all in Christ seek the totality of life also in the gift of sexuality.

I thank Rev. Dr. W. Koopmans for his insightful critique of this essay.

Essays done well, especially in collections, run the gamut-with variations in substance and length-with one more interesting than another. This sort of communication enriches, ennobles the Faith, and makes the walk in Christ more purposeful.

TH

www.ingramcontent.com/pod-product-compliance
Lightning Source LLC
Chambersburg PA
CBHW062025220426
43662CB00010B/1479